CompTIA
Project+™
Study Guide

Kim Heldman
William Heldman

WILEY

Wiley Publishing, Inc.

Acquisitions Editor: Jeff Kellum
Development Editor: Alexa Murphy
Technical Editors: Vanina Mangano and Jared Rundell
Production Editor: Rachel McConlogue
Copy Editor: Kim Wimpsett
Editorial Manager: Pete Gaughan
Production Manager: Tim Tate
Vice President and Executive Group Publisher: Richard Swadley
Vice President and Publisher: Neil Edde
Media Project Manager: Laura Moss-Hollister
Media Associate Producer: Marilyn Hummel
Media Quality Assurance: Shawn Patrick
Book Designers: Judy Fung and Bill Gibson
Proofreader: Candace English
Indexer: Ted Laux
Project Coordinator, Cover: Lynsey Stanford
Cover Designer: Ryan Sneed

Copyright © 2010 by Wiley Publishing, Inc., Indianapolis, Indiana

Published simultaneously in Canada

ISBN: 978-0-470-58592-4

For general information on our other products and services or to obtain technical support, please contact our Customer Care Department within the U.S. at (877) 762-2974, outside the U.S. at (317) 572-3993 or fax (317) 572-4002.

Wiley also publishes its books in a variety of electronic formats. Some content that appears in print may not be available in electronic books.

Library of Congress Cataloging-in-Publication Data
Heldman, Kim.
  CompTIA project+ study guide (PK0-003) / Kim Heldman, William Heldman.—1st ed.
    p. cm.
  Includes bibliographical references and index.
  ISBN 978-0-470-58592-4 (paper/cd-rom : alk. paper)
  1. Electronic data processing personnel—Certification. 2. Project management—Examinations—Study guides. 3. Information technology—Management—Study guides. I. Heldman, William. II. Title.
  QA76.3.H423 2010
  004.068'8—dc22

                                                                          2010005947

10 9 8

The logo of the CompTIA Authorized Quality Curriculum (CAQC) program and the status of this or other training material as "Authorized" under the CompTIA Authorized Quality Curriculum program signifies that, in CompTIA's opinion, such training material covers the content of the CompTIA's related certification exam. CompTIA has not reviewed or approved the accuracy of the contents of this training material and specifically disclaims any warranties of merchantability or fitness for a particular purpose. CompTIA makes no guarantee concerning the success of persons using any such "Authorized" or other training material in order to prepare for any CompTIA certification exam.

The contents of this training material were created for the CompTIA Project+ exam covering CompTIA certification objectives that were current as of 2010.

How to become CompTIA certified:

This training material can help you prepare for and pass a related CompTIA certification exam or exams. In order to achieve CompTIA certification, you must register for and pass a CompTIA certification exam or exams.

In order to become CompTIA certified, you must:

1. Select a certification exam provider. For more information please visit

   `http://www.comptia.org/certification/general_information/exam_locations.aspx`.

2. Register for and schedule a time to take the CompTIA certification exam(s) at a convenient location.

3. Read and sign the Candidate Agreement, which will be presented as the time of the exam(s). The text of the Candidate Agreement can be found at `http://www.comptia.org/certification/general_information/candidate_agreement.aspx`.

4. Take and pass the CompTIA certification exam(s).

For more information about CompTIA's certifications, such as its industry acceptance, benefits or program news, please visit `http://www.comptia.org/certification/`.

CompTIA is a not-for-profit trade information technology (IT) trade association. CompTIA's certifications are designed by subject matter experts from across the IT industry. Each CompTIA certification is vendor-neutral, covers multiple technologies and requires demonstration of skills and knowledge widely sought after by the IT industry.

To contact CompTIA with any questions or comments, please call 630-678-8300 or email `question@comptia.org`.

Dear Reader,

Thank you for choosing *CompTIA Project+ Study Guide* from Sybex, a proud Authorized Gold Partner in the CompTIA Authorized Partner Program (CAPP) for content developers. The learning material in this book, which meets the exacting standards of CompTIA's content assurance program, was written by an outstanding author who combines practical experience with a passion for teaching.

Sybex was founded in 1976. More than 30 years later, we're still committed to producing consistently exceptional books. With each of our titles, we're working hard to set a new standard for the industry. From the paper we print on to the authors we work with, our goal is to bring you the best books available.

I hope you see all that reflected in these pages. I'd be very interested to hear your comments and get your feedback on how we're doing. Feel free to let me know what you think about this or any other Sybex book by sending me an email at `nedde@wiley.com`. If you think you've found a technical error in this book, please visit `http://sybex.custhelp.com`. Customer feedback is critical to our efforts at Sybex.

Best regards,

Neil Edde
Vice President and Publisher
Sybex, an Imprint of Wiley

WILEY
Wiley Publishing, Inc.

To Kate and Juliette, project managers in the making.

Acknowledgments

Thank you for buying the *CompTIA Project+ Study Guide* to help you study and prepare for the CompTIA Project+ exam. We believe this book is a good introduction to the in-depth world of project management and certification and will open up many opportunities for you.

We would like to thank all the great team members at Sybex who were part of this project: Jeff Kellum, acquisitions editor; Alexa Murphy, development editor; Rachel McConlogue, production editor; and all those behind the scenes who helped make this book a success. They are terrific to work with, as always, and we appreciate their keen eyes and insightful ideas and suggestions.

Special thanks goes to Vanina Mangano for her work as technical editor. We appreciate her diligence and great suggestions that helped make the content stronger. Thank you to Jared Rundell as well for providing the final technical review.

And a thank-you, as always, goes to our family for their understanding of our crazy schedules. Kate and Juliette, you're the best!

About the Authors

Kim Heldman, MBA, PMP, is the chief information officer for the Colorado Department of Transportation. Kim is responsible for managing projects with information technology (IT) components ranging from small in scope and budget to multimillion-dollar, multiyear projects. She has more than 20 years experience in IT project management. Kim has served in a senior leadership role for more than 12 years and is regarded as a strategic visionary with an innate ability to collaborate with diverse groups and organizations, instill hope, improve morale, and lead her teams in achieving goals they never thought possible.

Kim has extensive experience in the government sector managing projects of various size and scope. Currently, Kim is working with the Governor's Office of Information Technology assisting in the oversight of one of the largest projects ever undertaken in the State of Colorado.

In addition to her project management experience, Kim also has experience managing application development, web development, network operations, infrastructure, security, and customer service teams.

Kim is the author of the *PMP Project Management Professional Exam Study Guide*, *Project Management JumpStart*, and *Project Manager's Spotlight on Risk Management*, as well as coauthor of *Excel 2007 for Project Managers*. Kim has also published several articles and is currently working on a leadership book.

Kim writes on project management best-practices and leadership topics, and she speaks frequently at conferences and events. You can contact Kim at `Kim.Heldman@comcast.net`. She personally answers all her email.

Bill Heldman teaches computer science, game programming, and 2D/3D digital animation at a career- and technical-education high school in Lakewood, Colorado, called Warren Tech. You can find more information about Warren Tech at `www.warrentech.org`.

Prior to becoming a schoolteacher, Bill had a long career in information technology with progressively responsible positions. Thanks to the volatility of the IT marketplace (read: frequent layoffs), Bill decided to pursue a different career path and was very, very lucky to find work as a teacher, a career path he loves.

In addition to teaching school, Bill is working on new ideas for digital-technology academies and game-programming camps and pursuing his PhD in educational leadership and educational technology.

You can reach Bill at `billheldman@gmail.com`, read his blogs at `blog.billheldman.com`, or connect with him on Facebook.

Contents at a Glance

Contents

Introduction

Have you ever wondered how the pyramids were built? Or the Eiffel Tower? How did someone have the organizational skills to put all those people together and create such magnificent structures? Coming forward to recent times—how is Microsoft capable of putting together the literally *millions* of lines of code that became Windows Server 2008? The answer to all of these is project management.

The CompTIA Project+ exam will test your knowledge of the concepts and processes involved in project management. There are several project management methodologies you can follow, each with their own processes and procedures, but at the foundation of each one is sound project management principles and techniques. This edition of the *CompTIA Project+ Study Guide* reflects CompTIA's commitment to the Project Management Institute (PMI) and its associated project management practices. These project management practices are detailed in PMI's publication, *A Guide to the Project Management Body of Knowledge (Guide to the PMBOK), Fourth Edition*. The five domains measured in CompTIA's 2010 version of the Project+ exam map to the five process groups that are the foundation of the *PMBOK Guide*: Initiating, Planning, Executing, Monitoring and Controlling, and Closing.

In the *CompTIA Project+ Study Guide*, you'll find plenty of discussion of project management concepts such as defining the requirements, creating the project charter document, creating the scope document, planning the project, assessing and managing risk, and closing out the project. You'll also find exam questions in categories such as team building and personnel management, quality management, status reporting, and more, and we discuss these areas as well.

The Project+ certification used to be centered on information technology (IT) projects and was called the IT Project+ exam. Many projects involve IT in one way or another, so you'll find references in this book to IT-related projects. We should also mention that both of our backgrounds are firmly rooted in IT, and many of our examples are drawn from real-life experiences. Regardless of the industry you work in, it's likely some segment of IT software and hardware directly affects your business.

Where should you go beyond taking your Project+ test? If you find that you're interested in all things project management, you should enroll in a good university-level class that takes you through the heavier stages of project management. This book and this test only touch the surface of project management techniques. You'll find there is much more to learn and that it's possible to make a career out of managing projects.

WARNING Don't just study the questions and answers in this book; the questions on the actual exam will be different from the practice ones included in the book and on the CD-ROM. The exam is designed to test your knowledge of a concept or objective, so use this book to learn the objective behind the question.

What Is the Project+ Certification?

CompTIA's mission is to create tests and certifications that aren't company-specific. For example, you can take a server test that deals with the elements of servers and server operation but doesn't ask you specifics about Dell, HP, or IBM equipment. CompTIA got its start with what is now an industry standard, the A+ exam. This is a test designed to quiz you on your understanding of the guts of a PC and its associated connection to a network. But there are other tests as well: Network+, Linux+, and others.

Why Become Project+ Certified?

Certification in project management has increasingly become a requirement for those interested in full-time careers in this field. It improves your credibility with stakeholders and customers. Becoming certified demonstrates your intent to learn the processes associated with project management and provides you with opportunities for positions and advancements that may not otherwise be possible.

Here are some reasons to consider the Project+ test and this study guide:

Demonstrates proof of professional achievement   Certification demonstrates to current and potential employers that you are knowledgeable and well grounded in project management practices and have taken the initiative to prove your knowledge in this area.

Increases your marketability   If you take a moment to surf job postings for project management positions, you'll often find that certification is either highly desirable or required. The CompTIA Project+ certification will help you stand out from other candidates and demonstrate that you have the skills and knowledge to fulfill the duties required of a project manager.

Provides opportunity for advancement   You may find that your Project+ certification is just what you need to get that next step up the ladder. People who study and pass certification tests prove, if nothing else, that they have the tenacity to get through a difficult subject and to prove their understanding by testing on the subject.

Provides a prerequisite for advanced project management training   If you're considering a project management career, the Project+ exam is a great way to start. Studying for this exam gives you the background on what project management is really all about, not simply what one company or organization thinks it's about. After passing the exam, you should consider obtaining the Certified Associate Project Management (CAPM) or the Project Management Professional (PMP) certification through the Project Management Institute. This study guide follows the principles and processes outlined by PMI and is a great introduction to its certifications.

Raises customer confidence because it raises your confidence   Customers who know you're certified in project management and who hear you speak and act with confidence are more confident in the company you represent. If you're able, for example, to identify and describe the four categories of risks to prepare for on a project, your customer gains confidence in you.

How to Become Project+ Certified

First, study the topics and processes outlined in this book, and make certain to answer all the end-of-chapter questions and take the extra bonus exams included on the CD.

Then go to the CompTIA website (www.comptia.org) to find the list of testing sites where the exam is currently conducted. At the time of this printing, Pearson VUE centers and Prometric offer the Project+ exam. You can find links to both of them at www .comptia.org. See the website for details regarding the price of the exam.

 Prices and testing centers are subject to change at any time. Please visit CompTIA's website for the most up-to-date information: www.comptia .org.

You'll need a driver's license and one other form of ID when you arrive at the testing center. No calculators, computers, cell phones, or other electronic devices are allowed in the testing area. You're allowed 90 minutes to take the exam, and there are 80 multiple-choice questions. You'll be notified of your grade as soon as you finish the test.

Who Should Buy This Book?

You should buy this book if you're interested in project management and would like to learn more about the topic. The Project+ exam is an ideal way to introduce yourself to project management concepts and techniques, and this book will immerse you in the basics of those techniques.

If you've never taken a certification test before, you'll find that the Project+ exam is a very pleasant way to get your feet wet. The test isn't overly complicated or riddled with trick questions; it simply covers the basics of project management. Once you pass the exam and gain confidence in your project management knowledge and skills, you'll be ready to progress to other certifications and eager to learn the more in-depth topics involved in project management.

How to Use This Book and CD

We've included several testing features, found both in the book and on the companion CD-ROM. At the beginning of the book (right after this introduction) is an assessment test. Take this exam before you start reading the book. It will help you determine the areas you understand well and the areas where you may need more study. The answers to the Assessment test questions are on a separate page after the last question of the test. Each answer also includes an explanation and a note telling you where this material appears.

To test your knowledge as you progress through the book, there are review questions at the end of each chapter. As you finish each chapter, answer the review questions, and then check your work—the correct answers appear on the page following the last review question.

Every question on the Project+ exam is a multiple-choice format. We used this same format for all the questions and practice exams in this study guide.

In addition to the assessment test and chapter review questions, you'll find two bonus exams on the book's companion CD-ROM. Take these exams just as if you were actually taking the exams (that is, without any reference material). When you have finished the first exam, move on to solidify your test-taking skills with the second exam.

Also on the CD, you'll find more than 150 flashcard questions for on-the-go review. Download them right onto your handheld device for quick and convenient reviewing.

Additionally, if you are going to travel but still need to study for the Project+ exam, you can take this entire book with you on your laptop computer. This book is in PDF (Adobe Acrobat) format on the CD so it can be easily read on any computer.

The majority of the examples used to demonstrate practical application of the material in this book focus on IT projects, because IT project managers were the original target audience for this exam. However, the techniques and concepts discussed in this book are not limited to IT projects. The information discussed in this book can be applied to projects in any industry.

Tips for Taking the Project+ Exam

Here are some general tips for taking your exam successfully:

- Bring two forms of ID with you. One must be a photo ID, such as a driver's license. The other can be a major credit card or a passport. Both forms must have a signature.
- Arrive early at the exam center so you can relax and review your study materials, particularly tables and lists of exam-related information.
- Read the questions carefully. Don't be tempted to jump to an early conclusion. Make sure you know exactly what the question is asking.
- Don't leave any unanswered questions. Unanswered questions are scored against you.
- There will be questions with multiple correct responses. When there is more than one correct answer, there will be a statement at the end of the question instructing to you select the proper number of correct responses, as in "Choose two."

- When answering multiple-choice questions you're not sure about, use a process of elimination to remove the incorrect responses first. This will improve your odds if you need to make an educated guess.

- For the latest pricing on the exam and updates to the registration procedures, refer to the CompTIA site at www.comptia.org.

The Exam Objectives

Behind every certification exam, there are exam objectives. The objectives are competency areas that cover specific topics of project management. The introduction section of each chapter in this book lists the objectives that are discussed in the chapter.

Exam objectives are subject to change at any time without prior notice and at CompTIA's sole discretion. Please visit the Certification page of CompTIA's website (www.comptia.org) for the most current listing of Project+ exam objectives.

The Project+ exam will test you on five domains, and each domain is worth a certain percentage of the exam. The following is a breakdown of the domains and their representation in the exam.

Domain	% of Examination
1.0 Pre-Project Setup/Initiating	12%
2.0 Project Planning	29%
3.0 Project Execution and Delivery	23%
4.0 Change, Control and Communication	27%
5.0 Project Closure	9%
Total	**100%**

Assessment Test

1. Which of these terms describes a critical path task?

   A. Hammock

   B. Zero float

   C. Critical task

   D. Mandatory task

2. When would you use your negotiation skills on a project that's in the Executing process group?

   A. When you want a certain individual to work on your project team

   B. When you're running a high-level project in which you could augment the outcome by adjusting certain tasks

   C. As a conflict-resolution technique with the team

   D. When you're attempting to get better hardware for the same money

3. This tool is often used in the vendor selection process to pick a winning bidder.

   A. Weighted scoring model

   B. Bidder conference

   C. IFB

   D. SOW

4. From the following list of options, select three of the five common stages of development that cohesive project teams progress through. Choose three.

   A. Forming

   B. Acquiring

   C. Storming

   D. Founding

   E. Inventing

   F. Norming

   G. Constraining

5. In this organizational structure, you report to the director of project management, and your team members report to their areas of responsibility (accounting, human resources, and IT). You will have complete control of the project team's assignments once the project is underway. Which type of organization does this describe?

   A. Strong matrix

   B. Functional

   C. Weak matrix

   D. Projectized

6. This describes how you will know the completed deliverables are satisfactory.

    A. Acceptance criteria

    B. KPIs

    C. Metrics

    D. EVM

7. Which of the following describes the responsibilities of the project sponsor?

    A. Provides or obtains financial resources

    B. Monitors the delivery of major milestones

    C. Runs interference and removes roadblocks

    D. Provides the project manager with authority to manage the project

    E. All of the above

8. Project managers may spend up to 90 percent of their time doing which of the following?

    A. Interacting with the project stakeholders

    B. Interacting with the project sponsor

    C. Interacting with the project team members

    D. Communicating

9. This type of estimate is predicated on historical data and expert judgment.

    A. Top-down

    B. Bottom-up

    C. Parametric

    D. Appraisal

10. Which of these is not an example of a project selection method?

    A. Cost-benefit analysis

    B. Expert judgment

    C. Top-down estimating

    D. Scoring model

11. You're the project manager on a project where the scope has expanded. The change has been approved by the change control board (CCB). What steps must you take to acknowledge the expansion? Choose two.

    A. Modify the project scope statement.

    B. Modify the project charter document.

    C. Obtain a new sign-off on the project scope statement.

    D. Obtain a new sign-off on the project charter document.

12. Some team members on your team are driving each other crazy. They have different ways of organizing the tasks they are both assigned to, and the disparity in styles is causing them to bicker. Which of the following describes this situation?

   A. This is a situation the project manager should resolve as soon as possible.

   B. This should be escalated to the project sponsor.

   C. This is a common cause of conflict.

   D. This is a team formation stage that will pass as they get to know each other better.

13. Ishikawa diagrams, Pareto diagrams, trend analysis, flowcharts, statistical sampling, and run charts are tools and techniques used in which process?

   A. Risk Monitoring and Control

   B. Quality Control

   C. Cost Budgeting

   D. Scope Verification

14. Which of the following project documents created in the project Closing process group describes what went well and what didn't go well on the project?

   A. Project close report

   B. Post-mortem

   C. Lessons learned

   D. Post-project review

15. This document authorizes the project to begin.

   A. Customer request

   B. Concept document

   C. Project charter

   D. Project scope statement

16. Which of these can convey that you've achieved the completion of an interim key deliverable?

   A. Completion criteria

   B. Milestone

   C. Gantt chart

   D. Project sign-off document

17. When should you seek recommendations from the sponsor to either kill a project or come up with alternative strategies? Choose three.

   A. When costs far outreach the budgeted amount that the project was originally given

   B. When an activity is insurmountable

   C. When the elapsed time used for one or more tasks far exceeds time estimates

   D. When the enthusiasm of the project sponsor wanes

18. This process defines what people or groups need information regarding the project, when the information should be distributed, how often it should be distributed, and the format it should be delivered in.

    A. Information distribution

    B. Communications planning

    C. Communications distribution

    D. Information planning

19. This type of analysis is performed during procurement planning to determine cost effectiveness.

    A. Monte Carlo

    B. Decision tree

    C. Make-or-buy

    D. Quantitative analysis

20. What is one important step that new project managers might overlook when faced with a possible scope change?

    A. Telling the customer no

    B. Determining an alternative solution

    C. Alerting vendors

    D. Communicating with the CCB

21. What signals the end of the Planning phase?

    A. The project team begins to execute the tasks in the project plan.

    B. The project scope document is formally signed.

    C. The vendor delivers the materials, equipment, or supplies.

    D. The project management plan is approved and signed.

22. The last document you'll prepare during scope definition is which of the following?

    A. Scope document

    B. Work breakdown structure (WBS)

    C. Scope management plan

    D. Project plan

23. Which cost-estimating technique relies on estimating work packages and then rolling up these estimates to come up with a total cost estimate?

    A. Top-down

    B. Parametric

    C. Bottom-up

    D. Analogous

24. In project management, the process of taking high-level project requirements and breaking them down into the tasks that will generate the deliverables is called what?

   A. Analyzing

   B. Decomposing

   C. Entity-relationship diagramming

   D. Documenting

25. Who is responsible for assembling the project's team members?

   A. Project sponsor

   B. Project stakeholders

   C. Project customer

   D. Project manager

26. All of the following represent a category of contract most commonly used in procurement except for which one?

   A. Time-and-materials

   B. Cost-reimbursable

   C. Fixed-price

   D. Fixed-price plus incentive

27. A well-written change control process should include which of the following components? Choose three.

   A. A description of the type of change requested

   B. The amount of time the change will take to implement

   C. The cost of the change

   D. How to update the affected project planning documents

   E. The stages at which changes are accepted

28. Your project sponsor has lost interest in the current project and has focused all their attention on a new project. The equipment originally intended for your project has been redistributed to other parts of the organization. What type of project ending does this describe?

   A. Integration

   B. Starvation

   C. Addition

   D. Extinction

29. All of the following are true regarding CPI except for which one?

   A. If CPI is greater than one, you've spent more money than anticipated at the measurement date.

   B. CPI is the most critical of all the EVM measurements.

   C. The CPI formula is EV/AC.

   D. Performance indexes are primarily used to calculate performance efficiencies.

30. Risk analysis includes all of the following except for which one?

   A. Qualitative risk analysis

   B. Quantitative risk analysis

   C. Avoid, transfer, mitigate, and accept

   D. Probability and impact

31. Which of the following are project management process groups? Choose three.

   A. Scheduling

   B. Planning

   C. Executing

   D. Communicating

   E. Documenting

   F. Budgeting

   G. Closing

32. When taking over an incomplete project, what item should be of most interest to the new project manager?

   A. Project concept document

   B. Project charter

   C. Project scope document

   D. Project plan

33. All of the following describe the purpose for the Distribute Information process except for which one?

   A. This is where the communications management plan is put into action.

   B. Information may take the form of status reports, project meetings, and so on.

   C. Lessons learned and feedback are gathered from the stakeholders.

   D. Barriers such as cultural differences, geographical locations, and technology should be taken into account when administering this process.

34. You are performing the Close Procurements process and have just verified that the work completed on contract is not accurate and does not meet with your satisfaction. What procedure did you use to determine this?

   A. Scope verification

   B. Post-project review

   C. Vendor analysis

   D. Product verification

35. What key meeting is held at the beginning of the Executing processes?

    A. Project kickoff

    B. Project review

    C. Project overview

    D. Project status meeting

36. What is the best way to prevent scope creep?

    A. Make sure the requirements are thoroughly defined and documented.

    B. Put a statement in the charter that no additions to the project will be allowed once it's underway.

    C. Alert the sponsor that you will not be taking any change requests after the project starts.

    D. Inform stakeholders when they sign the project scope statement that no changes will be accepted after the scope statement is published.

37. Which of these statements describes an assumption?

    A. Our most senior web developer will be available to work on this project.

    B. The electrical capacity at the site of the project event may not be adequate.

    C. The project's due date is June 27.

    D. There's a potential for server administrator to receive a promotion during the course of this project.

38. Your subject matter expert tells you that her most likely estimate is 40 hours, her pessimistic estimate is 65 hours, and her optimistic estimate is 24 hours. What is the final three-point estimate?

    A. 129 hours

    B. 42 hours

    C. 40 hours

    D. 43 hours

39. This is the final, approved version of the project schedule. All of the following are true regarding this term except for which of the following?

    A. It will prevent future schedule risk.

    B. It's approved by the stakeholders, sponsor, and functional managers.

    C. It's used to monitor project progress throughout the remainder of the project.

    D. This describes a schedule baseline.

40. What are the two types of charts that you might utilize to display the project schedule? Choose two.

    A. Gantt

    B. GERT

    C. Milestone chart

    D. CPM

    E. Histogram

41. All of the following describe types of project endings except for which one?

   A. Integration

   B. Starvation

   C. Addition

   D. Extinction

   E. Attrition

42. The project kick-off meeting should ideally occur when?

   A. After the project scope statement is completed

   B. Once the scope management plan is approved

   C. Before you begin creating the WBS

   D. After the project charter is signed

43. This element of the Executing process group encompasses standards compliance, internal process compliance, decision oversight, and phase gate approvals.

   A. Project oversight

   B. Project governance

   C. Organizational oversight

   D. Organizational governance

44. "Install an Interactive Voice Response System that will increase customer response time by an average of 15 seconds and decrease the number of customer service interactions by 40 percent" is an example of which of the following elements of the project charter?

   A. High-level requirements

   B. Goals and objectives

   C. Project description

   D. Milestone

45. The network communication model is a visual depiction of what?

   A. Lines of communication

   B. Participant model

   C. Communication model

   D. Participant communication model

46. Select the component that is not a member of the Planning process group.

   A. Risk identification

   B. Risk quantification

   C. Risk response development

   D. Risk control

47. This EVM figure represents the money that's been expended during a given time period for the completed work.

    A. PV

    B. EV

    C. BAC

    D. AC

48. Which of the following is not a true statement about cost estimating?

    A. Cost estimates are provided by team members.

    B. Cost estimates make up the project budget.

    C. Cost estimates have a quality factor built into them.

    D. You should average all cost estimates.

49. You're the project manager for a small project that is in the Closing phase. You prepare closure documents and take them to the project sponsor for sign-off. The project sponsor says that the documents are not needed because the project is so small. What should you tell the sponsor?

    A. You're sorry to have bothered them and will close the project without sign-off.

    B. The sponsor is the one who needs to sign off on the documents, showing that the project is officially closed.

    C. You offer to have a stakeholder sign off in the sponsor's place.

    D. You offer to sign off on the documents yourself.

50. This EVM figure represents the value of the work completed to date compared to the budget.

    A. PV

    B. EV

    C. BAC

    D. AC

Answers to Assessment Test

1. B. Tasks with zero float are critical path tasks, and if delayed, they'll cause the delay of the project completion date. For more information, please see Chapter 4.

2. C. In most situations, the team members would have been chosen during the Planning processes and assembled together for the first time during the Executing stage, so you wouldn't be negotiating for resources in this phase. The same is true for option D in that the procurement planning and negotiating would have taken place during Planning. Adjusting tasks would have also occurred during Planning or could potentially occur as the result of change requests during the Controlling processes. Negotiating in Executing is used as a conflict-resolution technique. For more information, please see Chapter 7.

3. A. A weighted scoring model is a tool that weights evaluation criteria and provides a way to score vendor responses. Bidder conferences, IFB, and SOW are all used during vendor solicitation. For more information, please see Chapter 5.

4. A, C, F. The five stages of team development are forming, storming, norming, performing, and adjourning. For more information, please see Chapter 7.

5. A. This describes a strong matrix organization because the project manager works in a division whose sole responsibility is project management, and once the team members are assigned to the project, the project manager has the authority to hold them accountable to their tasks and activities. For more information, please see Chapter 1.

6. A. Acceptance criteria describe how to determine whether the deliverables are complete and meet the requirements of the project. For more information, please see Chapter 3.

7. E. A project sponsor is responsible for obtaining financial resources for the project, monitoring the progress of the project, and handling escalations from the project manager. For more information, please see Chapter 2.

8. D. Project managers may spend up to 90 percent of their time communicating. For more information, please see Chapter 1.

9. A. A top-down estimate relies on historical data and expert judgment. It's also known as *analogous estimating*. For more information, please see Chapter 6.

10. C. Cost-benefit analysis, expert judgment, and scoring are all project selection techniques. Top-down estimating is a type of cost estimating. For more information, please see Chapter 1.

11. A, C. Any time there's a significant expansion or modification to the project, the project scope statement must be modified and agreed to in writing by obtaining sign-off. For more information, please see Chapter 8.

12. C. This situation describes varying work styles that are a common cause of conflict. Competing resource demands and expert judgment are also common causes of conflict. This isn't a situation the project manager should jump into immediately. It's better if the project team members can work this out on their own first. And issues like this should almost never have to be escalated to the project sponsor. For more information, please see Chapter 7.

13. B. .Quality Control concerns reviewing project results and determining whether they comply with the standards documented in the quality management plan. This process uses several tools and techniques, as stated in the question. For more information, please see Chapter 9.

14. C. Lessons learned describe what went well and what didn't go well on the project. Lessons learned are included in the project close report, the post-mortem report, and the post-project review. For more information, please see Chapter 10.

15. C. The project charter authorizes the project to begin. For more information, please see Chapter 2.

16. B. Milestones signal that you've completed one of the key deliverables on the project. For more information, please see Chapter 4.

17. A, B, C. When the project's costs exceed its budget, you have to go to the sponsor and get input on what to do next. When the elapsed time taken for one or more tasks far exceeds your initial time estimates or you find that the project activity is insurmountable, it's time to visit with the stakeholders and project sponsor to see whether you need an extension or whether it's time to kill the project. If the sponsor loses interest, it's time to talk with the sponsor, not necessarily to pull the plug on the project. For more information, please see Chapter 8.

18. B. Communications planning defines the type of information, frequency, format, and method of distribution the project stakeholders require during the course of the project. For more information, please see Chapter 5.

19. C. Make-or-buy analysis is performed during procurement planning to determine the cost-effectiveness of either making the goods and services in-house or procuring them from an outside vendor. For more information, please see Chapter 5.

20. B. When faced with the possibility of a scope change, the project manager should determine whether there are alternatives that would lessen the impact of the proposed change. For more information, please see Chapters 8.

21. D. After the sponsor has formally signed the project management plan, you've finished the Planning stage and now move into the Executing process. For more information, please see Chapter 6.

22. B. The WBS is a deliverables-oriented hierarchy that defines all the project work and is completed after the scope management plan and scope statement are completed. For more information, please see Chapter 3.

23. C. The bottom-up cost-estimating method is the most precise because you begin your estimating at the activities in the work package and roll them up for a total estimate. For more information, please see Chapter 6.

24. B. Decomposition is the process of analyzing the requirements of the project in such a way that you reduce the requirements down to the steps and tasks needed to produce them. For more information, please see Chapter 2.

25. D. The project manager assembles the team members for the project. The project manager may get input from the sponsor, stakeholders, or customers, but it is the project manager who decides what the formation of the team should be. For more information, please see Chapter 1.

26. D. The three categories of contracts most often used to procure goods and services are time-and-materials, cost-reimbursable, and fixed-price. Fixed-price plus incentive is a type of cost-reimbursable contract. For more information, please see Chapter 5.

27. A, D, E. The amount of time and money a change will require are outcomes of a change control process, not inputs to the process. For more information, please see Chapter 8.

28. A. Integration occurs when resources are distributed to other areas of the organization, and addition occurs when projects evolve into ongoing operations. Starvation is a project ending caused by resources being cut off from the project. Extinction occurs when the project work is completed and is accepted by the stakeholders. For more information, please see Chapter 10.

29. A. If CPI is greater than one, you've spent less money than anticipated (not more, as the option states) at the measurement date. For more information, please see Chapter 9.

30. C. Avoid, transfer, mitigate, and accept are negative risk strategies used in the risk response process. For more information, please see Chapter 6.

31. B, C, G. Initiating, Planning, Executing, Monitoring and Controlling, and Closing are the five project management process groups. For more information, please see Chapter 2.

32. C. The project's scope document should be of most interest to the new project manager. The scope statement describes the product description, key deliverables, success and acceptance criteria, key performance indicators, exclusions, assumptions, and constraints. For more information, please see Chapter 3.

33. D. Barriers such as cultural differences, geographical locations, and technology, along with time zones and hierarchical barriers, are taken into account when managing project teams. For more information, please see Chapter 9.

34. D. Product verification determines whether the work of the contract was completed accurately and satisfactorily. Scope verification is performed for project work that is produced by the internal project team (not performed on contract), and the post-project review is performed at the end of the project to capture lessons learned. For more information, please see Chapter 10.

35. A. The project kickoff meeting is held at the beginning of the Executing process group and serves to introduce team members, review the goals and objectives of the project, review stakeholder expectations, and review roles and responsibilities for team members. For more information, please see Chapter 7.

36. A. The best way to avoid scope creep is to make sure the project's requirements have been thoroughly defined and documented. For more information, please see Chapter 3.

37. A. Assumptions are those things we believe to be true. Options B and D describe risks, while option C describes a constraint. For more information, please see Chapter 2.

38. D. Three-point estimates are an average of the most likely, pessimistic, and optimistic estimates. For more information, please see Chapter 4.

39. A. The schedule baseline is the final, approved version of the schedule and is signed by the stakeholders, sponsor, and functional managers. Having a schedule baseline will not prevent future schedule risk. For more information, please see Chapter 4.

40. A, C. Gantt charts and milestone charts are the most commonly used formats to display a project schedule. For more information, please see Chapter 4.

41. E. Integration occurs when resources are distributed to other areas of the organization, and addition occurs when projects evolve into ongoing operations. Starvation is a project ending caused by resources being cut off from the project. Extinction occurs when the project work is completed and is accepted by the stakeholders. For more information, please see Chapter 10.

42. D. The project kick-off meeting should be held after the project charter is signed and ideally before the project scope statement is written. For more information, please see Chapter 3.

43. D. Organizational governance includes standards compliance, internal process compliance, decision oversight, and phase gate approval. For more information, please see Chapter 7.

44. B. Goals and objectives are specific and measurable. Project descriptions describe the key characteristics of the product, service, or result of the project. These are characteristics, but the clue in this question is the quantifiable results you're looking for at the conclusion of the project. The project description describes the project as a whole and milestones describe major deliverable or accomplishments for the project. For more information, please see Chapter 2.

45. A. Lines of communication describe how many lines of communication exist between participants. The network communication model is a visual depiction of the lines of communication. For more information, please see Chapter 5.

46. D. Risk identification, quantification, and risk response development occur in the Planning process of the project. Risk control occurs in the Monitoring and Controlling process group. For more information, please see Chapter 8.

47. D. AC represents the actual costs expended during a given time period for the completed work. PV is the planned value, EV is the earned value, and BAC is the budget at completion. For more information, please see Chapter 9.

48. B. Cost estimates do not make up the project budget; they act as an input to the budget. Cost estimates are provided by the team members who will be performing the task they're estimating. For more information, please see Chapter 6.

49. B. The sponsor is the one who must sign off on the completion of the project, whether successful or unsuccessful. Just as the sponsor is authorized to expend resources to bring forth the project's deliverables, the sponsor must also close the project and sign off. For more information, please see Chapter 10.

50. B. EV is the earned value and represents the value of the work completed to date compared to the budget. AC is the actual cost, PV is the planned value, and BAC is the budget at completion. For more information, please see Chapter 9.

Chapter

1

Initiating the Project

THE COMPTIA PROJECT+ EXAM TOPICS COVERED IN THIS CHAPTER INCLUDE

✓ **1.1 Explain the requirements to complete a pre-project setup**

- Identify the project

- Validate the project

- Prepare a project charter

- Obtain approval (signature) for project charter

✓ **1.2 Identify the characteristics of a project**

- Temporary endeavor

- Delivers a unique product or service

- Constrained by time

- Resources and quality

✓ **1.3 Summarize the steps required to validate a project**

- Validate business case (Feasibility analysis, Justification for project, Alignment to strategic plan)

- Identify and analyze stakeholders

✓ **1.6 Explain the different types of organizational structures**

- Functional

- Weak matrix

- Matrix

- Strong matrix

- Project Based

Your decision to take the CompTIA Project+ exam is an important step in your career aspirations. Certification is becoming more important for project managers, and many employers look for real-life experience and evidence of formal education, as well as project management certification from job applicants. This book is designed to provide you with the necessary concepts to prepare for the Project+ exam. Much of the information here will be based on the Knowledge Areas documented in *A Guide to the Project Management Body of Knowledge (PMBOK Guide)* published by the *Project Management Institute (PMI)*. We will include tips on how to prepare for the exam, as well as examples and real-world scenarios to illustrate the concepts.

This chapter will cover the definitions and characteristics of a project, a high-level overview of project management, how organizations are structured, and pre-project setup.

Defining the Project

Projects exist to bring about or fulfill the goals of the organization. Most projects benefit from the application of a set of processes and standards known as *project management*. Let's start with some fundamental questions:

- What makes a new assignment a project?
- How do you know if you are working on a project?
- What distinguishes a project from an operational activity?

Projects involve a team of people, and so do day-to-day business activities. They both involve following a process or a plan, and they both result in activities that help reach a goal. So, what is so different about a project? We'll answer these questions in the following sections.

Identifying the Project and Pre-project Setup

A *project* is a temporary endeavor that has definite beginning and ending dates, and it results in a unique product, service, or result. Projects are considered a success when the goals they set out to accomplish are fulfilled and the stakeholders are satisfied with the results.

Projects also bring about a product, service, or result that never existed before. This may include creating tangible goods, implementing software, writing a book, planning and executing an employee appreciation event, and more. There is no limit to what can be considered a project as long as it fits the following criteria:

Unique   A project is typically undertaken to meet a specific business objective. It involves doing something new, which means that the end result should be a unique product or service. These products may be marketed to others, may be used internally, may provide support for ongoing operations, and so on.

Temporary   Projects have definite start and end dates. The time it takes to complete the work of the project can vary in overall length from a few weeks to several years, but there is always a start date and an end date.

Resources and quality   According to CompTIA, the characteristics of a project include assigning resources to complete the work of the project and assuring the results of the project meet the quality standards outlined in the project plan. We'll talk about quality standards in more depth in Chapter 6, "Defining the Cost, Risk, and Quality Plans."

Stakeholder satisfaction   A project starts once it's been identified, the objectives have been outlined in the project charter, and appropriate stakeholders have approved the project plan. A project ends when those goals have been met to the satisfaction of the stakeholders.

Identifying the project is the first step in the pre-project setup. Once you've identified the project, you'll validate the project (we'll cover this topic in the section "Validating the Project" later in this chapter) and then write the project charter and obtain approval for the charter. We'll talk in more detail about the project charter in Chapter 2, "Project Process Groups and the Project Charter."

Understanding Operations

Operations are ongoing and repetitive. They don't have a beginning date or an ending date, unless you're starting a new operation or retiring an old one. Operations typically involve ongoing functions that support the production of goods or services. Projects, on the other hand, come about to meet a specific, unique result and then conclude.

It's important to understand that projects and operations go hand in hand in many cases. For example, perhaps you've been assigned to research and implement state-of-the-art equipment for a shoe manufacturing plant. Once the implementation of the equipment is complete, the project is concluded. A handoff to the operations team occurs, and the everyday tasks the equipment performs become an ongoing operation.

Don't be confused by the term *service* regarding the definition of a project. Providing janitorial services on a contract is operations; providing contract Java programmers for 18 months to work on an IT project is a project.

Another term you may come across regarding projects is *program*. A program is a group of related projects that are managed together using coordinated processes and techniques. The collective management of a group of projects can bring about benefits that wouldn't be achievable if the projects were managed separately. For example, the defense industry often utilizes program management to manage the sometimes hundreds of projects related to one over-arching goal such as placing a computerized rover on Mars.

Many organizations have project management offices (PMOs) in place that manage projects and programs. PMOs are responsible for maintaining standards, processes, and procedures related to the management of projects. They are responsible for identifying the various projects across the organization and including them within a program, where appropriate, to capitalize on the collective benefits of all the projects within the program. For example, your PMO may have a program that manages all projects for the accounting functions within the organization. This doesn't mean the projects affect accounting personnel only. Let's say your organization wants to implement a new reporting system for accounting data. This will involve the accounting department personnel, the information technology personnel, and the recipients of the reports.

Let's look at the definition of two more terms. *Project management* brings together a set of tools and techniques—performed by people—to describe, organize, and monitor the work of project activities. *Project managers* are the people responsible for applying these tools to the various project activities. Their primary purpose is to integrate all the components of the project and bring it to a successful conclusion. Managing a project involves many skills, including dealing with competing needs for your resources, obtaining adequate budget dollars, identifying risks, managing to the project requirements, interacting with stakeholders, staying on schedule, and ensuring a quality product.

 We'll spend the remainder of this book describing the tools and techniques you'll use to accomplish the goals of the project, including the key concepts you'll need to know for the exam. Many of the standards surrounding these techniques are documented in the *PMBOK Guide*.

Using the *PMBOK Guide*

Project management standards are documented in *A Guide to the Project Management Body of Knowledge* (*PMBOK Guide*), published by the Project Management Institute. PMI sets the global de facto standard in project management. It's a large organization with more than 400,000 members from countries around the globe.

In addition to publishing the *PMBOK Guide*, PMI also manages two rigorous certification exams for individual project managers: the Certified Associate in Project Management (CAPM) and the Project Management Professional (PMP). The *PMBOK Guide* is the basis for the exam portion of the CAPM and PMP certifications. If you continue in a career in project management, you may decide to study and sit for the CAPM or PMP certification exams. The material you will study to prepare for the Project+ exam is an excellent foundation on which to build your project management knowledge.

Understanding Organizational Structures

The structure of your organization has an impact on many aspects of project management, including the authority of the project manager and the process to assign resources.

Project managers are often frustrated by what appear to be roadblocks in moving the project forward, but in many cases, the root issue is the organizational structure itself and how it operates. In the following sections, we'll cover the different types of organizational structures and how they influence the way projects are conducted.

Functional Organization

The classic organizational structure is the *functional organization*, as shown in Figure 1.1. In this structure, the staff is organized along departmental lines, such as IT, marketing, sales, network, public relations, customer support, and legal. Each department is managed independently with a limited span of control. This organizational type is hierarchical in nature, with each staff member reporting to one supervisor, who in turn reports to one supervisor, and so on up the chain. Figure 1.1 shows a typical functional organization.

FIGURE 1.1   The functional organization

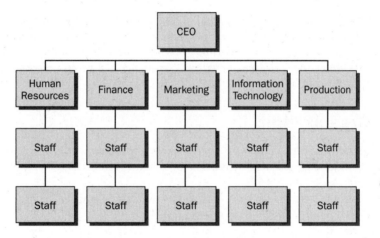

A functional organization often goes about the work of the project in a siloed fashion. That is, the project deliverables are worked on independently in different departments. This can cause frustration among project managers, because they are the ones held accountable for the results of the project, but they have no means of holding team members from other departments accountable for completing project deliverables.

A project manager in a functional organization should develop strong working relationships with the functional managers. Functional managers are responsible for assigning work to the employees who report to them. They are also responsible for rating the performance of the employees and determining their raises or bonuses. This, as you can imagine, sets up a strong loyalty between the employee and the functional manager as opposed to the employee and the project manager. However, that doesn't mean project managers can't be successful in this type of organization. Building a relationship with the functional managers and maintaining open communications is the key to successful projects in this type of structure. It also helps a great deal if you can contribute to the employee's performance ratings by rating their work on the project.

> **NOTE** Project managers have little formal authority in this type of structure, but it doesn't mean their projects are predestined for failure. Communication skills, negotiation skills, and strong interpersonal skills will help assure your success in working within this type of environment.

The functional organization is the most common organizational structure and has endured for centuries. The advantages of a functional organization include the following:

- Growth potential and a career path for employees
- The opportunity for those with unique skills to flourish
- A clear chain of command (each staff member has one supervisor)

The typical disadvantages of a functional organization include the following: the project managers have limited authority, multiple projects compete for the same limited resources, resources are generally committed part-time to projects rather than full-time, issue resolution must follow the department chain of command, and project team members are loyal to the functional manager.

Matrix Organization

The next organizational structure we'll cover is a *matrix organization*. There are three types of matrix organizations, as discussed in a moment. Figure 1.2 shows a balanced matrix organization.

FIGURE 1.2 The balanced matrix organization

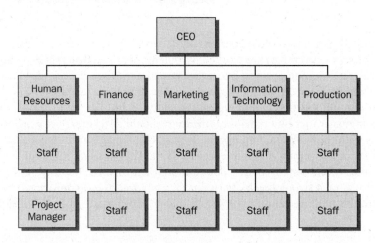

Matrix organizations typically are organized along departmental lines, like a functional organization, but resources assigned to a project are accountable to the project manager for all work associated with the project. The project manager is often a peer of the functional staff managers. The team members working on the project often have two or more supervisors—their functional manager and the project manager(s) they are reporting to.

Project managers working in a matrix organization need to be very clear with both the project team members and their respective functional managers about assignments and results regarding the following:

- Those outcomes for which the team member is accountable to the project manager
- Those outcomes for which the team member is accountable to the functional manager

The team member should be accountable to only one person for any given outcome so as to avoid confusion and conflicting direction.

Another trouble area in a matrix organization is availability of resources. If you have a resource assigned 50 percent of the time to your project, it's critical that the functional manager, or other project managers working with this resource, is aware of the time commitment this resource has allocated to your project. If time-constraint issues like this are not addressed, project managers may well discover they have fewer human resources for the project than first anticipated. Addressing resource commitments at the beginning of the project, both during pre-project setup and again during the planning phase, will help prevent problems down the road.

 In a typical matrix organization, functional managers assign employees to the project, while project managers assign tasks associated with the project to the employee.

The following are the typical characteristics of a matrix organization:

- Low to moderate authority for the project manager
- A mix of full-time and part-time project resources
- Better interdepartmental communication

Matrix Organizations Times Three

There are three types of matrix organizations:

Strong matrix   The strong matrix organization emphasizes project work over functional duties. The project manager has the majority of power in this type of organization.

Weak matrix   The weak matrix organization emphasizes functional work over project work and operates more like a functional hierarchy. The functional mangers have the majority of power in this type of organization.

Balanced matrix   A balanced matrix organization shares equal emphasis between projects and functional work. Both the project manager and the functional manager share power in this type of structure.

> Matrix organizations allow project managers to focus on the work of the project. The project team members, once assigned to a project, are free to focus on the project objectives with minimal distractions from the functional department.

It is important that you understand what type of matrix organization you're working in because the organizational type dictates the level of authority you'll have. But don't be fooled into thinking you will have your way more easily in a strong matrix environment. It is still essential that you keep the lines of communication open with functional managers and inform them of status, employee performance, future needs, project progress, and so on.

Project-Based Organization

The last type of organizational structure we'll cover is the *project-based organization*, which is shown in Figure 1.3. This organizational structure is far less common than the other two we've discussed. In this environment, the focus of the organization is projects, rather than functional work units.

FIGURE 1.3   The project-based organization

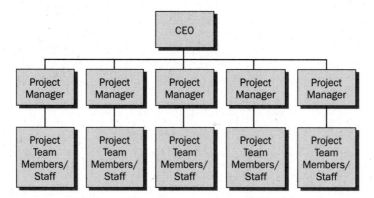

Project managers almost always have the majority of power in this type of structure. They are responsible for making decisions regarding the project and for acquiring and assigning resources from inside or outside the organization. Support staff, such as human resources, administrative support, accounting, and so on, often report to the project manager in a project-based environment.

One of the advantages of this type of organization is that team members are *co-located*, meaning they work together at the same physical location. Other advantages of this structure include the following: the project manager has a high authority level, full-time resources are assigned to the project, loyalty is established with the project manager rather than a functional manager, and you have a dedicated project support staff.

One of the biggest drawbacks of a project-based organization is reassigning project team members once the project ends. There may not always be a new project waiting for these resources. Again, it's essential that communication is occurring among project managers across the organization so that the complex timing of increasing or decreasing resources is managed as efficiently as possible.

Validating the Project

Stakeholders have many reasons for bringing about a project. Most organizations don't have the resources or time to execute every project that every stakeholder would like implemented. Validating the project involves two steps: preparing the business case and identifying and analyzing the project stakeholders. But there are some steps along the way you need to understand before and after the business case is written. First, the organization needs to have an understanding of the business need or demand for the project. Then, the business case is created, which includes a justification for the project, and finally, project selection methods are used to determine which projects the organization should implement.

The first step in validating a project is preparing and validating the business case. The business case typically documents the reasons the project came into existence. Before we dive into the business case specifics, we'll cover some of the needs and demands that bring about projects.

How Projects Come About

Projects come about for many reasons. For example, some organizations exist to generate profits, and many create projects specifically designed to meet this goal. Other organizations exist to provide services to others with no regard for profits. And they may bring about projects to enhance their ability to meet the demand for their services. No matter what the reason for bringing about a project, most of them will fall into one of the seven needs or demands described next:

Market demand   The demands of the marketplace can drive the need for a project. For example, the proliferation of handheld devices has created a need for rechargeable batteries that are capable of holding a charge for 12 hours or more.

Strategic opportunity/business need   Business needs often drive projects that involve information technology solutions. For example, the organization's accounting system is outdated and no longer able to keep up with current technology. A new system is implemented to help the organization become more efficient and create reports in a timelier manner.

Customer request   Customer requests can generate an endless supply of potential projects. For example, perhaps the discussions at a recent customer focus group brought about the idea for a new product offering.

Technological advance   Technology and business needs sometimes strike us as a chicken-and-egg scenario. Is it the technology that drives the business to think it needs a new product or service, or does the business need drive the development of the new technology? Both scenarios exist, and both bring about the need for new projects.

Legal requirement   Local, state, and federal regulations change during every legislative session and may drive the need for a new project. For example, a city may pass an ordinance allowing photos of red-light violations at busy intersections. The new equipment must then be procured and installed. Federal regulations requiring the encryption and secure storage of private data may bring about the need for a project to fulfill these requirements.

⊕ Real World Scenario

Assessing the Impact of Regulations and Legal Requirements

Projects often have legislative, regulatory, or other third-party restrictions imposed upon their processes or outputs. For example, suppose that you are managing a project that will create a new information technology system for a funds management company, one that's in the business of managing individual stock portfolios. You can imagine that this company is heavily regulated by the Securities and Exchange Commission (SEC) and that your new system, in turn, will encounter several regulatory guidelines that you must follow. The security aspect of your new system is especially pertinent. You must be able to assure the SEC and your shareholders that the system is hack-proof.

It's important that a project manager be able to not only recognize the need to investigate specific industry regulations and requirements but also communicate this need and its associated impact on the project scope and project plan to the stakeholders. Here are a few examples of the many external considerations you need to account for when implementing a technology-based project:

Legal and regulatory conditions   Know the statutes covering the type of activity your deliverable involves. If you collect information about customers, are you complying with privacy laws? Do you know which types of encryption can be exported legally? Also, you may face government reporting and documentation requirements or public-disclosure rules.

Licensing terms   Suppose that part of your project requires that developers write some code according to a Microsoft application programming interface (API). You need to be well aware of the licensing ramifications associated with using a Microsoft API. Trademark, copyright, and intellectual property issues all enter into this category.

Industry standards   Your project may utilize various interfaces between systems. Is there some standard that governs such things? For example, Microsoft uses the Web-Based Enterprise Management (WBEM) standards to move management data from one place to another. You will need to find out how your new system can use the Windows Management Instrumentation (WMI) interface to provide support for a heterogeneous system that you're developing. Theoretically, you would need to determine what, if any, specific methodologies or approved coding practices should be used in the implementation of your project.

Considerations such as these must be accounted for in the project plan and budget.

Ecological impact   Many organizations today are actively involved in green efforts to protect the environment. For example, perhaps a new Environmental Protection Agency (EPA) mandate requires extra equipment and processes to be implemented in your production assembly line to minimize pollution output. Therefore, a project is required.

Social need   Social needs or demands can bring about projects in a variety of ways. For example, a small developing country may have the need for safe, clean drinking water, so a project is initiated to purchase and install a new filtering system. Another example may include bringing about a project to develop a vaccine for a new flu virus that's predicted to hit the nation.

The needs or demands that bring about a project are usually stated in the business case. We'll look at the business case next.

Business Case Validation and Stakeholder Identification

Validating the project occurs by preparing a business case and indentifying and analyzing stakeholders. There are several steps to validating a business case as well. We'll cover all these project validation steps next.

Validating the Business Case

One of the first things a project manager can do at the onset of a project is to determine the business reason for the project. The business case, which is often based on one of the needs or demands we discussed in the previous section, is a written document or report that helps executive management and key stakeholders determine the benefits and rewards of the project. It documents the business need or justification for the project and will often include high-level details regarding estimated budgets and timelines for completing the project.

Feasibility study   A *feasibility study* is a formal endeavor that is undertaken to determine whether there is a compelling reason to perform the proposed project. Feasibility studies can examine the viability of the product, service, or result of the project. They may also examine technical issues related to the project and determine whether it's feasible, reliable, and easily assimilated into the organization's existing infrastructure. Not all business cases will or should include a feasibility study. Feasibility studies are usually conducted when the proposed project is highly complex, has a high potential for risk, or is a new type of project the organization has never undertaken before. Feasibility studies may be conducted as separate projects, as subprojects, or as a pre-project phase. It's best to treat this activity as a project when the outcome is uncertain.

Justification   Justification describes the benefits to the organization for undertaking the project. These benefits can include tangible and intangible benefits and should include the reasons for bringing about the project. Justification can be a section within the business case or an independent document.

Alignment to the strategic plan   Alignment to the strategic plan can also be included within the business case, and it should describe how the project and its outcomes will align to the organization's overall strategic plan. If the reason for the project doesn't support the strategic plan, there's really no reason to undertake the project.

Identifying and Analyzing Stakeholders

Stakeholders are anyone who has a vested interest in the project. Stakeholders can include individuals as well as organizations, and both the project sponsor and the project manager are considered stakeholders. The project sponsor is the executive in the organization who authorizes the project to begin and is someone who has the ability to assign funds and resources to the project. Identifying stakeholders is also a component of the project charter. We'll spend most of Chapter 2 talking about the project charter, and we'll go into much more detail about stakeholders in that chapter as well.

Project Selection

After the business case is created, you'll need some method to decide how you or the project selection committee will choose among competing projects.

Project selection methods are used to determine which proposed projects should receive approval and move forward. This process usually includes the allocation of high-level funding as well. Project selection may take place using formal documented guidelines, or it may be informal, requiring only the approval of a certain level of management.

Typically, a high-level board or committee will perform project selection. This committee may be cross-functional in nature and accountable for corporate-wide project selection, or selection may be determined on a departmental basis. A committee at the corporate level is composed of representatives from all departments, such as information technology, sales, marketing, finance, and customer service.

Project Selection Methods

A project selection committee uses a set of criteria to evaluate and select proposed projects. The selection method needs to be applied consistently across all projects to ensure the company is making the best decision in terms of strategic fit as well as the best use of limited resources.

Project selection methods will vary depending on the mission of the organization, the people serving on the selection committee, the criteria used, and the project itself. These methods could include examining factors such as market share, financial benefits, return on investment, customer satisfaction, and public perception. The exact criterion varies, but selection methods usually involve a combination of decision models and expert judgment.

Decision Models

A *decision model* is a formal method of project selection that helps managers make decisions regarding the use of limited budgets and human resources. Requests for projects can span a large spectrum of needs, and it can be difficult to determine a priority without a means of comparison. Is an online order entry application for the sales team more important than the addition of online help for the customer-support team? To the impacted departments, each project is probably viewed as a number-one priority. The problem is there may not be adequate budget or staffing to complete both requests, and a decision must be made to approve one request and deny the other. Unless you can make an "apples-to-apples" comparison of the two requests, the decision will be very subjective. A decision model uses a fixed set of criteria agreed on by the project selection committee to evaluate the project requests. By using the same model to evaluate each project request, the selection committee has a common ground on which to compare the projects and make the most objective decision. You can use a variety of decision models, and they range from a basic ranking matrix to elaborate mathematical models.

There are two primary categories of decision models: benefit measurement methods and constrained-optimization models.

Benefit Measurement Methods

Benefit measurement methods provide a means to compare the benefits obtained from project requests by evaluating them using the same criteria. Benefit measurement methods are the most commonly used of the two categories of decision models. Four common benefit measurement methods are cost-benefit analysis, scoring model, payback period, and economic model.

Cost-benefit analysis   A *cost-benefit analysis* compares the cost to produce the product or service to the financial gain (or benefit) the organization stands to make as a result of executing the project. You should include development costs of the product or service, marketing costs, technology costs, and ongoing support, if applicable, when calculating total costs.

Let's say your proposed project involves developing and marketing a new product. The total costs are projected at $3 million. Based on market research, it appears the demand for this product will be high and that projected revenues will exceed the organization's goals. In this case, the cost-benefit analysis is positive and is a strong indicator you should select this project provided the business case justifies it as well.

The cost-benefit model is a good choice if the project selection decision is based on how quickly the project investment will be recouped from either decreased expenses or increased revenue. The weakness of using a cost-benefit analysis is that it does not account for other important factors, such as strategic value. The project that pays for itself in the shortest time is not necessarily the project that is most critical to the organization.

Scoring model   A *scoring model* has a predefined list of criteria against which each project is rated. Each criterion is given both a scoring range and a weighting factor. The weighting factor accounts for the difference in importance of the various criteria. Scoring models can include financial data, as well as items such as market value, organizational expertise to complete the project, innovation, and fit with corporate culture. Scoring models have a combination of objective and subjective criteria. The final score for an individual project request is obtained by calculating the rating and weighting factor of each criteria. Some companies have a minimum standard for the scoring model. If this minimum standard is not obtained, the project will be eliminated from the selection process. A benefit of the scoring model is that you can place a heavier weight on a criterion that is of more importance. Using a high weighting factor for innovation may produce an outcome where a project with a two-year time frame to pay back the cost of the project may be selected over a project that will recoup all costs in six months. The weakness of a scoring model is that the ranking it produces is only as valuable as the criteria and weighting system the ranking is based on. Developing a good scoring model is a complex process that requires a lot of interdepartmental input at the executive level.

Payback period   The *payback period* is a cash flow technique that identifies the length of time it takes for the organization to recover all the costs of producing the project. It compares the initial investment to the expected cash inflows over the life of the project and determines how many time periods elapse before the project pays for itself. Payback period is the least precise of all the cash flow techniques we'll discuss in this section.

You can also use payback period for projects that don't have expected cash inflows. For example, you might install a new call-handling system that generates efficiencies in your call center operations by allowing the call center to grow over the next few years without having to add staff. The cost avoidance of hiring additional staff can be used in place of the expected cash inflows to calculate payback period.

Gustave Eiffel

The extraordinary engineer Gustave Eiffel put up the majority of the money required to build the Eiffel tower, nearly $2 million, himself. This was quite a sum in 1889. Tourism revenues exceeded the cost of constructing the tower in a little more than one year. That's a payback period any project manager would love to see. And Eiffel didn't stop there. He was wise enough to negotiate a contract for tourism revenues from the tower for the next 20 years.

Economic model   An *economic model* is a series of financial calculations, also known as cash flow techniques, which provide data on the overall financials of the project. A whole book can be dedicated to financial evaluation, so we will give you a brief overview of some of the common terms you may encounter when using an economic model: discounted cash flow, net present value, and internal rate of return.

Discounted cash flow   The *discounted cash flow* technique compares the value of the future worth of the project's expected cash flows to today's dollars. For example, if you expected your project to bring in $450,000 in year 1, $2.5 million in year 2, and $3.2 million in year 3, you'd calculate the present value of the revenues for each year and then add up all the years to determine a total value of the cash flows in today's dollars. Discounted cash flows for each project are then compared to other similar projects on the selection list. Typically, projects with the highest discounted cash flows are chosen over those with lower discounted cash flows.

Net present value   *Net present value (NPV)* is a cash flow technique that calculates the revenues or cash flows the organization expects to receive over the life of the project in today's dollars. For example, let's say your project is expected to generate revenues over the next five years. The revenues you receive in year 2, 3, and so on are worth less than the revenues you receive today. NPV is a mathematical formula that allows you to determine the value of the investment for each period in today's dollars. Each period's resulting sum in present-day dollars is added together. The initial investment is subtracted from that sum to come up with an overall value for the project. The rule for NPV is that if NPV is greater than zero, you should accept the project. If it's less than zero, you should reject the project.

The difference between NPV and discounted cash flows is that NPV subtracts the total cash flow in today's dollars from the initial project investment. Discounted cash flow totals the value of each period's expected cash flow to come up with a total value for the project in today's terms.

Internal rate of return   *Internal rate of return (IRR)* is the discount rate when the present value of the cash inflows equals the original investment. IRR states the profitability of an investment as an average percent over the life of the investment. The general rule is that projects with higher IRR values are considered better than projects with lower IRR values.

Constrained Optimization Models

Constrained optimization models are mathematical models, some of which are very complicated. They are typically used in very complex projects and require a detailed understanding of statistics and other mathematical concepts. A discussion of these models is beyond the scope of this book.

Expert Judgment

Expert judgment relies on the expertise of stakeholders, subject matter experts, or those who have previous experience to help reach a decision regarding project selection. Typically, expert judgment is used in conjunction with one of the decision models discussed previously.

Companies with an informal project selection process may use only expert judgment to make project selection decisions. Although using only expert judgment can simplify the project selection process, there are dangers in relying on this single technique. It is not likely that the project selection committee members will all be authorities on each of the proposed projects. Without access to comparative data, a project approval decision may be made based solely on who has the best slide presentation or who is the best salesperson.

Political influence can also be part of the expert judgment. An executive with a great deal of influence may convince the selection committee to approve a particular project.

Once your selection committee has selected and approved a list of projects, the project manager will move forward with the project management processes. We'll look at one way these processes are organized in the next section.

Understanding the Project Management Knowledge Areas

The project manager is the person who oversees all the work required to complete the project by using a variety of tools and techniques. The *PMBOK Guide* categorizes these tools and techniques into processes. For example, the Develop Project Charter process outlines inputs, tools and techniques, and outputs for producing the fully documented project charter, which is an output of this process.

The *Project Management Knowledge Areas* are collections of individual processes that have elements in common. For example, the Project Human Resource Management area is comprised of four processes that are all used to help establish, acquire, and manage project resources.

According to the *PMBOK Guide*, these are the nine Project Management Knowledge Areas:

- Project Integration Management
- Project Scope Management
- Project Time Management
- Project Cost Management
- Project Quality Management
- Project Human Resource Management
- Project Communications Management
- Project Risk Management
- Project Procurement Management

As you move through subsequent chapters, we will cover these areas in more detail. Keep in mind that these Knowledge Areas may not have equal importance on your next project. For example, if you are performing a project with internal resources and require a minimum amount of goods or supplies for the project, the Project Procurement Management area will have less emphasis in your project planning activities than the Project Scope Management area.

Understanding the Role of the Project Manager

Like we stated earlier in this chapter, the project manager is the person responsible for integrating all the components of a project and applying the various tools and techniques of project management to bring about a successful conclusion to the project. The project manager's role is diverse and includes activities such as coaching, planning, negotiating, solving problems, and more.

Good soft skills are as critical to the success of a project as good technical skills. We'll examine many of the technical skills needed as they relate to the project management processes in the coming chapters, but we can't neglect talking about the soft skills as well. These are skills any good manager uses on a daily basis to manage resources, solve problems, meet goals, and more.

You probably already use some of these skills in your day-to-day work activities. Here's a partial list:

- Leadership
- Communicating
- Listening
- Organization
- Time management
- Planning
- Problem solving
- Consensus building
- Resolving conflict
- Negotiating
- Team building

Let's examine a few of these skills in a little more detail.

Leadership

A project manager must also be a good leader. Leaders understand how to rally people around a vision and motivate them to achieve amazing results. They set strategic goals, establish direction, and inspire and motivate others. Strong leaders also know how to align and encourage diverse groups of people with varying backgrounds and experience to work together to accomplish the goals of the project.

Leaders possess a passion for their work and for life. They are persistent and diligent in attaining their goals. And they aren't shy about using opportunities that present themselves to better their team members, to better the project results, or to accomplish the organization's mission. Leaders are found at all levels of the organization and aren't necessarily synonymous with people in executive positions. We've known our share of executive staff members who couldn't lead a team down the hall, let alone through the complex maze of project management practices. It's great for you to possess all the technical skills you can acquire as a project manager. But it's even better if you are also a strong leader that others trust and are willing to follow.

Communication

Most project managers will tell you they spend the majority of their day communicating. PMI suggests that project managers should spend up to 90 percent of their time in the act of communicating. It is by far the number-one key to project success. Even the most detailed project plan can fail without adequate communication. And of all the communication skills in your tool bag, listening is the most important. Ideally, you've finely honed your leadership skills and have gained the trust of your team members. When they trust you, they'll tell you things they wouldn't have otherwise. As the project manager, you want to know everything that has the potential to affect the outcomes you're striving for or anything that may impact your team members.

Project managers must develop a communication strategy for the project that includes the following critical components:

- What you want to communicate
- How often you'll communicate
- The audience receiving the communication
- The medium used for communicating
- Monitoring the outcome of the communication

Keeping these components in mind and developing a comprehensive communication plan early in the project will help prevent misunderstanding and conflict as the project progresses.

We'll discuss communication in more detail in Chapter 5, "Communicating the Plan."

Problem Solving

There is no such thing as a project that doesn't have problems. Projects always have problems. Some are just more serious than others. We'll discuss some specific techniques you can use to help with problem solving and conflict resolution in Chapter 7, "Executing the Project."

Early recognition of the warning signs of trouble will simplify the process of successfully resolving problems with minimal impact. Many times, warning signs come about during communications with your stakeholders, team members, vendors, and others. Pay close attention not only to what your team members are saying but also to how they're saying it. Body language plays a bigger part in communication than words do. Learn to read the real meaning behind what your team member is saying and when to ask clarifying questions to get the heart of the issue on the table.

Negotiating

Negotiation is the process of obtaining mutually acceptable agreements with individuals or groups. Like communication and problem-solving skills, this skill is used throughout the life of the project.

Depending on the type of organizational structure you work in, you may start the project by negotiating with functional managers for resources. If you will be procuring goods or services from an outside vendor, you will likely be involved in negotiating a contract or other form of procurement document. Project team members may negotiate specific job assignments. Project stakeholders may change the project objectives, which drives negotiations regarding the schedule, the budget, or both. As you execute the project, change requests often involve complex negotiations as various stakeholders propose conflicting requests. There is no lack of opportunity for you to use negotiating skills during the life of a project, and we'll be talking about many of these examples in more detail in the coming chapters.

🌐 Real World Scenario

Negotiating with the Business Unit

You're working on a software development project for a business unit in your company. You've gotten past the initial project request steps, and you're now in the process of honing in on the details of the requirements for the project.

You require subject matter expertise from the business unit in order to more fully understand and appreciate the business processes that your software is going to automate.

You set up a meeting with the director of the business unit. At the meeting you ask her two things. First, you want to know whether you can use someone from the business unit to assist you in understanding the business process flows. You make it clear that the assigned individual must be a subject matter expert (SME) in the business process. Second, you ask whether you can have this individual full-time for a minimum of two weeks. You suggest the name of someone whom you think will perform very adequately as a business SME.

The director is surprised that you require so much time from one of her people. She asks you to more thoroughly explain your needs. You explain to her that in order for you to develop software that fully meets the business need, you must understand the flows involved in the business process. Further, you describe the process of generating a data flow diagram, which is a block diagram that shows, at a very high, nontechnical level, the process as you see it, noting that you'll need the SME to validate the data flow diagram.

After some bantering back and forth, the two of you come to an agreement that you can have a week and a half of someone's time and that you'll use not one but two different business SMEs, splitting their efforts accordingly so that neither one has to fully dedicate their time to the business flow discovery process. The director stresses repeatedly to you that her people are busy, and she is being very generous in letting you have them at all.

You agree to the specifications, thank her for her time, and get to work figuring out the best questions to ask the SMEs in order to complete the business flow discovery process in as efficient and timely a manner as possible.

Organization and Time Management

As we've stated earlier in this chapter, the project manager oversees all aspects of the work involved in meeting the project goals. The ongoing responsibilities of a typical project manager include tracking schedules and budgets and providing updates on their status, conducting regular team meetings, reviewing team member reports, tracking vendor progress, communicating with stakeholders, meeting individually with team members, preparing formal presentations, managing change requests, and much more. This requires excellent organizational skills and the ability to manage your time effectively. We've found that most project managers are good time managers as well, but if you struggle in this area, we strongly recommend taking a class or two on this topic.

Meetings consume valuable project time, so make certain they are necessary and effective. Effective meetings don't just happen—they result from good planning. Whether you conduct a formal team meeting or an individual session, you should define the purpose of the meeting and develop an agenda of the topics to be discussed or covered. It's good practice to make certain each agenda item has a time limit in order to keep the meeting moving and to finish on time. In our experience, the only thing worse than team members coming late to a scheduled meeting is a meeting that goes past its allotted time frame.

Clear documentation is critical to project success, and you'll want a system that allows you to put your hands on these documents at a moment's notice. Technology comes to the rescue with this task. Microsoft's SharePoint product is an excellent tool to help you organize project documents. Other tools are available to you as well. Find one that works, even if it's a manual system, and keep it up-to-date.

Summary

A project is a temporary endeavor that produces a unique product service or result. It has definitive start and finish dates. Project management is the application of tools and techniques to organize the project activities to successfully meet the project goals. A project manager is responsible for project integration and applying the tools and techniques of project management to bring about a successful conclusion to the project.

Organizational structures impact how projects are managed and staffed. The primary structures are functional, matrix, and project-based. The traditional departmental hierarchy in a functional organization provides the project manager with the least authority. The other end of the spectrum is the project-based organization, where resources are organized around projects; in these types of organizations, the project manager has the greatest level of authority to take action and make decisions regarding the project. The matrix organization is a middle ground between the functional organization and the project-based organization.

Project selection techniques involve the use of decision models, such as a cost-benefit analysis and expert judgment, to allocate limited resources to the most critical projects.

Project managers are individuals charged with overseeing every aspect of a given project from start to finish. A project manager needs not only technical knowledge of the product or service being produced by the project, but also a wide range of general management skills. Key general management skills include leadership, communication, problem solving, negotiation, organization, and time management.

Exam Essentials

Be able to define a project.　A project brings about a unique product, service, or result and has definite beginning and ending dates.

Be able to identify the difference between a project and ongoing operations.　A project is a temporary endeavor to create a unique product or service. Operational work is ongoing and repetitive.

Name the three types of organizational structures.　The three types of organizational structures are functional, matrix, and project-based structures. Matrix organizations may be structured as a strong matrix, weak matrix, or balanced matrix organization.

Be able to define the role of a project manager.　A project manager's core function is project integration. A project manager leads the project team and oversees all the work required to complete the project goals to the satisfaction of the stakeholders.

Be able to identify the most common project selection methods.　The most common project selection methods are benefit measurement methods such as cost-benefit analysis, scoring models, payback period, and economic models (which include discounted cash flows, NPV, and IRR), as well as expert judgment.

Understand what skills are needed to manage a project beyond technical knowledge of the product.　Key general management skills include leadership, communication, problem solving, negotiation, organization, and time management.

Key Terms

Before you take the exam, be certain you are familiar with the following terms:

A Guide to the Project Management Body of Knowledge (PMBOK Guide)

benefit measurement methods

co-located

constrained optimization methods

cost-benefit analysis

decision model

discounted cash flow

economic model

expert judgment

feasibility study

functional organization

internal rate of return (IRR)

matrix organization

net present value (NPV)

operations

payback period

program

project

project-based organization

project management

Project Management Institute (PMI)

Project Management Knowledge Areas

project managers

project selection methods

scoring model

Review Questions

1. What is the definition of a project? Choose two.

   A. A group of interrelated activities that create a unique benefit to the organization

   B. Through the use of project management techniques, which are repeatable processes, a series of actions that are performed to produce the same result multiple times

   C. A temporary endeavor undertaken to create a unique product, service, or result

   D. A process used to generate profit, improve market share, or adhere to legal requirements

   E. A time-constrained endeavor with assigned resources responsible for meeting the goals of the project according to the quality standards

2. What organization is recognized worldwide for setting project management standards?

   A. PMC

   B. PMI

   C. PMP

   D. CompTIA

3. What is the term for a group of related projects managed in a coordinated fashion?

   A. Life cycle

   B. Phase

   C. Process group

   D. Program

4. Which of the following are the requirements to complete a pre-project setup? Choose three.

   A. Conduct a feasibility analysis.

   B. Identify the project.

   C. Validate the project.

   D. Validate the business case.

   E. Prepare a project charter and obtain approval of the charter.

   F. Identify and analyze stakeholders.

5. Which of the following general management skills does a project manager employ up to 90 percent of their time?

   A. Programming

   B. Communications

   C. Leadership

   D. Problem solving

6. You receive a request from customer service to develop and implement a desktop management system for the customer-support staff. What type of project request is this?
   A. Business need
   B. Market demand
   C. Legal requirement
   D. Technological advance

7. You are working in a matrix organization. Choose two responses that describe this type of structure.
   A. Project resources are members of another business unit and may or may not be able to help you full-time.
   B. Matrix organizations can be structured as strong, weak, or balanced.
   C. Project managers have the majority of power in this type of structure.
   D. This organizational structure is similar to a functional organization.
   E. Employees are assigned project tasks by their project manager in this type of structure.

8. A project manager has the most authority under which organizational structure?
   A. Project-based
   B. Functional
   C. Balanced matrix
   D. Strong matrix

9. Your project has expected cash inflows of $7.8 million in today's dollars. Which cash flow technique was used to determine this?
   A. Discounted cash flow
   B. IRR
   C. NPV
   D. Cost-benefit analysis

10. Which of the following are the steps required to validate a project? Choose two.
    A. Analyze the feasibility.
    B. Justify the project.
    C. Align it to the strategic plan.
    D. Validate the business case.
    E. Identify and analyze stakeholders.

11. This general management skill concerns obtaining mutually acceptable agreements with individuals or groups.
    A. Leadership
    B. Problem solving
    C. Negotiating
    D. Communicating

12. Frederico, the director of the marketing department, has approached you with an idea for a project. What are the steps you'll take for the pre-project setup of this project? Choose three.

   A. Write a business-case analysis.

   B. Identify the project.

   C. Determine the strategic opportunity/business need that brought about the project.

   D. Determine the project selection methods you'll use to justify the project.

   E. Validate the project.

   F. Write a project charter and obtain approval for the charter.

13. Your project has expected cash inflows of $1.2 million in year 1, $2.4 million in year 2, and $4.6 million in year 3. The project pays for itself in 23 months. Which cash flow technique was used to determine this?

   A. IRR

   B. NPV

   C. Discounted cash flow

   D. Payback period

14. You've been given an idea for a project by an executive in your organization. After writing the business-case analysis, you submit it to the executive for review. After reading the business case, he determines that the project poses a significant amount of risk to the organization. What do you recommend next?

   A. Proceed to the project selection committee.

   B. Reject the project based on the analysis.

   C. Proceed to writing the project plan.

   D. Perform a feasibility study.

15. You're a project manager working on a software development project. You are working hand in hand with a systems analyst who is considered an expert in her field. She has years of experience working for the organization and understands not only systems development but also the business area the system will support. Which person should make the decisions about the management of the project?

   A. Project manager

   B. Systems analyst

   C. Project manager with input from systems analyst

   D. Systems analyst with input from project manager

16. What is one disadvantage of a project-based organization?

    A. The organization doesn't work on anything that isn't project-related.

    B. Costs are high because specialized skills are required to complete projects in this type of structure.

    C. The functional managers have control over which team members are assigned to projects.

    D. Once the project is completed, the project team members may not have other projects to work on.

17. Which of the following are reasons for bringing about a project? Choose three.

    A. Feasibility study

    B. Market demand

    C. Business case justification

    D. Strategic opportunity

    E. Stakeholder needs

    F. Social needs

18. Your project has expected cash inflows of $7.8 million in today's dollars. The project's initial investment is $9.2 million. Which of the following is true?

    A. The discounted cash flows are lower than the initial investment, so this project should be rejected.

    B. The discounted cash flows are lower than the initial investment, so this project should be accepted.

    C. NPV is less than zero, so this project should be rejected.

    D. NPV is greater than zero, so this project should be accepted.

19. The executives in your organization typically choose which projects to perform first by reviewing the business case and then determining, based on their experience with similar projects, which will likely perform well and which will not. What form of project selection method is this?

    A. Business case analysis

    B. Expert judgment

    C. Feasibility analysis

    D. Decision model technique

20. Which two elements should always be included in a business case analysis? Choose two.

    A. Feasibility study

    B. Project selection methodology

    C. Alignment to the strategic plan

    D. Justification

    E. Cash flow techniques to determine financial viability.

Answers to Review Questions

1. **C, E.** A project creates a unique product, service, or result and has defined start and finish dates. Projects must have resources in order to bring about their results, and they must meet the quality standards outlined in the project plan. Interrelated activities are not projects because they don't meet the criteria for a project. Project management processes are a means to manage projects, and processes used to generate profits or increase market share do not fit the definition of a project. Processes are typically ongoing; projects start and stop.

2. **B.** The Project Management Institute (PMI) is the leading professional project management association, with more than 400,000 members worldwide.

3. **D.** A program is a group of related projects that can benefit from coordinated management. Life cycles are the various stages a project goes through, and process groups consist of Initiating, Planning, Executing, Monitoring and Controlling, and Closing.

4. **B, C, E.** The steps in pre-project setup include the following: identifying the project, validating the project, preparing a project charter, and obtaining approval of the charter.

5. **B.** Project managers can spend up to 90 percent of their time communicating. The other skills listed here are important as well, but the clue in this question is the 90 percent figure that relates to the amount of time project managers may spend communicating.

6. **A.** A request to develop a product for use by an internal department is a business need. Market demands are driven by the needs of the market, legal requirements come about because of rules or regulations that must be complied with, and technological advances are because of improvements in expertise or equipment.

7. **B, E.** A matrix organization can be structured as a strong, weak, or balanced matrix. Employees are assigned to projects by their functional managers, and the project tasks are assigned to them by the project manager. The project manager has the majority of power in a project-based organization.

8. **A.** A project-based organization is designed around project work, and project managers have the most authority in this type of structure. Project managers have the least amount of authority in a functional organization, they have some authority in a balanced matrix, and, a little more authority in a strong matrix, but not as much authority as they have in a project-based organization.

9. **A.** The discounted cash flow technique compares the total value of each year's expected cash inflow to today's dollar. IRR calculates the internal rate of return, NPV determines the net present value, and cost-benefit analysis determines the cost of the project versus the benefits received.

10. **D, E.** The steps required to validate a project are validating the business case (which encompasses a feasibility analysis, justification for the project, and alignment to the strategic plan) and identifying and analyzing stakeholders.

11. C. Negotiating involves obtaining mutually acceptable agreements with individuals or groups. Leadership involves imparting a vision and motivating others to achieve the goal. Problem solving involves working together to reach a solution. Communicating involves exchanging information.

12. B, E, F. The steps in pre-project approval are identifying the project, validating the project, and writing the project charter and obtaining approval of the project charter. A business case is part of the project validation process, the strategic opportunity or business need is typically documented in the business case, and project selection methods are used after pre-project setup, not as part of the pre-project setup.

13. D. Payback period is a technique that calculates the expected cash inflows over time to determine how many periods it will take to recover the original investment. IRR calculates the internal rate of return, NPV determines the net present value, and discounted cash flows determine the amount of the cash flows in today's dollars.

14. D. The next best step to take in this situation is to perform a feasibility study. Feasibility studies are typically undertaken for projects that are risky, projects that are new to the organization, or projects that are highly complex. Projects of significant risk to the organization shouldn't be taken to the selection committee without having a feasibility study first and writing the project plan doesn't make sense at this point because you don't know if the project will be chosen or not. You also can't reject the project because there isn't enough information to determine if it should be rejected until the feasibility study is completed.

15. C. The project manager is ultimately responsible for managing the work of the project. That doesn't mean that they should work without the benefit of input from others.

16. D. The key problem with a project-based organization is that there may not be a new project in place at the conclusion of the one team members were released from. This leaves specialists "sitting on the bench" with no work to do and is costly to the organization. It's an advantage to a project-based organization to work on projects. Costs aren't necessarily any higher in this type of organization than others. Costs will depend on the type of project you're working on, not the organizational structure. And the project managers have control over who works on the projects in a project-based organization.

17. B, D, F. The needs or demands that bring about a project include the following: market demand, strategic opportunity/business need, customer request, technological advances, legal requirements, ecological impacts, and social needs. A feasibility study is conducted to determine the viability of a project, and the business case documents the reasons for the project and the justification for the project. Stakeholder needs may bring about a project, but their needs will fall more specifically into one of the seven needs or demands that bring about a project.

18. C. NPV is calculated by subtracting the total of the expected cash inflows stated in today's dollars from the initial investment. In this question, the initial investment is higher than the cash flows, so the resulting NPV is less than zero, and the project should be rejected. Discounted cash flows tell you the value of the cash flows in today's dollars.

19. B. This question describes the expert judgment form of project selection. The question states the executives already read the business case analysis. The feasibility study is a study conducted to determine the risks and potential benefits to the project, and decision models are mathematical models that use differing variables to determine a decision.

20. C, D. The business case analysis may include the feasibility study but should always include the justification for the project and the alignment to the strategic plan. It's a good idea to also include high-level timelines and estimated budgets.

Chapter

2

Project Process Groups and the Project Charter

THE COMPTIA PROJECT+ EXAM TOPICS COVERED IN THIS CHAPTER INCLUDE

✓ **1.4 Explain the components of a project charter**

- Key project deliverables

- High level milestones

- High level cost estimates

- Identify stakeholders

- General project approach

- Problem statement

- High level assumptions

- High level constraints

- High level risks

- Project objectives

✓ **1.5 Outline the process groups of the project life cycle**

- Initiating/Pre-Project Setup

- Planning

- Executing

- Monitoring/controlling

- Closing

Project Life Cycles and Process Groups

Most projects are divided into phases that consist at a minimum of a beginning phase, middle phase, and ending phase. These phases are typically segments of work that allow you to more efficiently manage, plan, and control the work of the project. A *project life cycle* is the total composition of these multiple phases. The life cycle of a project encompasses all the work of the project and can be represented on a timeline.

Ideally, the *deliverables* from one phase of the project are completed and approved prior to the start of the next phase. A deliverable is an output or result that must be completed and approved before moving to the next phase of the project or before you can declare the project complete. In reality, for most projects, the deliverables are completed throughout the life of the project, and the life cycle phases overlap.

Project life cycles vary widely between different industries and to some degree even within an organization. However, even though project life cycles are diverse, you will find several key elements common to each. At the highest level, a project life cycle should describe the deliverables for each phase and list the categories of resources involved. A high-level timeline for the phase might be constructed as well. A project life cycle should also explain how the output of the project will be incorporated into the organization's operational business upon completion.

It is possible to overlap phases to speed up the project schedule and to perform what's called *fast tracking*. This is where you start the next project phase before the prior phase has completed. These techniques are almost always used to shorten the project schedule.

Project Process Groups

PMI defines project management as a series of processes that are executed to apply knowledge, skills, tools, and techniques to the project activities to meet the project requirements. These processes have been organized into five process groups called Initiating, Planning, Executing, Monitoring and Controlling, and Closing. Each process group contains at least two individual processes (some have many more) that have their own inputs to the process, tools and techniques, and outputs. For example, the Develop

Project Charter process is grouped within the Initiating process group. It has five inputs, one tool and technique, and one output (the project charter).

The process groups are tightly linked. Outputs from one group usually become inputs to another group. The groups may overlap, or you may find you have to repeat a set of processes within a process group. For example, as you begin executing the work of the project, you may find that changes need to be made to the project plan. So, you may repeat some of the processes found in the Planning process group and then re-perform many of the Executing processes once the changes to the plan are made. This is known as an *iterative* approach. Figure 2.1 shows the links between the groups.

FIGURE 2.1 PMI process groups

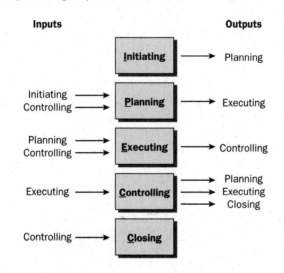

As we discuss each group, notice the correlation between the process groups and the domains covered in the CompTIA Project+ exam. The process groups are the foundation of project management. You need to understand each group, its characteristics, and how it contributes to delivering the final product, service, or result of the project.

Initiating Processes

Initiation is the formal authorization for a new project to begin or for an existing project to continue. The Initiating process group is the first of the five process groups that PMI describes in the *PMBOK Guide*.

The *Initiating* processes include all the activities that lead up to the final authorization to begin the project, starting with the original project request. This process can be formal or informal, depending on the organization. We've already covered a couple of the activities associated with project initiation in Chapter 1. Identifying the project and the business need, documenting the business justification, performing business case validation, and using the project selection methods are all performed during the Initiating process.

In addition to these activities, you'll also document the high-level requirements definitions and perform a cost justification during this process.

You'll take a closer look at high-level requirements in the "Receiving a Project Request" section later in this chapter.

Planning Processes

Planning processes are where the project goals, objectives, and deliverables are refined and broken down into manageable units of work. Project managers create time and cost estimates and determine resource requirements for each activity. Planning involves several other critical areas of project management, including communication, risk, human resources, quality, and procurement.

The Planning process group is unquestionably one of the most critical elements of managing a project. For that reason, the Planning process group will be covered in detail in Chapters 3 through 6.

Executing Processes

Executing processes are where the work of the project is performed. The project manager must coordinate all the project team members as well as other resources assigned to the project.

Executing processes include the actual execution of the project plan, team development, quality assurance, information distribution, and more. We will cover this more closely in Chapter 7, "Executing the Project."

Monitoring and Controlling Processes

Monitoring and Controlling processes are the activities that monitor the progress of the project to identify any variances from the project plan. Requests for changes to the project scope are included in this process. This area is also where corrective actions are taken to get the work of the project realigned to the project plan.

Other areas of the Monitoring and Controlling process group include scope control, cost control, schedule control, quality control, performance reporting, and risk control. In Chapters 8 and 9, we will spend considerable time discussing the various methods for monitoring progress: specifically, change control and quality control.

Closing Processes

The primary purpose of the *Closing* processes is to document the formal acceptance of the project work and to hand off the completed product to the organization for ongoing maintenance and support.

Closing processes include the sign-off, archive of project documents, turnover to a maintenance group, release of project team members, and review of lessons learned. This process group is the one most often skipped in project management. And although some of these activities may seem fairly straightforward, several elements of this process group deserve close attention. Chapter 10, "Closing the Project," will explore the last stages of a project.

Use the old poison antidote, syrup of ipecac, to help you remember the process groups in order: Initiating, Planning, Executing, (Monitoring and) Controlling, and Closing.

Receiving a Project Request

The Initiating process group covers the receipt of a project request through the authorization to start a project. Authorization is established through the publication of the project charter.

As we stated previously, there are several steps accomplished in the Initiating process group. We've already talked about identifying the project, developing the business case, validating the business case, and using project selection techniques in Chapter 1. Now we'll cover the project request process and documenting the project requirements.

Project Request Process

The project request process can be formal or informal, depending on the organization. You may have a process that requires a formal written document describing the project goals and justification, or you may experience what we like to call *drive-bys*—the project your boss tells you about in the 30-second elevator ride to the lobby. Regardless of who initiates a project request or how it's initiated, the organization must review it and make a decision on a course of action. To do that, you'll need to gather enough information to adequately evaluate the request and determine whether the project is worth pursuing.

After receiving a request, your next step involves meeting with the requestor to clarify and further define the project needs, identify the functional and technical requirements, and document the high-level requirements.

Several needs or demands bring about the reasons for a project. Refer to Chapter 1, "Initiating the Project," if you need a refresher.

High-Level Requirements

To clarify the project request, you need to develop what the *PMBOK Guide* refers to as a *product description*. In some industries, a product description is often referred to as *high-level requirements*.

High-level requirements explain the major characteristics of the product or service of the project and describe the relationship between the business need and the product or service requested. Before you jump into completing your high-level requirements, you need to make certain the problem or need that generated the project request is clearly defined and understood. That means you'll need to meet with the person requesting the project to clarify the project goals and understand what problem they're trying to solve. If the problem is unclear, the solution may be off-target, so it's critical you understand the problem before you move on to defining requirements. You'll also need to understand the different categories of requirements and the importance of obtaining both functional requirements and technical requirements.

Defining the Problem

A project can get off to a bad start if the project manager does not take the time to clearly define the problem or need generating the project request. Have you ever been on a project where people are working furiously to meet a deadline but no one appears to know why the work is being done? Then halfway through the project everything changes or, worse yet, the whole thing gets canceled? If this sounds familiar, it may be that a solution was being developed without clarifying the problem.

The customer is not always able to articulate what the problem is, and their request may be vague and loosely worded. Your job as project manager is to figure out what the customer really means. We've worked on many IT-related projects that were developed and implemented to the precise requirements of the customer only to hear them exclaim, "You delivered what I asked for but not what I wanted!"

    It's your responsibility to investigate the customer request and communicate your understanding of the request. This may result in the creation of a project concept document, or perhaps the business case, which represents your first attempt at restating the customer request to demonstrate understanding of the project.

Problems can also arise when project requests are proposed in the form of a solution. It is not uncommon for clients to come to you with a very specific request and a solution they've already discovered that satisfies the request. You may be thinking this is great news, because there is no need to tie up your calendar with a lot of requirements-gathering meetings. The problem is, your client may not be asking for the right solution. As a project manager, you need to make certain that the problem has been identified before the solution is proposed.

Let's say that you get a request for a new billing system, which is a fairly major undertaking. The first thing you should do is meet with the person making the request to get more information. Why do they need a new billing system? What functionality is the current billing system not providing? What business need or opportunity do they believe this new system will solve? These kinds of questions will help you understand what is behind the new billing system request. If your project requestor is concerned about the number of customer calls related to general billing questions, the best solution might not be a new billing system but rather a clearer explanation of the charges or a bill insert explaining each line item on the bill. If they are interested in a new look and feel for the bill, you may be dealing with requirements that range from reformatting the current bill data to using a different paper to print bills. Numerous business needs may cause your customer to want a "new billing system," but many of them may have nothing to do with developing an entirely new application. That is why a good project manager asks questions to uncover what is behind a request. Lack of up-front clarification and problem definition has been the downfall of numerous projects. Do not assume that a customer-requested solution is always the best solution until you understand the business need. Clearly defining the problem up front will give you and the client a better starting point for identifying the functional and technical requirements.

Requirement Categories

Once you have a clear idea of the problem generating your client's request, you must also understand what the client's requirements, objectives, and expectations are for the project outcomes. You'll need to identify three types of requirements: functional, business, and technical requirements.

Functional Requirements

Remember from Chapter 1 that a project produces a unique product. *Functional requirements* define what the product, service, or result of the project will do. Functional requirements focus on how the end user will interact with the product. The requirements for a client whose business need is a new billing format are going to be very different than the requirements of a client who wants to introduce a new product or feature. This is why it is so important to have the problem defined before you start looking at specific requirements. Knowing the problem will assist you in asking the right questions to identify the client requirements. For a new billing statement, you need to know how the client wants the bill to appear. Will this be a one-time fee or a recurring rate or both? If there is a monthly fee, is it a fixed rate, or does it vary by usage? Are there discount periods? Is there a contract period or a penalty for breaking the contract? What are the categories of charges and credits? For a new product or feature, you will need very different data.

Applications used by business units internal to the organization are an area where you should use extra caution in defining the requirements. Your client may assume things will work in a certain fashion without explicitly stating that assumption as a requirement. We'll use a new order entry system for sales consultants as an example. Your client has told you that the system needs to display product availability, generate sales reports, and include a help feature. Although these may sound like good requirements, they are missing some critical data. What drives the product availability? How will the sales reports be generated? What information is included in the help feature? By asking these questions, you come up with the following requirements:

- The system should display product availability by geographic location.
- Users can generate sales reports online in real time.
- Each product should include a help feature that provides detailed information on the cost, benefits, and usage of the product.

Although functional requirements can be stated in more general terms than technical requirements, as a project manager, you must ask questions to drive out ambiguity. If your customer requirement states that a new sales system must be easy for the sales consultants to use, do you know what that means? If the answer is no, you do not have a clear requirement, and you need to define what "easy to use" means to the customer. It could be the flow of the screens, built-in help, or other criteria. The requestor needs to clarify the meaning so the requirement defines the functionality that will make the system easy to use. If you are not sure whether you have a clearly defined requirement, ask yourself how you would create a test scenario to validate the requirement. If there is no way to validate that the requirement has been met, you need to get more data.

Business Requirements

An organization's *business requirements* are the big-picture results of fulfilling a project. Business results can be anything from a planned increase in revenue to a decrease in overall spending to increased market awareness.

Technical Requirements

Technical requirements, also known as nonfunctional requirements, are the product characteristics needed for the product to perform the functional requirements. Technical requirements typically refer to information technology–related projects. You can think of technical requirements as the elements that happen behind the scenes of a project or program to meet the client's request.

There are many categories of technical requirements, and the need to include a specific type varies based on the product being developed. Some of the more common technical requirements include usability requirements, maintainability requirements, legal requirements, performance requirements, operational requirements, and security requirements.

The following are examples of technical requirements for an IT project:

- System response time can be no greater than five seconds.
- The system must be available Monday through Saturday from 7 A.M. to 7 P.M.
- The system must run on both PCs and Macs.

Industry or corporate standards may also impact your technical requirements if you are developing an application with interfaces to existing systems. The application interface may require a specific programming language or methodology. These restrictions need to be documented in the requirements, because they may impact activity duration or cost estimates that are completed in later planning processes.

 If you work in a regulated industry, make sure you address the question of whether any specific government- or industry-related regulations impact the design or delivery of your product. Regulatory noncompliance is a serious offense, and correcting infractions can be both time-consuming and costly.

Your client may be more prepared to discuss the functional requirements than the technical requirements, so come prepared with a list of standard questions. If your company has a requirements template or checklist, use it in your meetings with the client group.

Documenting the Requirements

Once you have clarified what problem your customer is trying to solve and have defined the functional, business, and technical requirements, you are ready to start documenting the requirements and completing the product description.

The high-level requirements document is part of the formal request for project approval. It is also the basis for defining the project scope, estimating the cost of the project, identifying the resources required, and developing the schedule. The high-level requirements should contain the following information:

Problem Statement:

What issue or problem generated this request?

What is the specific business need that the client wants to address?

Objectives:

How do you define project success?

What is the end result?

What are the deliverables leading to the end result?

What are the goals?

How are the goals measured?

Strategic Value:

How does this product fit the strategic vision of the corporation?

Is there a link to other proposed or ongoing projects?

Requirements:

What work functions are required?

Are there interfaces to existing systems?

What are the performance criteria?

What are the support requirements?

Timing:

When does the customer need the project completed?

Are there market windows involved?

Are there significant business expenses to be incurred if the project is not complete?

Is there an impact to corporate revenue if the project is delayed?

Historical Data:

Have there been similar projects in the past?

Were they successful?

Can pieces of previous projects be reused for this project?

Clearly defined high-level requirements with measurable objectives and good supporting data regarding strategic value, timing, and relevant historical information on similar projects is critical to project approval as well as ongoing communications throughout the project.

Decomposing Requirements

Project managers must possess the ability to incorporate systems thinking so that they are able to *decompose*, or break down, the initial project requirements into manageable units of work. This means you take the requirements initially given to you and examine every facet of them until their meaning is clear. Then you make a determination as to whether the requirement is functional, business, or technical in nature. Then you can further break down the requirements during the Planning processes into small units of work or activities. It's important that the requirements are stated in clear and concise terms so that there's no misunderstanding among the stakeholders. Let's look at an example.

Stakeholder requirement   Users throughout a company's *53 campuses* will be able to connect to a *centralized database system via browsers* in order to *manage sales and inventory information.* You and the stakeholders have agreed upon this *high-level* requirement, and you are now ready to decompose this complex requirement into its baser elements.

Decomposition   To decompose the stakeholder requirement, you pick out the main elements and determine the types of requirements these entail:

Fifty-three campuses   This element of the stakeholder requirement is a business requirement because the company has 53 campuses and you're *required* to have all of them connect to a central database.

Centralized database   This element is a technical requirement. You'll use a centrally located database for all transaction activity.

Via browsers   This is a functional requirement. The stipulation is that all users will use a browser to connect to the system.

To manage sales and inventory information   This is also a functional requirement. You might confuse this with a business requirement, but in actuality you're saying here that the users are functionally going to do something with the system—they're going to manage sales and inventory information.

Once you have an understanding of the requirements in the Planning process group, you'll define tasks, dependencies, milestones, and resources based on these requirements.

Vendor Bids

Sometimes, projects are performed by external organizations. This situation may occur if the project request involves a new technology the organization can't satisfy internally. It may also involve services that require specialized expertise from outside sources.

If your project, or a key component of your project, will be completed outside your organization, you may be involved in writing or providing input for a *request for proposal (RFP)*. An RFP is a procurement document that is advertised to the vendor community requesting vendors provide a written proposal outlining how they will meet the requirements of the project and how much it will cost.

Once a vendor is selected, a *statement of work (SOW)* is completed. The SOW is a description of what product or service the vendor will provide and is generally included as part of the contract.

The use of an outside vendor involves unique considerations that don't apply to internally developed projects. A contract is a legal document between the buyer and vendor that needs to be taken into consideration as you move forward to complete the project scope and the overall project plan.

RFPs, SOWs, and contracts are part of Procurement Planning, which will be covered in more detail in Chapter 5, "Communicating the Plan."

Project Stakeholders

While refining the high-level requirements in the project selection process, you will first interact with a very important group of people: your stakeholders. What exactly is a stakeholder, and why is it important to identify all your key stakeholders?

> Remember from Chapter 1 that identifying and analyzing stakeholders is one of the steps in validating a project, along with preparing a business case.

A *stakeholder* is a person or an organization that has something to gain or lose as a result of performing the project. Stakeholders are key to the success of your project. They typically have a lot of influence in the organization, and let's face it, most stakeholders are concerned about the needs of their own departments (or organizations) first. So, they'll be looking to you as the project manager to help them understand what they'll gain as a result of this project. If you are successful at winning the confidence and support of the project's major stakeholders, it will go a long way toward assuring the success of the project overall.

> It's your responsibility as the project manager to manage stakeholder expectations regarding the project.

Unfortunately, some stakeholders may not support your project for any number of reasons. They may not like the person who requested the project, they may not like the goal of the project, it might create major change in their business unit, it might change their operational procedures, and so on. A project that creates a major impact on operational procedures may be viewed as a threat. And any project that brings about a major change in the organization can cause fear and generate resistance. The key is to get to know your stakeholders as soon as possible. Meet with them one-on-one to gain an understanding of their concerns and issues and also to begin to set expectations and help them see the benefits of performing the project.

The general management skills we talked about in Chapter 1 will come in handy when dealing with your stakeholders, particularly your communication and negotiation skills. Individual stakeholders may have very different priorities regarding your project, and you may have to do some negotiating with your stakeholder groups to bring them to a consensus regarding the end goal of the project. Building consensus among a group with diverse viewpoints starts with up-front negotiation during the Initiating process group and continues with ongoing communication throughout the life of the project. In Chapter 5 we will discuss Communications Planning in detail, including how you define and implement a communications plan geared to the needs of individual stakeholders.

Set up individual meetings or interviews early in the project to get to know your stakeholders and understand their perspectives and concerns about the project. They aren't going to go away, and if you ignore some of your stakeholders, the issues they raise will become more and more difficult to resolve.

Project Sponsor

The project *sponsor* is usually an executive in the organization who has the authority to assign money and resources to the project. The sponsor may also serve as a champion for the project within the organization. The sponsor is an advisor to the project manager and acts as the tie-breaker decision maker when consensus can't be reached among the stakeholders. One of the primary duties of a project manager is keeping the project sponsor informed of current project status, including conflicts or potential risks. The project sponsor typically has the following responsibilities:

- Provide or obtain financial resources
- Authorize assignment of human resources to the project
- Assign the project manager and state their level of authority
- Serve as final decision maker for all project issues
- Negotiate support from key stakeholders
- Monitor delivery of major milestones
- Run interference and remove roadblocks
- Provide political coaching to the project manager

 A *project champion* is usually one of your key stakeholders, and they spread the great news about the benefits of the project and act as a cheer-leader of sorts, generating enthusiasm and support for the project.

Other Project Stakeholders

A complete list of stakeholders varies by project and by organization. The larger and more complex your project is, the more stakeholders you will have. Sometimes you will have far more stakeholders than you want or need, especially on high-profile projects. We recommend that you define who you think the other stakeholders are on the project and review the list with your project sponsor. The project sponsor is often in a better position to identify what we refer to as *political stakeholders*—influential people in the organization who have expressed a desire to be involved in this project, without a direct or obvious connection. You do not want to ignore these people just because their role is not obvious, and your sponsor can assist you in identifying the needs of these stakeholders.

Some stakeholders are more obvious and much easier to identify. In addition to the project sponsor, the following are the other types of stakeholders you'll find on most projects:

Project manager   We have already talked about the project manager in detail. This is the person responsible for managing the work associated with the project.

Project team members   These are the experts who will be performing the work associated with the project. Depending on your organizational structure, these people may report directly to the project manager, may report to a functional manager within the organization, or may participate in a matrix-managed team. Project team members may be assigned to the project either full-time or part-time. Most projects have a combination of dedicated and part-time resources. If you have part-time resources, you need to understand their obligations outside the project and make certain they are not over-allocated.

Functional managers   If your resources are supplied by another organization, the functional managers who assign those resources are critical stakeholders. You need to establish a good relationship with your functional managers and brush up on those negotiation skills because you'll need them. Normally, multiple projects compete for the same resource pool. So, it's a good idea to document your agreements with the functional manager regarding the amount of time the resource will be available for your project, as well as the deliverables they're accountable for, in order to prevent future misunderstandings. You should also obtain prior agreement regarding your input to the employee's annual performance appraisal, salary increase, and bonus opportunity.

Customer or client   The *customer* is the recipient of the product or service created by the project. In some organizations this stakeholder may also be referred to as the *client*. A customer is often a group or an organization rather than a single person. Customers can be internal or external to the organization.

End user   The term *end user* denotes the person who directly uses the product produced as a result of an IT project. This term is often seen in IT projects to distinguish between the organization purchasing the output of the project and the group that will use it on a daily basis. As an example, the sales department is the customer for an online order entry system, while the frontline sales consultants are the end users of this system.

End users usually participate at some level in requirements gathering and review and in functional testing of the product.

As you can see from this list, your stakeholders represent a wide range of functional areas and a diverse set of wants and needs relative to your project. To keep track of everyone, you may want to develop a stakeholder matrix. We'll look at what that entails next.

Stakeholder Matrix

If you have a large project with multiple stakeholders, it may be appropriate to create a stakeholder matrix to help you keep track of everyone. You can use a simple spreadsheet to create the matrix. At a minimum, it should include a list of all the project stakeholders with the following information for each one:

- Name
- Department
- Contact information
- Role on the project

- Needs, concerns, and interests regarding the project
- Level of involvement on the project
- Level of influence over the project
- Notes for your own reference about future interactions with this stakeholder, political issues to be aware of, or individual quirks you want to remember about this stakeholder

Since project stakeholders can move on and off the project at different times, it's important that the project manager reviews and updates the matrix on a periodic basis.

IT Projects and Stakeholders

Computer systems and software are often integrated into projects. These projects may involve a single business unit, or several business units, and very rarely the entire organization. We'll look at this topic next and then examine the types of stakeholders you'll likely have on an IT-related project.

Single Business Unit Project

Projects within a single business unit, for example the accounting or human resources department, typically involve requesting a project to help design and build, or purchase, a software system that meets a specific business requirement.

In many cases, business unit stakeholders have already done some research regarding systems that will meet their new requirements, and they may recommend a commercial off-the-shelf (COTS) application. As the project manager, you should scrutinize the software or ask a trusted source in IT to recommend whether the software meets the needs of the business unit and also meets the standards of the IT department.

 This situation can turn into a cart-before-the-horse scenario very quickly. We have seen stakeholders become so enamored with a software system a vendor has demoed for them that they won't even acknowledge there are other possibilities to explore. Even worse, the system they have their hearts set on may not meet the bulk of their requirements. This is why it's imperative you document the requirements first and then begin the search for the solution. If your stakeholder has already jumped ahead of you, explain the importance of the requirements-gathering activity, and insist on completing this document before continuing with further product investigations.

IT projects often involve replacing an old or outdated computer system that no longer meets their needs. It can be tricky to determine the requirements for a new system because your stakeholders will find it difficult to think outside the bounds of the old system. You'll hear them say, "The old system does it this way." That may no longer be a requirement. You need to ask a lot of "why" questions for a project like this. Why does the system need to perform this way? Why do you need this functionality? And so on.

Real World Scenario

The Importance of Requirements Gathering

Bill worked for a large gas and electric utility for several years and at one point found himself working in the human resources IT department with the specific charge of supporting HR software and associated services.

The payroll system in use at the time was old and outdated, and the manager of the department was looking for a suitable, scalable, and up-to-date replacement. There weren't a lot of choices at the time: you had systems developed on IBM mainframe computers or PC software, which was just coming into the forefront of people's thinking about how software systems should operate and be utilized in corporate offices. This was in the early 1990s and long before we had web-based systems and the sophistication of today's PCs.

The manager of the department found some software written by a large utility company in another part of the country. This software ran on the mainframe and satisfactorily performed the department's payroll functions. This utility company was willing to sell the program, and the manager was seriously considering the offer.

This scenario has some very interesting requirements issues associated with it. For example, what would happen if Bill's company purchased the code and found that, for whatever reason, it didn't work correctly on their mainframe? This would be akin to you buying some software a next-door neighbor had written: a program that ran perfectly fine on his computer but didn't run well at all on yours. What kind of support could you expect going forward?

Further, what about payroll software being developed for PCs and networks at the time? Although we realize 1993 was way back in the dark ages of computing, nevertheless strong networking companies like Novell existed, and there were huge players in the networking and business software markets. Had the manager found a satisfactory PC- and network-based payroll product, would it have been a wise choice to go with it instead? In our experience in the industry, early adopters of such technology often wind up being beta testers and regret their decisions.

Moreover, suppose that the adopted system had some bells and whistles other business units might desire. Would the chosen system be able to support scalability going forward?

This is one example of why you need a sound requirements methodology when you're evaluating business unit requests and systems. You must think about the current situation—what are the needs and issues you have today?—as well as future possibilities as you implement the new project.

Multiple Business Unit Project

Sometimes two or more business units can use a system in order to meet business objectives or solve a business problem. For example, procurement, accounting, and human resources tend to generate a lot of documents. They might want to consider a content management system that allows them to create, manage, and store their documents electronically so they may get together and pool their funding to purchase a system they can all use.

Now your task has gotten more difficult because you have a variety of stakeholders involved, all with different agendas but similar interests. Gaining consensus in such stakeholder environments will be the most important aspect of this project.

Additionally, it's important that you understand each business unit's logical workflows in order to make collective sense out of the system that you design and build or purchase. For example, one business unit may not require quality control procedures for incoming documents because they're already quality checked by the sender. But another participating business unit may have a quality control step that they need the new system to employ.

Enterprise Project

Another interesting project is one that impacts the entire enterprise. What we mean by the word *enterprise* is the complete array of business units—almost everyone in the company or division is affected.

You may not be aware of it, but you've probably been part of or at least interacted with an enterprise project. Two distinct examples come to mind: your organization's email system and its corporate intranet. Almost everyone in the company interacts with each of these enterprise systems.

Enterprise projects bring about interesting stakeholder issues and a critical need to document requirements. Since everyone is impacted by an enterprise project, they are all potential stakeholders. But you can't have all employees participate in the project, so you'll need representatives from each business area to serve as project stakeholders. For example, a new email system will require decisions about document retention. In other words, how long we retain email, how often it is up, whether it is permanently deleted after a certain period of time, and so on. The person responsible for making these decisions, perhaps your records retention manager, must be a key stakeholder on the project.

🌐 Real World Scenario

The Enterprise Resource Planning Implementation

Your organization is considering implementing an enterprise resource planning (ERP) system. This system will handle all the back-office functions for your organization, including procurement, human resources, materials inventory, fleet management, budgeting, and accounting. Currently, your organization has 14 disparate systems that handle these functions.

Identifying your stakeholders for this project turns out to be a daunting task. Within each of the departments, there are executives with their own ideas regarding the system requirements, and there are also functional managers who are much closer to their processes and business unit functions on a day-in and day-out basis. For the most part, their requirements match those of the executives, but you are having some difficulty reconciling the day-to-day processing requirements with some functionality the executives have requested.

Project success or failure can rest on any one of these stakeholders. As the project manager, your best course of action is to meet individually with each stakeholder and understand their individual requirements and concerns about the project. Next, you'll document those requirements and concerns and then bring the key stakeholders together to discuss where they agree and gain consensus regarding the differences.

Project Team Members in IT Projects

An IT project should include several IT stakeholders from various positions within the department. The makeup of the project team for an IT-related project is much different from a team you'd assemble for other types of projects. For example, construction workers have specific times to perform their functions during the course of the project. A plumber doesn't necessarily need to know what the electrician is doing. And it makes no difference to a roofer how the drywall finisher is texturing the wall boards. In an IT project, not only do you have individuals who are specialized in their respective areas of IT, but they must also have some idea about the other team members' functions. For example, a software developer needs to have a solid knowledge of how databases function because data from user input screens must end up in the database so that other functions or reports can use the data for other purposes.

Likewise, database administrators (DBAs) must be knowledgeable about software development, and they need to understand how servers work and how users connect to databases across the network. Server administrators must understand that their servers support business functions and that the underlying network operating system isn't the sum total of what the server is about.

 The Project+ exam used to be called the IT Project+ exam and focused primarily on projects within the information technology arena. As a result, you may encounter a question or two concerning IT-related topics, so we'll spend time throughout the book explaining IT-related subject matter where appropriate.

The following are the types of IT stakeholders or team members you may encounter on your project:

Software developers   Software developers specialize in writing software or web-based programs that provide computer-related solutions to business problems, productivity issues, entertainment, and more.

Server administrators   These team members are responsible for configuring and supporting the servers that will host your project.

Database administrators (DBAs)   DBAs are responsible for creating the database schema and their associated requirements. They also plan the backup and recovery methodologies for the data.

Internetworking specialists   Internetworking specialists are the folks who handle the routers, switches, LAN cabling, and WAN connections.

Telephony specialists   The people who manage the company's telephone equipment and operations are telephony specialists. Think of a telephone-based menu system such as an interactive voice-response system, realizing that a software developer had to write the code that intercepts the incoming call, that provides a menuing system for the user to choose from, and that then routes the call to the appropriate party.

Systems analysts   Systems analysts operate at the functional level of taking the system requirements and breaking them down into a system design specification that the system developers can use to build the project.

Business analysts   Business analysts understand the workflow processes and the needs of the business unit but are also able to interface with the IT folks to help them understand what it is the business unit really wants. Business analysts can be IT-savvy folks who come from the business unit or business-savvy people who are in the IT shop.

System architects   System architects have a very technical level of knowledge about systems and are able to draft the blueprint for infrastructure of the proposed system.

Security analysts   The security analyst is the person who makes certain that all security requirements for the project are implemented. Security is a unique specialty and requires someone who has a firm background and understanding of the subject.

Technical writers   A technical writer is responsible for writing all of the documentation for the system. This includes training documents as well as user manuals, help-desk cheat sheets, and other documentation.

These team members should have a solid understanding of their technical areas and stay updated on the latest trends and information. It's also important that team members feel a sense of freedom to question something that's being done and to work closely with one another in making sure that the right decisions are made going forward. There is little room for superstars or "lone rangers" (those who prefer to work alone and not associated with project teams) in efforts such as these. The project team must consist of a group of people who understand the project's goals and who come together with a cohesive purpose. Otherwise, chaos will occur.

Additionally, people on project teams must be great self-starters and able to work on their tasks with little guidance apart from the system design specification. System project teams are usually not a good place for a beginner to start out because you need folks who have expertise in their area and a decent basis of experience.

🌐 Real World Scenario

Matching the Requirements to the Project Team

The project you've just been assigned has the following requirements: it will create a set of computer programs and databases that will allow the vehicle service department to track all warranty work performed on any given vehicle. The system will be intranet-based and accessible via a browser from any computer in the environment. The database will contain all the relevant pieces of information for warranty work performed by the department. Reports will be generated that can be electronically shipped to the vehicle manufacturer for reimbursement. Drop-downs using lookup tables will be provided on the user interface wherever possible to minimize data entry time and incorrect data entry. Consistency checking will be performed on key fields that require double-checking of the data (such as VIN).

You can tell from this short description that you're going to need at least one web programmer. You also know that you're going to need a DBA, and you'll need a server administrator to assist with the databases and software that you'll be developing. You'll also need the assistance of a business analyst to help you understand the business processes and translate them into the computer programs.

As you drill into the project a little more, you'll discover how many of each type of resource will be needed, but for now you've at least identified the relevant technology skills needed for the project.

As the project manager of a technical project team, you'll be working with a wide variety of personality types. Information technology personnel are typically well educated and can have a mind-set that they know best. While you need to have a firm grasp on all the technological ramifications of the deliverables being created, you must also understand team dynamics and how humans interact with one another in high-stress settings. You should be prepared to handle grievances, to mediate arguments, to gather around a whiteboard and draw out the functions so all stakeholders understand them, to communicate in one person's lingo what the other person is trying to say, and so on. Clear, concise, and adequate communications are essential in IT project management.

Creating the Project Charter

The result of the Initiating process is the *project charter*. This document provides formal approval for the project to begin and authorizes the project manager to apply resources to the project. The project sponsor is the one who publishes, signs, and approves the project charter. Publishing the charter is a major milestone, because it is the first official document of your approved project.

 For the exam, remember that the project sponsor is the person who authorizes and approves the project charter. In reality, the project manager or the person who requested the project is the one who writes the project charter and makes certain it's distributed to all the key stakeholders, but the sponsor is the one who approves it.

Organizational standards may drive the specific format of the project charter and the information it contains. As a project manager, you should check with the PMO to determine whether there is a template or a required format for the project charter.

The following are the key elements that should be included in your project charter. We'll cover several of these elements in the next section.

- Project goals and objectives
- Project description
- Problem statement
- Key project deliverables
- High-level milestones
- High-level cost estimates
- Stakeholders
- High-level assumptions
- High-level constraints
- High-level risks
- General project approach
- Name of the project manager and their authority level
- Name of the sponsor
- Other Contents

Goals and Objectives

The charter documents the high-level goals and objectives of the project. This is the first communications document to explain what the project is all about. A project charter needs to include a clear statement as to what end result the project will produce and how success will be measured. Goals and objectives must be clear and stated in such a manner that the end result is easily measured against the objective. Instead of stating, "Install a fast customer record retrieval system," a goal should state a measurable outcome like, "Install a customer records system that will retrieve records in an average of three seconds."

Working with the sponsor (and/or customer) to document quantifiable and measurable goals is key to the project success. It gives the customer, sponsor, key stakeholders, project manager, and team members the same common understanding of the end result of the project.

Project Description

The *project description* documents the key characteristics of the product, service, or result that will be created by the project. The description in the charter starts out at a high level, and more details are added once you develop the project scope statement, which is discussed in Chapter 3. The project description documents the relationship between the product being created and the business need that drove the project request. This description needs to contain enough detail to be the foundation for the Planning process group, which begins once the charter is signed.

Problem Statement

The problem statement answers the question, "Why are we embarking on this project in the first place? What is it we hope to gain in undertaking this project? What problem are we trying to solve?" This question is often addressed in the business case, and it is acceptable to reference the business case in the project charter.

Key Deliverables

Deliverables are measurable outcomes or results or are specific items that must be produced in order to consider the project complete. Deliverables are tangible and are easily measured and verified. For example, if your project involves implementing a new software system, one of the key deliverables may include installing a server to house the system.

Requirements may describe the characteristics of the deliverables, or they may be thought of as elements that are necessary to complete the project. For example, the new accounting system must adhere to Sarbanes-Oxley legislation, which is a type of requirement. The deliverables section can list both the deliverables and the high-level requirements we talked about earlier in this chapter.

High-Level Milestones

Milestones are major events in a project that are used to measure progress. They may also mark when key deliverables are completed and approved. Milestones are also used as checkpoints during the project to determine whether the project is on time and on schedule. Milestones will be further defined in the Planning process section of Chapter 4.

High-Level Cost Estimates

The detailed project budget is prepared later during the Planning processes. But for purposes of the project charter, you need to have a high-level estimate of the project's costs. You can use historical information from past projects that are similar in size, scope, and complexity to the current project. Or, you may ask your vendor community to help you with some high-level figures for the project.

Stakeholder Identification

You should have a fairly comprehensive understanding of who your stakeholders are by the time the project charter is complete. You could include a scaled-down version of the stakeholder matrix we talked about earlier in this chapter in the project charter. This doesn't mean you won't discover other stakeholders as you progress into the project planning process. However, you'll have increased chances for a successful project if you take the time as early as possible in the project to discover and interview all the key stakeholders on the project.

High-Level Assumptions

Assumptions are events, actions, concepts, or ideas you believe to be true. For example, you may have a resource need for the project with a highly specialized skill. Someone with this skill set resides in your IT department, and since you've worked with both the functional manager and this resource on past projects, you assume they'll be available for this project. You can make assumptions about many elements of the project, including resource availability, funding, weather, timing of other related events, availability of vendors, and so on. It's important to always document and validate your project assumptions.

High-Level Constraints

Constraints are anything that either restricts or dictates the actions of the project team. For example, you may have a hard due date that can't be moved. If you're developing a trade show event that occurs on September 25, this date is a constraint on the project because you can't move it. Budgets, technology, scope, quality, and direct orders from upper management are all examples of constraints.

The term *triple constraint* is one you'll hear often in project management circles. According to CompTIA, the triple constraints are time, budget, and quality. However, most project managers and industry experts agree the triple constraints are time, budget, and scope, all of which affect quality.

High-Level Risks

Risks pose either opportunities or threats to the project. Most of the time, we think of risks as having negative impacts and consequences.

You should include a list of high-level risks in the project charter. These may cover a wide range of possibilities, including budget risks, scheduling risks, project management process risks, political risks, legal risks, management risks, and so on. The difference between a risk and a constraint is that a constraint is a limitation that currently exists. A risk is a potential future event that could impact the project. Beginning the project with a hard due date of September 25 is a constraint. The potential for a vendor missing an important delivery on September 15 is a risk.

Project Approach

This is the section of the charter where you formulate the approach you and your project team will take in bringing about the deliverables of the project. This also describes the types of project management processes you'll use to manage the project.

Other Contents

Other elements you should describe in your charter include the name and authority level of the project manager, the name of the project sponsor, and any team members you've committed ahead of time to serve on the project team.

Formal Approval

The project sponsor should sign the project charter. This sign-off provides the project manager with the authority to move forward, and it serves as the official notification of the start of the project. This approval is usually required prior to the release of purchase orders or the commitment by functional managers to provide resources to support the project.

Issuing the project charter moves the project from the Initiating phase into the Planning phase. All of the stakeholders should receive a copy of the charter. It is also a good idea to schedule a meeting to review the charter, review the next steps, and address any questions or concerns they may have.

Next we'll begin a case study that we'll continue throughout the remainder of the book. The case study will outline the concepts you've learned in the chapter and walk you through a simulated project based in a fictitious business.

🌐 Real World Scenario

Chaptal Wineries

This case study will appear throughout the remainder of the book. It's designed to review the use of most of the project management elements we talk about, using information from each chapter you read.

You work for a midsize winery called Chaptal (named for the process of adding sugar to wine to increase its alcohol level—*chaptalization*) in the Sonoma County region of California. Business has been very, very good! Wine is hot, hot, hot all over the country, and your wine maker, Juliette Rene, has gained prominence throughout major wine circles.

The owner of the winery, Kate Cox, has decided to set up shop in other interesting parts of the world: western France, Chile, and southeastern Australia. She has established strong partnerships in these areas and is now ready to connect the three sites together into one network so that she can keep track of the daily activities of each winery. The prospective new wineries are as follows:

France   LaCroix is in the Bordeaux region of France. Chaptal's partner is Guillaume Fourche, a long-time Bordeaux *negociant*. A *negociant* is someone who buys wine from the various smaller wine merchants to blend into interesting *cuvees* that are then bottled and sold. Kate wants to set up an international distributorship with this individual, utilizing Juliette's wine-making skills to improve the quality of the wines that LaCroix distributes.

Chile   Fernando Sanchez, in the Aconcagua Valley, has been making wonderful Chilean red wines for several years now. Fernando Sanchez is interested in branching out internationally and understands that a partnership such as the one with Chaptal would be beneficial for both wineries.

Southeastern Australia   In Adelaide, Australia, a new renegade winery has sprung up. Roo Wines, headed up by a young new upstart wine maker, Jason Jay, awes Kate with the luscious dark Shiraz wines that they release.

Kate has entered into financial agreements and working partnerships that give her a partial stake in the profits of each of the wineries, while allowing them to retain their original look and feel and maintain the management of their day-to-day operations. The people who work for each entity will ultimately report to Kate, but each winery is free to continue doing what it does best. Kate has committed to not interfere.

You have been with Chaptal, serving as the head of IT, since the installation of one small file server on which Kate kept the spreadsheets for the various accounts and Juliette kept track of the residual sugar readings of the grapes.

Today Kate told you that she wants you to install an email server in each of the other three locations, connecting them so that everyone can communicate with one another and all employees' email addresses are in the global address list. She also wants an intranet site set up so that the new wine releases and other communications are available to everyone for comment and approval.

Having just recently passed the CompTIA Project+ test, you understand that there are some basic elements you need to capture in this first meeting.

Basic requirements   You have two requirements that you must fulfill:

- Set up an email system for all four sites.

- Set up an intranet.

Stakeholders   Kate is the project sponsor. In addition to her, there are three primary stakeholders:

- Guillaume Fourche

- Fernando Sanchez

- Jason Jay

Other key staff members within each of the wineries are stakeholders on the project as well. They most likely include the vintner, viticulturists, general manager, director of sales, accounting director, and human resources director.

Now that you have identified the stakeholders and understand the requirements for the project, you set about gathering the goals for the project, including the due date, high-level milestones, key deliverables, estimated costs, assumptions, constraints, and high-level risks. You note the following:

Assumptions   IT personnel are available at each winery (or you are able to hire consultants) to assist with all the technical aspects of implementing this project.

English will be the primary language for all communications.

Constraints   This project has a budget of $250,000. Each site requires new hardware, a backup solution, ISP, licensing fees, contract help, and so on.

High-level risks   Downtime at one or more of the sites. Security intrusions. Improper training of users on the use of the intranet site.

You document the project charter, and Kate signs it, authorizing the project to begin.

Summary

Collectively, project management consists of five process groups: Initiating, Planning, Executing, Monitoring and Controlling, and Closing. Each of these process groups consists of individual processes that each have inputs, tools and techniques, and outputs. The primary output of the Initiating process group is the project charter.

Initiation is the formal authorization for the project to begin. It starts with a project request that outlines the high-level requirements, or the product description. There are three types of requirements: functional, business, and technical.

Project stakeholders are anyone who has a vested interest in the outcomes of the project. Some project stakeholders you will likely encounter include the project sponsor, team members, functional managers, customers (both internal and external), and end users. A project sponsor is an executive in the organization who has the authority to assign budget and resources to the project. Project sponsors serve as final decision makers on the project and sign and approve the project charter.

The output from the Initiating process is the project charter. This document becomes the basis for more-detailed project planning. It should contain the project description, project approach, stakeholders, goals and objectives, problem statement, high-level deliverables, milestones, costs, assumptions, constraints, and risk.

Exam Essentials

Be able to define the Initiating process.   Initiation authorizes the project to begin.

Understand the three categories of requirements.   Functional requirements define how the user will interact with the system. Business requirements are the big picture of what the business wants from the system. Technical requirements define what the system does to perform the functional requirements.

Be able to define a project sponsor and the stakeholders common to most projects. A project sponsor is an executive in the organization who has the authority to allocate dollars and resources to the project.

A stakeholder is an organization or someone who has a vested interest in the project and has something to gain or lose from the project. Stakeholders include the sponsor, project manager, project team members, functional managers, customer, end users, and others with an interest in the project.

Be able to describe a project charter and list the key components.   A project charter provides formal approval for the project to begin and authorizes the project manager to apply resources to the project. The key components are the problem statement, deliverables, milestones, costs, assumptions, constraints, risks, stakeholders, and project description.

Key Terms

Before you take the exam, be certain you are familiar with the following terms:

assumptions	Monitoring and Controlling
business requirements	Planning
closing	product description
customer	project champion
decompose	project charter
end user	project description
enterprise	project life cycle
Executing	request for proposal (RFP)
fast tracking	sponsor
functional requirements	stakeholder
high-level requirements	statement of work (SOW)
Initiating	technical requirements

Review Questions

1. The Initiating process includes which task?
    A. Assigning work to project team members
    B. Sequencing project activities
    C. Approving a project and authorizing work to begin
    D. Coordinating resources to complete the project work

2. This person is responsible for authorizing the project to begin and signing the project charter.
    A. Project sponsor
    B. Executive in the organization who requested the project
    C. Project champion
    D. Project manager

3. Beginning one phase of a project before another has finished is an example of what?
    A. Sequencing
    B. Compression
    C. Fast tracking
    D. Constricting

4. A primary role of the project manager includes informing this person of changes, status, conflicts, and issues on the project.
    A. The project requestor
    B. The project sponsor
    C. The project champion
    D. The most influential project stakeholder

5. Which of the following is not a component of a high-level requirements document or product description?
    A. Historical data
    B. Problem statement
    C. Technical requirements
    D. Testing scenarios

6. Which stakeholder assigns employees to the project?
    A. Project manager
    B. Functional manager
    C. Customer
    D. Sponsor

7. Which three of the following options are process groups in the project management process groups?

   A. Risk

   B. Initiating

   C. Monitoring and Controlling

   D. Procurement

   E. Scope

   F. Planning

8. This process is where the work of the project is performed.

   A. Planning

   B. Monitoring and Controlling

   C. Initiating

   D. Executing

9. Which of the following is true concerning the project charter?

   A. Describes the project schedule

   B. Contains cost estimates for each task

   C. Authorizes the start of the project work

   D. Lists the responsibilities of the project selection committee

10. You receive a confusing request from the marketing department to develop a new billing system. What is the first step you should take?

   A. You meet with the marketing person to identify and clarify the request.

   B. You write the project charter.

   C. You submit a request to the project selection committee.

   D. You request the finance department to do a cost-benefit analysis.

11. Jack is a stakeholder on the project. He's quite enamored with the project and serves to provide enthusiasm, critiques, energy, communication, and motivation for your project. What is Jack's role?

   A. Project sponsor

   B. Project champion

   C. Project team member

   D. Business analyst

12. You're working on a project to develop a client-server application. Your company's collections department will equip their field personnel with wireless tablet PCs that will connect with the server and database. The manager of the collections department brought the request forward. You work for the PMO and are managed by the director of administrative services. The IT department is managed by the director of IT. The telecommunications segments, including wireless, are managed by the director of telecommunications. Who is the project sponsor?

    A. Manager of collections

    B. Director of administrative services

    C. Director of IT

    D. Director of telecommunications

    E. Not enough information

13. Identify the items that should not be included in a project charter. Choose two.

    A. Anticipated budget

    B. Project objectives

    C. High-level cost-benefit analysis

    D. Hardware needed

    E. Business case

    F. Project description

    G. Project title and description

14. Portions of the project will be performed by resources outside the organization. This requires a written document from an outside vendor indicating the type of work that needs to be done and the steps necessary to do them, along with the cost. What is this document called?

    A. SOW

    B. RFP

    C. RFI

    D. RFQ

15. You're undertaking a new project in which users will connect to an application running on a server and post information to a database. At first glance, what types of IT resources do you think you'll need? Choose three.

    A. Database administrator

    B. Application developer

    C. Telecommunications specialist

    D. Server administrator

    E. Graphic designer

16. Randy is a key technical resource for your project. You've worked with Randy on past projects and have identified him in the project charter as one of the team members who will work on the project. The charter has been published, and there is great excitement about this project. You've scheduled a meeting to talk to Randy's functional manager next week. Which of the following conditions does this describe?

    A. Risk

    B. Assumption

    C. Deliverable

    D. Constraint

17. From the following options, select those that best describe the definition of a deliverable. (Choose three.)

    A. Marks the completion of a project phase

    B. Has measurable outcomes or results

    C. Is a specific item that must be produced to consider the project complete

    D. Describes the characteristics of the product of the project

    E. Is documented in the project charter

    F. Is tangible and easily verified

18. From the following options, select the one that does not describe a constraint.

    A. Project team actions are dictated.

    B. It may regard budget, resources, or schedule.

    C. Project team actions are restricted

    D. Project situations are believed to be true.

19. This component of the project charter describes the characteristics of the product of the project.

    A. Milestones

    B. High-level deliverables

    C. Project description

    D. Goals and objectives

20. Your project is to be performed outdoors. You are only four days from the big event, and there is a hurricane headed for shore. This is an example of which of the following?

    A. Risk

    B. Assumption

    C. Deliverable

    D. Constraint

Answers to Review Questions

1. C. The Initiating process concerns the formal acceptance of the project and authorizes the project manager to start the project work. Assigning work to project team members, sequencing project activities, and coordinating resources occur in the Planning process.

2. A. The project sponsor authorizes the project to begin and approves and signs the project charter.

3. C. Fast tracking involves starting the next phase of the project before the prior phase is completed in order to shorten the project schedule.

4. B. A key role of the project manager is informing the sponsor of changes, status, issues, and conflicts on the project. The project requestor and stakeholders should be informed as well, but the primary role of the project manager involves informing the sponsor and keeping them updated.

5. D. A high-level requirements document contains the problem statement, objectives, strategic value, functional and technical requirements, timing, and historical data. Testing scenarios would not be created at this point in the project.

6. B. The functional manager provides the employees performing the work of the project. The project manager is accountable for overseeing the work required to complete the project. The customer is the person or group that is the recipient of the product or service created by the project. The project sponsor champions the project throughout the organization and acts as an advisor to the project manager.

7. B, C, F. The five process groups are Initiating, Planning, Executing, Monitoring and Controlling, and Closing. Options A, D, and E are Knowledge Areas.

8. D. The Executing process is where the work of the project is performed.

9. C. The project charter formally approves the project and authorizes work to begin. The project schedule and cost estimates are developed later in the planning process.

10. A. You must clarify the project request to determine exactly what the marketing person needs. You need to understand the problem that needs to be addressed so that you can define the high-level requirements and write the project charter.

11. B. The project champion is someone who understands the goals of the project and serves as a voice of enthusiasm throughout the organization regarding the benefits of the project.

12. E. The project sponsor is an individual who is authorized to expend the resources necessary to bring about the deliverables of the project. In this question, we really don't have enough information to make a good decision about identifying the project sponsor.

13. A, E. The project charter includes high-level costs for the project but not an anticipated budget. The business case is its own document and is not part of the project charter.

14. A. The statement of work (SOW) is a document that indicates the requirements of the project and outlines the type of work that needs to be completed. All the other options describe procurement documents that notify sellers of the option to bid on the project.

15. A, B, D. You will need someone who can handle the database, someone to program the application code, and someone who can manage the server for you.

16. B. Assumptions are things believed to be true. In this case, you have not verified Randy's availability and are assuming the functional manager will agree to assign him to the project.

17. B, C, F. Deliverables are measurable outcomes or results or are specific items that must be produced in order to consider the project complete. Deliverables are tangible and are easily measured and verified. It's possible that key deliverables may mark the completion of a project phase and that deliverables are documented in the project charter, but these options do not describe the definition of a deliverable.

18. D. Constraints restrict or dictate the actions of the project team and may take the form of budget, resources, schedules, or other limitations. Situations believed to be true are assumptions.

19. C. The project description describes the characteristics of the product, service, or result of the project.

20. A. Risks are potential future events that pose either opportunities or threats to the project. This is a potential event that would have negative consequences to the project if it were to occur.

Chapter

3

Planning a Project

THE COMPTIA PROJECT+ EXAM TOPICS COVERED IN THIS CHAPTER INCLUDE

✓ **2.1 Prepare a project scope document based on an approved project charter**

- Key Performance Indicators (KPIs)
- Scope boundaries
- Constraints
- Assumptions
- Detailed objectives
- Final project acceptance criteria
- Validate scope statement with stakeholders

✓ **2.2 Use a Work Breakdown Structure (WBS) and WBS dictionary to organize project planning**

- Explain the benefits of a WBS
- Explain the levels of a WBS
- Explain the purpose of a WBS
- Identify the planning processes which utilize the WBS as an input
- Critique a given WBS
- Explain the purpose of a WBS dictionary

Now that you have an approved project charter, it is time to talk about project planning. In many cases, we've seen that once a project is approved, people want to start working on the project activities immediately. The general consensus is, Who has time for planning? We need to get this project started!

As the project manager, it's your responsibility to write the project plan and make certain everyone, including team members and key stakeholders, understands the project plan. Starting with this chapter and continuing through Chapter 7, "Executing the Project," we'll cover all the aspects of project planning. The first planning topic is the project kick-off meeting, followed by the project scope document.

Project scope includes all the components that make up the product or service of the project and the results the project intends to produce. Scope planning will assist you in understanding what's included in the project boundaries and what is excluded.

You'll need to define and document three scope components to complete scope planning: the scope-management plan, the scope statement, and the work breakdown structure (WBS). The scope management plan documents how the project scope will be defined and verified and how scope will be monitored and controlled throughout the life of the project. The scope statement provides a common understanding of the project by documenting the project objectives and deliverables. And the final component of scope is the work breakdown structure, which breaks the project deliverables down into smaller components from which you can estimate task durations, assign resources, and estimate costs.

Holding the Kick-Off Meeting

Once the project charter is signed and approved, your next task is to hold a project kick-off meeting. This meeting should include the sponsor, your key project team members, and the key stakeholders on the project. You'll want to address and discuss most of the sections in the charter during this meeting. It's important that everyone understands the goals and objectives of the project, the project description, the high-level milestones, and the general project approach. This document, along with the project scope document that we'll talk about in this chapter, are the two documents you'll come back to when stakeholders try to steer you or the team in a different direction than what was originally outlined. We're not saying that stakeholders would ever do this on purpose, but trying to sneak in one more feature or making this "one little change" tends to make its way into most projects we've worked on. These documents are your safety net and the way to keep out-of-control requests at bay. The project sponsor signs the charter, but the key stakeholders on the project sign the project scope document. So, they can't say they didn't know!

Documenting the Scope Management Plan

The *scope management plan* describes how the project team will define project scope, verify the work of the project, and manage and control scope. The project scope management plan should contain the following elements:

- The process you'll use to prepare the project scope statement
- A process for creating the work breakdown structure (WBS)
- A definition of how the deliverables will be verified for accuracy and the process used for accepting deliverables
- A description of the process for controlling scope change requests, including the procedure for requesting changes and how to obtain a change request form

One of the most important elements of the scope management plan, the change request process, will help master that dreaded demon that has plagued every project manager at one time or another—*scope creep*. Scope creep is the term commonly used to describe the changes and additions that seem to make their way onto the project to the point where you're not managing the same project anymore. The solution, of course, is having a plan.

Project scope change is inevitable with the majority of projects. The key to dealing with scope change is describing how you'll handle it within the scope management plan. In our experience, you can save yourself a lot of pain during project execution if you take the time at the start of the project to define the basics of how the team will handle requests for any changes to the defined scope.

If the project team defines the basic scope management framework early in the planning process, each team member has a point of reference to communicate with stakeholders who may come to them with "something they forgot to mention" when the scope statement was approved. Everyone involved in the project needs to understand that the rules set up at project implementation time need to be followed to make a request to change the scope of any project. Without a documented plan, you will soon find that interested parties are talking to team members and changes are happening outside of your control. The team members will, understandably, want to try to accommodate the customer's needs. But without analysis of the impact of these changes, adding 10 or 20 minor code changes may put your schedule or your budget in jeopardy.

These are key items to consider when you are developing a scope management plan:

Stability of the scope   You probably have some indication at this point in the project as to how stable the scope is based on the work you have already done to define requirements, prepare and review the project charter, and define the scope statement. If you found major disagreement between stakeholders or gaps in the product description, you have a high probability for scope instability unless you resolve the issues and bring stakeholders to a consensus.

Impact of scope changes   If you are constrained with a dictated finish date, any scope change can be critical. Adding to the scope of the project may also impact the budget. You'll need to ask questions such as, Will you have available resources to add to the project to complete the additional work? What is the process for securing additional funding?

Scope change process   One of the primary reasons a project gets out of control is the lack of a documented process for scope changes. Clients and stakeholders will go directly to team members, and before you know it, people will be working on deliverables that were never included in the scope statement.

Your scope change process needs the following at a minimum:

- A change request form. Information required on a scope change request includes a description of the change, the reason for the change, what the impact is if the change is not implemented, and the originator of the request.

- An analysis of the impact of the request on the scope, budget, schedule, and quality of the project. The results of the analysis can be added to the form used to submit the request so that all pertinent data is in one location.

- An approval process to accept or reject requests. This can range from ad hoc meetings that are called as scope changes are received to a formal change review board that meets on a regular basis.

- A communication plan to keep stakeholders informed of the status of requests.

- A method to incorporate approved changes into the project plan.

We'll talk in more detail about changes, change request processes, and the impacts of change in Chapter 8, "Processing Change Requests."

Writing the Project Scope Statement

The project *scope* includes all the components that make up the product or service of the project and the results the project intends to produce. Although this sounds simple and straightforward, a poorly defined scope can lead to missed deadlines, cost overruns, and unhappy clients. Good scope planning helps ensure that all the work required to complete the project is agreed on and clearly documented.

Scope Planning builds on and adds detail to the high-level elements you've defined in the project charter. Depending on the detail of work completed for project initiation, scope planning may also include a more detailed analysis of the product, an additional cost/benefit analysis, and an examination of alternative solutions. You may find that some of the work required for scope planning has already been completed during the initiation process. If that's the case, congratulations: you are now ahead of the game.

The processes to define the scope elements are iterative, they do not always occur in sequence, and they can overlap. Regardless of the sequence, the primary outputs of these processes include the scope management plan, a scope statement, and a work breakdown structure.

The purpose of the *project scope statement* is to document the project objectives, the deliverables, and the work required to produce the deliverables. It is then used to direct the project team's work during the Executing processes and as a basis for future project decisions. The scope statement is an agreement between the project and the project customer that states precisely what the work of the project will produce. Simply put, the scope statement tells everyone concerned with the project exactly what they're going to get when the work is finished. Any major deliverable, feature, or function that is not documented in the scope statement is not part of the project. Typically, the scope statement includes a product description, key deliverables, success criteria, key performance indicators, exclusions, time and cost estimates, assumptions, and constraints. We've talked in detail about most of these elements in Chapter 2, "Project Process Groups and the Project Charter," so we'll recap them briefly next.

Product Description

The *product description* describes the features, functions, and characteristics of the product, service, or result of the project. You can use your existing product description from the project charter and make changes or refinements based on any additional information you have obtained.

Key Deliverables and Detailed Objectives

Deliverables, as you recall, are measurable outcomes, measurable results, or specific items that must be produced to consider the project or project phase completed. Deliverables should be specific and verifiable. It may be a good idea to include at least one deliverable from each business unit in the organization that's represented on the project team to show the big picture of what is involved in completing this project.

Objectives describe the overall goal the project hopes to achieve. Objectives, like deliverables, should also be measurable and verifiable. Objectives are often time-bound. For example, you may have a drop-dead date for the entire project or for critical due dates for some of the project's key objectives. It's also a good idea to include a major objective for each of the business organizations on the project.

Success Criteria and Key Performance Indicators (KPIs)

Success criteria, also known as *acceptance criteria*, include the process and criteria you'll use to determine that the deliverables are complete and satisfactorily meet expectations. This should include a definition of the specifications the deliverables must meet in order to fulfill the expectations of the stakeholders.

Final acceptance criteria is the criteria that describes how you'll determine whether the entire project is complete and meets expectations.

Key performance indicators (KPIs) help you determine whether the project is on track and progressing as planned. KPIs can be monitored incrementally to determine performance and alert you that you must take action to get the project back on track. Earned-value management is an example of a KPI. We'll talk about this topic in Chapter 9, "Controlling the Project."

Critical Success Factors

Deliverables and requirements are sometimes referred to as *critical success factors*. Critical success factors are those elements that must be completed accurately and on schedule in order for the project to be considered complete. They are often key deliverables on the project, and if they are not accurate or complete, they will likely cause project failure.

Exclusions from Scope

Exclusions are anything that isn't included as a deliverable or work of the project. It's important to document exclusions from scope so there is no misunderstanding about features or deliverables once the product is complete.

Time and Cost Estimates

Depending on the organization, you may come across scope statement templates that require time and cost estimates. In this section, you'll provide an estimate of the time it will take to complete all the work and the current high-level estimates for the cost of the project. These will be *order of magnitude* estimates based on actual duration and cost of similar projects or the expert judgment of someone familiar with the work of the project. order-of-magnitude estimates are usually wide ranging and do not have to be precise estimates at this stage in the project.

Assumptions

You'll recall from Chapter 2 that an assumption is an action, a condition, or an event that is believed to be true. The problem with assumptions is that you may not have a common understanding of them among all project team members or stakeholders. You may think something is obvious, but if it's not written down, chances are other team members will have a different opinion on the matter. Assumptions must be documented and validated. For example, say you're developing software for a new desktop support system and assume that the software will be deployed on the existing computers at the client site. The client assumes that new workstations are part of the project. If this assumption was left unchecked and undocumented, you'd have an unhappy customer at the end of this project.

Constraints

The last section of the scope statement is the constraints list. Remember that a constraint is anything that restricts or dictates the actions of the project team. Every project faces potential constraints regarding time, budget, scope, or quality. From the start of most projects, at least one of these areas is limited. If you are developing software to support a new product with a very short market window, time will be your biggest constraint. If you have a fixed budget, money will be the constraint. If both time and money are constrained, quality may suffer. A predefined budget or a mandated finish date needs to be factored into any discussion on project scope. Scope will be impacted if either time or budget is constrained. As the project progresses and changes to scope are requested, scope may become a constraint that in turn drives changes to time, cost, or quality.

As you can see, the scope statement contains a lot of important project information. Let's take a look at a sample scope statement to help you put all the pieces together.

🌐 Real World Scenario

Sample Project Scope Statement

You are a project manager for a rural wireless-telecommunications carrier in charge of a project for a new consumer product feature called Voice-Activated Dialing. The product is critical to the corporate strategy to become one of the top three carriers in the markets where your company offers wireless service. Using your high-level requirements, the project charter, and input from various team members and stakeholders, you are ready to create your project scope statement.

Here is what your project scope statement might look like:

Project justification (from the project charter)   Market research and customer feedback indicate that a demand for Voice-Activated Dialing (VAD) has increased 40 percent over the past three months. One of our competitors has already announced a launch date for this product, and two others are expected to follow within the next two months.

Our market share growth is expected to decline by 20 percent if we do not add VAD as part of our product mix.

Product description   Voice-Activated Dialing allows callers to dial their phone by speaking a phone number or name.

Major deliverables   The major deliverables are as follows:

■ Product requirements defined

■ System requirements defined

■ System requirements developed

- Sales training developed

- Customer-service training developed

- System enhancements implemented

- Sales consultants trained

- Customer-service technicians trained

- Marketing communication plans executed in all markets

- VAD available in all markets

Success criteria and KPIs The launch of VAD will generate $2.5 million in incremental annual revenue for the corporation over the next four years.

The additional VAD training required for sales consultants will require no more than two additional hours added to the existing sales consultant training course.

Exclusions Voice-Activated Dialing does not include the ability to add/edit/delete address book entries using voice commands or an interface to personal information managers.

Time and cost estimates VAD must be completed within six months for the company to be a viable player in this market.

The development and launch of VAD is estimated to cost $350,000. This includes all IT work, sales consultant training, customer brochures, and the marketing campaign. This is a high-level estimate based on the schedule and cost of a similar project. Estimates will be refined as more detailed data is available.

Assumptions IT has resources to implement system changes within the six-month time frame you need to start offering VAD.

Fifteen percent of your customers will add VAD to their current service option. The product will have a 15 percent take rate. VAD will be priced at $4.95/month.

Constraints The window to obtain a share of the VAD market is six months.

Validating the Scope Statement

Once you have completed the scope statement, your next step is to conduct a review session with your project team to make sure that everyone is in agreement and there are no unresolved issues or missing information. Individual team members may have worked on specific sections of the scope statement, and a formal team review of the entire document will confirm that everyone is on the same page and prevent later misunderstandings of the project scope. Once the project team has resolved any outstanding issues, you'll present the scope statement to all the stakeholders, including the project sponsor and the customer.

Attach a sign-off and approval sheet at the back of the scope statement with enough signature lines for the sponsor and each of the major stakeholders on the project. Their approval on this document should be required before any project work is undertaken.

If any changes are made to the scope statement during the review with the stakeholders, you'll need a follow-up meeting with the project management team to cover the changes and discuss the impact on the project. One of your most important duties as project manager is to keep your team informed.

Generally speaking, if you've done your due diligence and defined the scope of the project, gained stakeholder approval, and had all major stakeholders and the sponsor sign the scope statement, you're well on your way to a successful project outcome. Taking the time to create a well-documented scope statement will also help in establishing a solid basis for future change management decisions.

Creating the Work Breakdown Structure (WBS)

The final element of scope planning is the *work breakdown structure (WBS)*. The WBS is a deliverables-oriented hierarchy that defines all the work of the project. Each level of the WBS is a further breakdown of the level above it. *Decomposition* is the process of breaking down the high-level deliverables (and each successive level of the WBS) into smaller, more manageable work units. Once the work is broken down to the lowest level, you can establish time estimates, resource assignments, and cost estimates.

A WBS is one of the fundamental building blocks of project planning. It will be used as an input to numerous other planning processes. It's also the basis for estimating activity duration, assigning resources to activities, estimating work effort, and creating a budget. Because the WBS is typically displayed as a graphical representation, it can be a great way of visually communicating the project scope. It contains more details than the project scope statement does and helps further clarify the magnitude of the project deliverables.

The WBS puts boundaries around the project work because any work not included in the WBS is considered outside the scope of the project.

Decomposing the Major Deliverables

The quality of your WBS depends on having the right team members involved in its development. You won't want a large team of people to assist in this process, but it's helpful if you can involve some of your more experienced team members. Work with the functional managers to get representation from each business unit that has a major deliverable for the project.

A WBS is typically created using either a tree structure diagram or an outline form. The tree structure can be created using software, using a whiteboard, or using easel paper with sticky notes for each level and each component of the WBS. This allows the components to be moved around as you work though the process and get everything in proper order.

A typical WBS starts with the project itself at the topmost level. The next level consists of the major deliverables, project phases, or subprojects that support the main project. From there, each deliverable is decomposed into smaller and smaller units of work. The lowest level of any WBS is called the *work package level*. This is the level where resources, time, and cost estimates are determined. Work packages are assigned to team members or organizational units to complete the activities associated with this work.

Make sure that all the participants have reviewed the project charter and scope statement and have a clear understanding of all the deliverables. Have copies of these documents available as a reference. The team may go through several iterations of constructing the WBS before it's considered complete.

Figure 3.1 is an abbreviated example of a WBS for an application development project.

FIGURE 3.1   Sample WBS

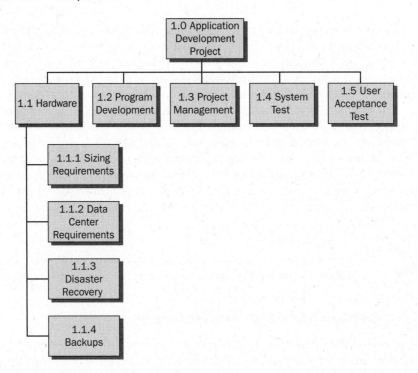

The second method for depicting a WBS is the outline form. Regardless of how you depict the WBS, each level in the WBS should have a unique identifier. This identifier is typically a number, and it's used to sum and track the costs, schedule, and resources associated with the WBS elements. These numbers are usually associated with the corporation's chart of accounts, which is used to track costs by category. Collectively, these numeric identifiers are known as the *code of accounts*. If you took the example from Figure 3.1 and converted it to outline form using the code of accounts, it would look like this:

Application Development Project

1. Hardware
   - 1.1 Sizing Requirements
   - 1.2 Data Center Requirements
   - 1.3 Disaster Recovery
   - 1.4 Backups
2. Program Development
3. Project Management
4. System Test
5. User Acceptance Test

🌐 Real World Scenario

The Office Move Project

Recently we had to move 2,000 employees from various places around a city into one centralized location—a new 11-story building. Each of the business units had a different function, with different managers and move timelines. IT had to make certain that all the employees' computers were moved into the new building the day before the business unit made its physical move, and IT had to assure that all the computer connections worked, the printers were installed and accessible, and the network was functioning properly.

Our project managers started this effort by getting various stakeholders into a room and then, as ideas were voiced, writing them down on sticky notes and pasting them to a whiteboard. Another person began to arrange the notes into some sort of logical order. One stakeholder might cry out, "Make sure all monitors work," while another would say, "We need our email to work when we come in on Monday." Each of these sticky notes had something to do with powering up the machine and validating that it was connected to the network.

In time, as we fleshed out various components of the project, the whiteboard looked just like a tree with yellow leaves all over it, and we had an almost fully complete WBS. A few minor adjustments later, work packages were assigned to members of the IT team, and the work of the project soon got underway.

Guidelines for Creating a WBS

Getting started creating a WBS can sometimes seem overwhelming. We've found that a lot of people who struggle with this process are actually taking on more work than they should. Once you start breaking down your deliverables into smaller units of work, there is a temptation to immediately put these work units in logical order or to determine time estimates so you can get people started working. You'll need to keep reminding the group that the purpose of the WBS is to make certain each deliverable is identified (usually as a level-two element) and that each subdeliverable is decomposed from there. This isn't the process where activities are put into logical order or where predecessor or successor work is determined. That will occur when the project schedule is developed. For now, focus on the deliverables and their decomposition.

Although there is no one right way to complete a WBS, there are some tips you can use to help be more successful. Here are some guidelines that we find helpful to review with the project team before diving into a WBS session:

Recruit knowledgeable resources.   Do not try to complete the WBS yourself in the interest of saving time. If you are not an expert on the deliverables, you will miss key elements. You also want the team members to assist in this process so that they buy in to the work of the project and can see the level of effort needed to bring about a successful conclusion. Involving knowledgeable team members in the creation of a WBS is far more effective at communicating what the project is about than handing someone a completed WBS.

Work though all level two items before proceeding to the next level.   You'll need to control the tendency the team may have to start decomposing a deliverable as soon as it's put up on the board. It's natural to start thinking about what work is required to meet the deliverable. As the project manager, you need to take control of the situation and remind the team to not decompose anything until all the high-level deliverables have been identified. Keep referring the group to the scope statement until everyone is confident that your high-level deliverables are represented on the WBS. Then you can start decomposing.

Each item in a lower level is a component of the level above.   Completing all the items at the lower levels of a WBS leads to the completion of the higher-level components. As a checkpoint, you should review the items at the lower level and ask the team whether completion of those items will result in completion of the components of the next higher level. If the answer to this question is no, then you have not identified all the lower-level tasks.

Define the work package level.   Make sure you work the WBS to a level where the team feels comfortable that resources can be assigned and held accountable for completing the work, and estimates can be determined. This is the primary goal of constructing the WBS. Sequencing, assigning resources, and estimating are all separate activities that you will complete after the WBS is complete.

Do not create a to-do list.   You should not decompose work components into individual activities. Otherwise, you will spend your entire project-management experience managing individual checklists and activities for the work packages. The person who is assigned to the work package level is the one responsible for determining and managing all the activities that make up the work package.

Use the appropriate number of levels.   Each major deliverable may have a different level of decomposition. It is not uncommon for one portion of the WBS to have three levels and another to have five levels. You should be concerned about getting to a manageable work package, not about balancing the WBS. If you try to force an even number of levels across all deliverables, you will end up with some deliverables that are not broken down in adequate detail and others that end up listing every minor activity to complete a simple task.

Benefits of the WBS

The WBS is often listed as one of the most important components of a successful project. As you will see in later chapters, the WBS is an input to numerous project management processes. In our experience, we've also found it invaluable in many other ways.

The WBS is an excellent tool for team building and team communication. A graphic representation of the major project deliverables and the underlying subcomponents allows team members to see the big picture and understand how their part in the project fits in. The direct link between a given work package and a major project deliverable can also help clarify the impact on individual team members. Additionally, as new resources are added to the project, the WBS can help bring these new team members up to speed.

If your organization typically undertakes projects that are similar in size, scope, and complexity, consider using your existing WBS as a template for future projects. It's a great starting point for the new project and can help kick off the brainstorming session with the project team. The other benefit is that you have a finished example that you can use to show the existing team and keep them focused on decomposing the deliverables rather than defining activities, putting them in logical order, and so on.

A detailed WBS will not only prevent critical work from being overlooked, but it will also help control change. If the project team has a clear picture of the project objectives and the map to reach these objectives, they are less likely to go down a path unrelated to the project scope. We don't mean to imply that a WBS will prevent change; there are always changes during the project life cycle. But a WBS will clarify that a request is a change and not part of the original project scope. The WBS is also useful when discussing staffing requirements or budgets.

The WBS is an excellent tool for communicating with customers and stakeholders. People don't always comprehend the magnitude of a project until they see the diagram of the project deliverables and the subcomponents required to reach the objectives of the project. Seeing the work of the project displayed on a WBS will help you convey to the project team and the stakeholders the need for communicating at all levels of the project, coordinating work efforts, and adhering to the project scope.

WBS Dictionary

There's one more component of the WBS, called the *WBS dictionary*. This is where the WBS levels and work component descriptions are documented. These are some of the elements you should list in the WBS dictionary:

- Code of accounts identifier
- Description of the work of the component

- Organization responsible for completing the component
- Resources
- Cost estimates
- Criteria for acceptance

All the WBS components should be listed in the dictionary. This serves as a reference for you and the team regarding the WBS and should be easily accessible to all project team members.

Real World Scenario

Chaptal Wineries

You've recently visited the French site to meet with Monsieur Fourche so that you can discuss the email server and intranet sites. You will be visiting each site so that you can understand what the physical connectivity elements are. You need to understand where the server could be placed, what the wide area network costs are, what the provision times are for connectivity, and where the demarcation point will be at the Fourche site.

You have to consider the same requirements for the Chile location and the Australia site.

On returning from your world travels, you create a scope document containing the following elements:

Business need   The owner of Chaptal Wineries, Kate Cox, has requested that the three new offshore acquisitions be connected to share email and calendar information as well as vital information such as residual sugar and other viticultural data, vintage charts, wine blends, regulatory updates, and so forth. Two systems are required: an email system that connects all four sites and a system that runs an intranet site.

Deliverables description   The deliverables will consist of the installation of at least one server at each site. The servers will connect via wide area networking technology. Email software will be installed on each server in such a way that all sites belong to a single email organization. Users will utilize conventional email software to keep their email and calendars online. Additionally, an intranet site will be created on a Chaptal Wineries server, and key users in each of the offshore sites will be trained on how to post important data to the intranet so that all employees have complete data at their fingertips.

Major deliverables   The deliverables include the following:

- Installation of high-quality servers at each site. Servers will all come from the same vendor, and each server will be identically equipped.

- Installation of well-known email software.

- Establish wide area networking connectivity between sites.

- Installation of appropriate internetworking gear such as routers and firewalls at each site.

- Creation of an intranet site.

- Training and documentation.

Success and acceptance criteria   Your success criteria includes the following:

- Server gear will be installed at each site, baselined, and certified 100 percent functional.

- Email software will be installed on each site server, and site connections with the other site servers will be validated.

- Connectivity between sites will be installed and baselined by a telecommunications company.

- The ISP for each site will be determined and contracted.

- Routers will be installed and router tables built. Firewalls will be installed, configured, and baselined. The administrator will be able to ping each site server within the network and send a test email to each site server.

- The intranet site will be created, and all initial elements requested by the business will be made operational.

- Users will be trained, and documentation will be provided.

- Users in all sites will be able to send email to one another and access viti-vital information 24/7.

Assumptions   You have the following assumptions:

- There is no variance in the behavior of like hardware.

- Telecommunications companies in each nation will have reasonable wide area network setup request procedures and installation timelines.

- Intranet development time is assumed to be approximately 60 person-days (30 working days, 2 people).

- All sites will provide reasonable access for installers, and a secure, climate-controlled, power-conditioned room for the electronic gear.

- Routers will use the Open Shortest Path First (OSPF) routing protocol.

- Contractual help will be used for the configuration of the routers.

Constraints   Your constraints for the email server and intranet sites are as follows:

- Language barriers

- Availability of people at any given site due to the winemaking schedules

- Can't install during harvest and crush seasons

Work breakdown structure (WBS)   This list represents your WBS. (The California site already has a wide area connection and the internetworking equipment.)

1. Hardware procurement

    1.1   Purchase servers and network operating system licenses.

    1.2   Purchase internetworking gear.

2. Wide area network telecommunications connection procurement

    2.1   Provision a wide area connection with French telco.

    2.2   Provision a wide area connection with Australian telco.

    2.3   Provision a wide area connection with Chilean telco.

3. Internetworking equipment installation

    3.1   Contractor installs router and switches at French site, configures, baselines, and tests.

    3.2   Contractor installs router and switches at Australian site, configures, baselines, and tests.

    3.3   Contractor installs router and switches at Chilean site, configures, baselines, and tests.

4. Server installation

    4.1   Install server at French site. Baseline and test.

    4.2   Install server at Australian site. Baseline and test.

    4.3   Install server at Chilean site. Baseline and test.

    4.4   Install server at California site. Baseline and test.

5. Email-software installation

    5.1   Install email software on French server. Baseline and validate the software is working correctly.

    5.2   Install email software on Australian server. Baseline and validate the software is working correctly.

    5.3   Install email software on Chilean server. Baseline and validate the software is working correctly.

    5.4   Install email software on California server. Baseline and validate the software is working correctly.

6. Intranet development

6.1 Develop intranet pages.

6.2 Test intranet.

7. Training of users

7.1 Train French users on the use of email.

7.2 Train French users on the use of intranet.

7.3 Train Australian users on the use of email.

7.4 Train Australian users on the use of intranet.

7.5 Train Chilean users on the use of email.

7.6 Train Chilean users on the use of intranet.

7.7 Train California users on the use of intranet.

7.8 Train California users on the use of email.

8. Unit, integration, and user acceptance testing

8.1 Perform unit testing.

8.2 Perform integration testing.

8.3 Perform user acceptance testing.

Summary

Scope planning uses the output of the Initiating process, the project charter, to create the scope statement and the scope management plan. The scope management plan documents the process you'll use to prepare the project scope statement and WBS, a definition of how the deliverables will be verified, and a description of the process for controlling scope change requests.

The project scope statement is the basis for many of the planning processes and future change decisions. It is also the basis for setting the boundaries of the project with the customer and stakeholders. A scope statement includes the product description, key deliverables, success and acceptance criteria, key performance indicators, exclusions, time and cost estimates, assumptions, and constraints.

The work breakdown structure (WBS) is created by taking the major deliverables from the scope statement and decomposing them into smaller, more manageable components. The breakdown continues through multiple levels until the components can be estimated and resourced. The lowest level of decomposition is the work package. The WBS includes all the work required to complete the project. Any deliverable or work not listed on the WBS is assumed to be excluded from the project. The WBS is a critical component of project planning. A WBS is the basis for time estimates, cost estimates, and resource assignments.

The WBS dictionary should list every deliverable and each of their components contained in the WBS. It should include a description of the component, code of account identifiers, responsible party, estimates, criteria for acceptance, and any other information that helps clarify the deliverables and work components.

Exam Essentials

Describe the purpose of a scope management plan.   A scope management plan documents the procedures for preparing the project scope statement and WBS, defines how the deliverables will be verified, and describes the process for controlling scope change requests.

Understand the purpose of the scope statement.   The scope statement is the basis of the agreement between the project and the customer concerning what comprises the work of the project. It defines the deliverables and success criteria that will meet those objectives.

Be able to list the components of a scope statement.   A scope statement includes a product description, key deliverables, success and acceptance criteria, key performance indicators, exclusions, assumptions, and constraints.

Know how to define and create a work breakdown structure (WBS).   The WBS is a deliverable-oriented hierarchy that describes the work required to complete the project. The WBS is a multilevel tree diagram that starts with the project, includes the major deliverables, and decomposes the major deliverables into smaller units of work to the point where time and cost estimates can be provided and resources assigned.

Understand the levels in a WBS.   The highest level of the WBS is the project name. The major deliverables, project phases, or subprojects make up the next level. The number of levels in a WBS will vary by project; however, the lowest level of the WBS is a work package.

Describe a WBS dictionary.   The WBS dictionary describes each of the deliverables and their components and includes a code of accounts identifier, estimates, resources, criteria for acceptance, and any other information that helps clarify the deliverables.

Key Terms

Before you take the exam, be certain you are familiar with the following terms:

acceptance criteria   scope creep

code of accounts   scope management plan

critical success factors   scope planning

decomposition   success criteria

order of magnitude   WBS dictionary

product description   work breakdown structure (WBS)

product scope statement   work package level

scope

Review Questions

1. Which of the following is not a key component of scope planning?
    - **A.** Work breakdown structure (WBS)
    - **B.** Scope statement
    - **C.** Project charter
    - **D.** Scope management plan

2. The scope statement provides which of the following?
    - **A.** A basis for a common understanding of the project and for making future decisions regarding the project
    - **B.** A detailed list of all resources required for project completion
    - **C.** A schedule of all the key project activities
    - **D.** A process for managing change control

3. Which of the following is a characteristic of a WBS?
    - **A.** A cost center structure of the project
    - **B.** An organization chart of the project team members
    - **C.** Used primarily on large complex projects involving multiple departments
    - **D.** A deliverables-oriented structure that defines the work of the project

4. Which of the following are components of a scope statement? Choose three.
    - **A.** General project approach
    - **B.** Product description
    - **C.** KPIs
    - **D.** Exclusions
    - **E.** Stakeholder list
    - **F.** High-level milestones
    - **G.** Change request process

5. A WBS is created using a technique called *decomposition*. What is decomposition?
    - **A.** Matching resources with deliverables
    - **B.** Breaking down the project deliverables into smaller, more manageable components
    - **C.** Estimating the cost of each individual deliverable
    - **D.** Creating a detailed to-do list for each work package

6. What is the lowest level of the WBS?
    - **A.** Work package
    - **B.** Level 10
    - **C.** Milestone
    - **D.** Activities

7. Which of the following is not a guideline for developing a WBS?

    A. Define the highest level of deliverables before you move to lower levels.

    B. Make sure that each item in a lower level is a component of the level above.

    C. Sequence the work packages.

    D. Involve project team members in the process.

8. Which of the following is not a benefit of a WBS?

    A. A WBS is an excellent tool for team building.

    B. A WBS helps prevents critical work from being overlooked.

    C. A WBS can become a template for future projects.

    D. A WBS can be used to describe how the deliverables will be verified

9. All of the following are true regarding code of accounts identifiers except for which one?

    A. These are unique numbers for each component on the WBS.

    B. They are documented in the WBS dictionary.

    C. They are tied to the organization's chart of accounts.

    D. They are assigned to the resources who are associated with each work package.

10. Your team is working on creating a WBS for phase 2 of the ABC software implementation project. Which of the following is an example of what might appear in the second level of your WBS?

    A. ABC Software implementation project

    B. Project deliverables

    C. Project phases

    D. Activities

11. Which element is not a component or function of the scope management plan?

    A. Describes the deliverables' acceptance criteria

    B. Describes how scope changes will be handled

    C. Describes the procedures for preparing the scope statement

    D. Describes the procedures for preparing the WBS

12. This element of the project scope statement helps you incrementally monitor project performance:

    A. Success criteria

    B. KPIs

    C. Exclusions

    D. Key deliverables

13. There are three primary constraints on most all projects. Your customer, or project sponsor, will stipulate which of the three is the most important to them. What are these three elements according to CompTIA? Choose three.

    A. Budget

    B. Team members

    C. Scope

    D. Quality

    E. Time

    F. Sponsors and stakeholders

    G. Scope management plan

14. Which element of the project scope statement describes the features, functions, and characteristics of the product of the project?

    A. Deliverables description

    B. Milestones description

    C. Product description

    D. KPIs

15. This term describes a characteristic of the planning processes:

    A. Looping

    B. Iterative

    C. Ongoing

    D. Repetitive

16. Your project is nearing completion of the first phase. Your key stakeholder for this phase reminds you that she will not accept the deliverable unless it measures 3 centimeters exactly. If the measurements are off, phase 2 will be delayed, and the entire project will be at risk. This is an example of which of the following?

    A. Delivery acceptance criteria

    B. Success criteria

    C. Critical success factor

    D. KPI

17. Elements of the project that are not listed on the WBS are considered what? Choose two.

    A. Work that will be completed in a future phase of the project.

    B. Exclusions from scope.

    C. They are considered scope creep.

    D. They are not considered part of the project.

18. You're developing a scope document for a customer request. A couple of the elements that the client wants could be difficult to accomplish, but after consulting with the project team, you think they can be done. These elements are not included in the product description. What should you do?

    A. Include these elements in the scope document, trusting your project team to deliver.

    B. Include these elements in the scope document, denoting them as a concern, and document how the issues were resolved.

    C. Discuss the problem elements with the project sponsor and the customer. Obtain sponsor sign-off.

    D. Note the elements in the exclusions section of the project scope statement, and state that they'll be included in phase 2.

19. What is the primary function of the project sponsor regarding the scope document?

    A. Signs off on the project scope document

    B. Has input into the project scope document

    C. Does not interact with the project scope document

    D. Authors the project scope document

20. You're developing the scope document and project plan for a new project. What process group are you in?

    A. Initiating

    B. Planning

    C. Executing

    D. Controlling

Answers to Review Questions

1.   C. The key components of scope planning are the scope management plan, scope statement, and work breakdown structure. The project charter is created during project initiation.

2.   A. The scope statement serves as a basis for understanding the work of the project and for future decision making.

3.   D. A WBS is a deliverables-oriented hierarchy that defines the work of the project and can be used on projects of any size or complexity.

4.   B, C, D. The sections of a project scope statement are product description, key deliverables, success and acceptance criteria, key performance indicators, exclusions, time and cost estimates, assumptions, and constraints.

5.   B. Decomposition breaks the major deliverables down into smaller, more manageable units of work that can be used estimate cost and time and perform resource planning.

6.   A. The lowest level of a WBS is the work package. The number of levels will vary by project and complexity.

7.   C. The purpose of a WBS is to identify all the work required to complete a project. Defining the order of the tasks will occur during the scheduling process.

8.   D. The scope management document, not the WBS, describes how the deliverables will be verified.

9.   D. The code of accounts identifier is a unique number assigned to each component of the WBS. It is documented in the WBS dictionary and is tied to the chart of accounts.

10. C. The first level of the WBS is the project name, in this case ABC software implementation. The second level of the WBS represents major project deliverables, project phases, or subprojects. If the project has phases or subprojects, these are listed at the second level, with deliverables listed at the third level. Since the question asks about phase 2 of the project and option C is project phases, this is the correct second-level entry for the WBS.

11. A. The scope management plan contains a definition of how the deliverables will be verified, but the acceptance criteria are documented in the project scope statement.

12. B. KPIs are key performance indicators that help you incrementally monitor project performance.

13. A, D, E. They are budget, quality, and time according to CompTIA.

14. C. The product description describes the features, functions, and characteristics of the product, service, or result of the project.

15. B. Project planning processes are iterative, meaning you'll define the scope statement and other planning documents, and as you create these documents, more information may come to light or you may discover an element you missed. So, you'll go back through processes you've already started and modify them with the new information.

16. C. Critical success factors are those elements of the project that must be completed accurately to consider the project a success. Without these elements, the project is likely in danger of failing.

17. B, D. Work that is not included in the WBS is not part of the project. Exclusions from scope are work components that are not included in the project and should not appear on the WBS.

18. C. Whenever problems arise on a project that are outside the authority or control of the project manager to resolve or when problems have the ability to affect project outcomes, the sponsor should always be informed.

19. A. The project sponsor, along with other key stakeholders, signs off on the project scope document. Project sponsors may have some input to scope, but the project manager is the author of the document, and the stakeholders are primary contributors to the scope document.

20. B. The Planning process group is where you begin to define important documents such as the scope document and project plan.

Chapter

4

Schedule Planning

THE COMPTIA PROJECT+ EXAM TOPICS COVERED IN THIS CHAPTER INCLUDE

✓ **2.4 Develop a project schedule based on WBS, project scope and resource requirements**

- Schedule to milestones
- Analyze Gantt chart
- Identify dependency types
- Determine the critical path of a project schedule
- Establish schedule baselines

✓ **2.5 Given a desired deliverable, apply the appropriate tool and/or method to produce the appropriate outcome**

- Tools
- PERT
- Gantt
  - Methods
- CPM

✓ **2.6 Given a scenario, interpret the results of using the following tools and/or methods**

- Tools
- GERT
  - Methods
- CPMNetwork diagram (ADM, PDM, CDM, CCM)

After the WBS is completed, the next planning document you'll develop is the project schedule. This chapter will cover all aspects of creating a project schedule, starting with defining activities, sequencing activities, estimating, and finally building the schedule.

You're probably familiar with project schedules and you've likely seen many of them during the course of your career. At first glance, it would seem that putting together a schedule is fairly basic. All you need to do is enter the work packages from the WBS into Microsoft Project, and you have the schedule. However, a sound project schedule takes a lot of planning. All the tasks must be identified, they must be sequenced in the order they can be completed, they need an estimated time frame for completion, and finally all this data must be organized to come up with the overall project schedule.

The schedule documents the planned start and finish of each of the activities included in the project, and the total project duration is calculated once the schedule is complete. Once finalized, checking the schedule becomes part of the project manager's weekly, if not daily, routine until the project is completed. Progress is reported against the schedule, and status updates regarding activities are provided to the stakeholders on a regular basis.

If you don't take the time up front to perform schedule planning and create an accurate schedule, you'll be spending a lot of time during project execution making changes to the schedule and explaining why deliverables are not being completed as anticipated.

The project schedule is another planning document that uses an iterative approach in its development. You'll want several subject matter experts to assist you with the estimating and planning of the schedule, and it's a good idea to let everyone know up front that it will probably take several sessions to finalize the schedule.

Defining Activities

The foundation for developing a project schedule is a list of the activities required to complete the project. Activity Definition is the process of breaking down the work packages from the WBS that we discussed in Chapter 3, "Planning a Project," into individual activities that make up all the work of the work package. Although the industry standards set by the *PMBOK Guide* define breaking down work packages into activities as a separate process, in reality Activity Definition is typically not a stand-alone process. It is part of the iterative process of further decomposing the WBS to a manageable level. It's a natural progression to break down the work packages into activities as you're decomposing the WBS because you've got all the right people in the room and you've got the momentum going.

According to industry standards, activities are not included on a WBS.

Many guidelines are available on how far you should break down an activity, and none of them is right for every situation. You don't want a schedule so large that you need a cart to carry it around on, but you don't want it too high-level, either, because you won't be able to accurately estimate times or due dates.

The key to Activity Definition is to identify all the tasks required to produce the work packages (and ultimately the deliverables). This needs to be balanced with keeping activities at a high enough level that they can be managed effectively. You do not want to end up trying to keep track of each team member's to-do list.

A good rule of thumb we use for most projects is to define activities at a level that will take one to two weeks to complete. If you have a very critical task that's shorter in duration than this, or a very small project, you may want to make an exception to this.

You'll want to list each activity you've defined on an *activity list*. This list should include every activity needed to complete the work of the project, along with an identifier or code so that you can track each activity independently. It's also good practice to list the WBS code this activity is associated with, along with a scope of work description.

Once you have all your activities defined, you're now ready to start putting them into the sequence in which they will be completed.

Activity Sequencing

Activity Sequencing is the process of identifying dependency relationships between project activities and sequencing them in proper order. First you need to identify the type of dependency, and then you need to determine the specific relationship between the activities. Using this data, you can then create a pictorial representation of the tasks that shows all the dependencies.

Dependencies are relationships between activities. For example, one activity may not be able to start until another has finished, or perhaps one activity is dependent on another activity starting before it can finish. We'll cover several types of dependencies next.

Types of Dependencies

There are three categories of dependencies in Activity Sequencing:

- Mandatory dependencies
- Discretionary dependencies
- External dependencies

A *mandatory dependency* is defined by the type of work being performed, and one activity is dependent on another activity. For example, a utility crew can't lay the cable for a new housing area until a trench has been dug.

A *discretionary dependency* is usually process- or procedure-driven and may include best-practice techniques. An example is a decision to require sign-off on certain types of activities to conform to an established corporate practice.

An *external dependency* is a relationship between a project task and some factor outside the project that drives the scheduling of that task. Installation of a new server depends on when the vendor can deliver the equipment.

It is important to know the type of dependency you're dealing with because you have more flexibility with a discretionary dependency than a mandatory dependency. This distinction becomes important later when you're looking at ways to complete a project in less time.

Logical Relationships

It isn't enough just to know there is a dependency between two activities. You need to answer several other questions: How does the dependency impact the start and finish of each of the activities? Does one activity have to start first? Can you start the second activity before the first activity is finished? All these variables impact what your overall project schedule looks like.

Once you identify a dependency between two activities, you need to determine what that logical relationship is so that you can sequence the activities properly. Before we cover those relationships, we'll present a few key terms that are critical to understanding task dependencies.

A *predecessor* activity is one that comes before another activity. A *successor* activity is one that comes after the activity in question. Figure 4.1 shows a simple predecessor/successor relationship between Activity A and Activity B.

FIGURE 4.1   Predecessor/successor relationship

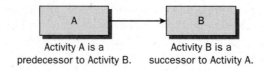

| Activity A is a | Activity B is a |
| predecessor to Activity B. | successor to Activity A. |

Four possible *logical relationships* can exist between the predecessor activity and the successor activity. Identifying the correct relationship between dependent activities is critical to developing an accurate schedule. Depending on the type of dependency relationship, you may be able to schedule the activity in parallel, or the successor activity may have to wait until the predecessor is completed. The four logical relationships are as follows:

Finish-to-start   In a finish-to-start relationship, the successor activity cannot begin until the predecessor activity has completed. This is the most frequently used logical relationship and is the default setting for most project-scheduling software packages.

Start-to-finish   In a start-to-finish relationship, the predecessor activity must start before the successor activity can finish. This relationship is seldom used.

Finish-to-finish   A finish-to-finish relationship is where the predecessor activity must finish before the successor activity finishes.

Start-to-start   In a start-to-start relationship, the predecessor activity depends on starting before the successive activity can start.

Once the activity dependency relationships have been identified, the project team has the data to create a picture of when the various project tasks can begin and end. This picture is a network diagram.

Creating a Network Diagram

One technique used by project managers for Activity Sequencing is a network diagram. Understanding activity relationships is fundamental to using this technique. A *network diagram* depicts the project activities and the interrelationships among these activities. A network diagram is a great tool to develop with the project team. Use a whiteboard, and label each sticky note with one activity. This will make it easy to see the workflow, and you can move the sticky notes around to make changes.

The most commonly used network diagramming method is the *precedence diagramming method (PDM)*. PDM uses boxes to represent the project activities and arrows to connect the boxes and show the dependencies. Figure 4.2 shows a simple PDM network diagram of tasks with finish-to-start dependencies.

FIGURE 4.2   Precedence diagramming method

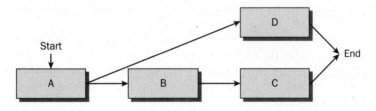

Two other types of network diagrams are not used as often as PDM. One is called the *arrow diagramming method* (ADM), and it's the exact opposite of the PDM. The PMD has the activities on nodes (or in boxes), and arrows connect each of the activities. In the ADM method, the arrows themselves represent the activities, and the nodes are the connecting points between the activities.

The second technique is the *conditional diagramming method* (CDM). This is a way to diagram activities that loop, or are repeated throughout the project, and is a way to diagram activities that are not in sequential order. You would use CDM in conjunction with the graphical evaluation and review technique (GERT). GERT allows for conditional loops in the project schedule as well. This analysis technique is rarely used in practice.

There's one more method called the *critical chain method* (CCM) that we'll talk about in the "Creating the Project Schedule" section of this chapter.

Now that the activities are sequenced based on their logical dependencies, you're ready to estimate how long it will take to complete each activity.

Activity Duration Estimates

You've defined your activities, identified all the dependencies between tasks, and developed a network diagram to depict the flow of the project work. You must be ready to complete the project schedule, right? Not quite yet—you still need a very critical component: how long each task will take to complete. *Activity Duration* is the process of estimating the time to complete each item on the activity list. The most common measurements used to define durations are days or weeks, but you can also use hours, months, or other increments of time, depending on the project.

Before we explain the techniques you can use to complete your duration estimates, let's make sure we have a common understanding of Activity Duration.

Defining Duration

When you are estimating duration, you need to make sure that you are looking at the total elapsed time to complete the activity. If you have a task that is estimated to take five days based on an eight-hour day fully dedicated to that task, the actual duration estimate would be ten days if the resource assigned to the task is spending only four hours a day on the task.

You also need to be aware of the difference between workdays and calendar days. If your workweek is Monday through Friday and you have a four-day task starting on Thursday, the duration for that task will be six calendar days, because no work will be done on Saturday and Sunday. Figure 4.3 illustrates this situation. The same concept applies to holidays or vacation time.

FIGURE 4.3   A four-day task separated by the weekend

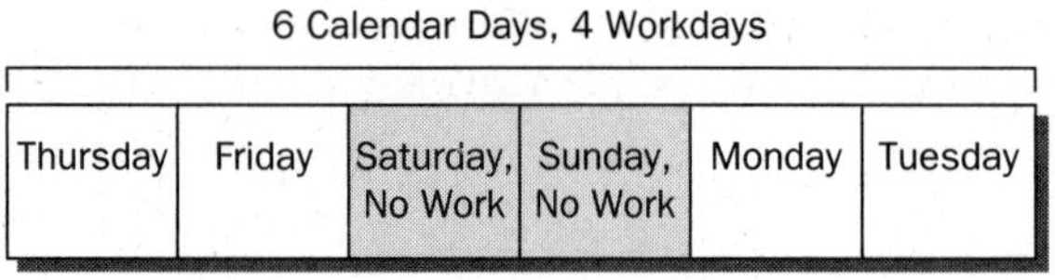

6 Calendar Days, 4 Workdays

Thursday	Friday	Saturday, No Work	Sunday, No Work	Monday	Tuesday

Make certain that everyone who is providing estimates is in agreement up front as to whether they will be provided in workdays or calendar days. We recommend using workday duration estimates. Most project management software packages allow you to establish a calendar that accounts for nonworkdays and will exclude these days when computing duration.

Now that we have a common understanding of duration, we'll discuss the different techniques used to create Activity Duration estimates.

Estimating Techniques

You can use several techniques to determine Activity Duration estimates. We'll explain five of the most common methods:

Analogous estimating, or top-down estimating   *Analogous estimating (top-down estimating)* is the use of actual durations from similar activities on a previous project. This is most frequently used at the early stages of project planning, when you have limited information regarding the project. Although analogous estimating can provide a good approximation of task duration, it is typically the least accurate means of obtaining an estimate. No two projects are the same, and there is the risk that the project used to obtain the analogous estimates is not as similar as it appears.

Results from analogous estimating are more accurate if the person doing the estimating is familiar with both projects and is able to understand the differences that could impact the activity durations on the new project.

Expert judgment   *Expert judgment* uses the people most familiar with the work to create the estimate. Ideally, the project team member who will be doing the task should complete the estimate. If all the team members haven't been identified yet, go recruit people with expertise for the tasks you need estimated. If you don't know who the internal experts are, research the documentation on team members from similar projects or solicit input from your stakeholders. Ask for people who have completed a similar task on a previous project to assist with the estimates for this project.

The most accurate estimates using expert judgment are those made by the person who'll be completing the task. Remember that people with more experience will likely provide a shorter estimate for an activity than someone who doesn't have as much experience. You should validate the estimate or ask other experts in the department to validate them for you.

Parametric estimating   *Parametric estimating* is a quantitatively based estimating method that multiplies the quantity of work by the rate. To apply quantitatively based durations, you must know the productivity rate of the resource performing the task or have a company or industry standard that can be applied to the task in question. The duration is obtained by multiplying the unit of work produced by the productivity rate. For example, if a typical cable crew can bury 5 miles of cable in a day, it should take 10 days to bury 50 miles of cable.

Three-point estimates   *Three-point estimates* are an average of the most likely estimate, the optimistic estimate, and the pessimistic estimate for the activity. The most likely estimate assumes that work proceeds according to plan. The optimistic estimate is the fastest time frame in which your resources can complete the activity. The pessimistic estimate assumes the work will take a long time to complete. This is a simple calculation. For example, let's say your most likely estimate is 10 days. The optimistic estimate is 7 days, and the pessimistic estimate is 14 days. The three-point estimate is calculated this way:

(10 + 7 + 14) / 3 = 10 days

PERT   *Program Evaluation and Review Technique (PERT)* is a method that the U.S. Navy developed in the 1950s. The Navy was working on one of the most complex engineering projects in history at the time—the Polaris Missile Program—and needed a way to manage the project and forecast the project schedule with a high degree of reliability. PERT was developed to do just that.

PERT   and three-point estimates are similar techniques. The difference is that three-point estimates use an average estimate to determine project duration, while PERT uses what's called *expected value* (or the weighted average). Expected value is calculated using the three-point estimates for Activity Duration and then finding the weighted average of those estimates.

The formula to calculate expected value is as follows:

(optimistic + pessimistic + (4 × most likely)) / 6

Using the same numbers used in the three-point estimates produces the following expected value:

(7 + 14 + (4 × 10)) / 6 = 10 days

Most projects use some combination of the estimating techniques explained here. Once you have determined which estimating technique works best for your project, assign a duration estimate to each task, as illustrated in Figure 4.4.

FIGURE 4.4   Network diagram with task duration

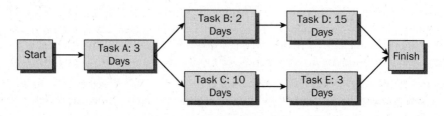

This will prepare you for the next step in this process, which is Schedule Development.

Real World Scenario

The Mandated-Reporting Project

The State of Bliss has received $2.5 billion in special grant monies from the federal government for health care, education, and transportation projects. Ordinarily, these departments don't work together, and they currently don't share any data. One of the requirements for receiving the grant money is that extensive reporting must be conducted on a monthly basis regarding the use of these funds, including how the money was spent, the vendors who participated in projects, and other related information. The catch is that the information must be reported from one central entity at the state. The information should include department-level data, but it must be reported in one format from one central location.

The transportation department volunteered to take the lead on this project. One of the deliverables on the critical path for this project is interface development. When this deliverable is completed, it will allow the new reporting system to receive data from each of the disparate grant systems that reside in the departments and produce reports from this data from one centralized reports system. Several activities are associated with this deliverable. One of them is verifying that the data received, calculated, and shown on the final report matches the data that resides on the grant system from which it originated. Your programming and business analyst experts give you three estimates on the time to complete this task. Most likely is 20 days, optimistic is 15 days, and pessimistic is 35 days. You calculate a three-point estimate and determine that the time estimate for this task should be 23 days. With this information in hand, you proceed to creating a project schedule and assigning resources to each task.

Creating the Project Schedule

Schedule Development involves establishing a start date and a finish date for each of the project activities. All the other work you've done so far, including defining the activities, sequencing the activities, and determining duration estimates, culminates in creating the final project schedule.

It may take several iterations to get the schedule finalized. Once it's approved, it serves as the schedule baseline for the project. You'll use this baseline to track actual progress against what was planned once you begin the work of the project.

We'll cover three of the most common techniques used for developing schedules next:

- The critical path method
- Duration compression
- Project management software

Critical Path Method

One of the most widely used techniques in Schedule Development is the *critical path method (CPM)*. CPM determines the amount of *float time* for each activity on the schedule by calculating the earliest start date, earliest finish date, latest start date, and latest finish date for each. Float is then calculated to determine the amount of time you can delay the earliest start of an activity without delaying the ending of the project. Activities with zero float are considered critical path activities. If a critical path task does not finish as scheduled, the project end date will be affected.

The *critical path* is the longest full path on the project. If you refer to Figure 4.4, you'll see the longest path for this project has a duration of 20 days. This is calculated by adding the durations for the A-B-D path (Task A, Task B, and Task D). We'll walk through a detailed example of how to calculate the critical path later in this section.

NOTE

For the exam, make certain you understand that the critical path is the longest full path on the project. The simplest calculation you can use for the exam is to add up the duration of each activity for each path on the project and determine which one is the longest.

In addition to calculating the overall time to complete the project and identifying tasks on the critical path, CPM provides other useful data. You will be able to determine which tasks can start late or can take longer than planned without impacting the project end date. During project execution, the project manager can use this information to focus attention on the tasks that have the most impact on the overall project completion date.

We'll now walk you through a CPM calculation. CPM is rarely done manually, since a variety of software tools will do these calculations for you. But unless you understand the fundamentals behind what the software is doing, you can't take advantage of what it's telling you.

The network diagram we created during Activity Sequencing and the task duration estimates are the key components of the CPM calculation. Refer to the precedence diagram shown in Figure 4.4 as we walk you through this example:

Forward pass   The first step in determining your critical path is to complete a *forward pass* through the network diagram. This means that you are working from the left to the right of your network diagram. This will give you two calculations for each activity: early start and early finish. *Early start* is the earliest date an activity can begin, as logically constrained by the network. *Early finish* is the earliest date an activity can finish, as logically constrained by the network.

In Figure 4.4, the early start for Task A is 0 since it is the first activity on the network. The duration for A is three days, so your early finish is 3. The early finish for A becomes the early start for its successor, Task B. Continue to calculate the early start and finish dates for each activity on the network, moving across the diagram until you reach the Finish box.

Table 4.1 shows the completed early start and early finish calculations for each of the tasks in the network diagram. Based on the calculations from this completed forward pass, the project is completed on day 20.

TABLE 4.1 Forward pass

Task	Early Start	Early Finish
A	0	3
B	3	5
C	3	13
D	5	20
E	13	16

Backward pass The next step to complete the critical path is to complete a *backward pass*. This means you start at the finish of your network diagram and work back though each path until you reach the start. This gives you two calculations, late finish and late start. *Late finish* is the latest date an activity can complete without impacting the project end date. *Late start* is the latest date you can start an activity without impacting the project end date.

In Figure 4.4, the final activity to complete is Task D. The latest it can finish is day 20. To calculate the late start for this activity, subtract the duration of 15 days from the late finish. Your late start is day 5. The late start for Task D becomes the late finish for its predecessor, Task B. Continue backward through the network, calculating the late start and late finish for each task on the network diagram.

Then compute the second path, starting with Task E. Since the project finish date is day 20, the late finish for Task E is also day 20. By subtracting the duration of three days, you obtain the late start of day 17. Continue to calculate the late start and finish dates for each activity on the network.

Table 4.2 shows the completed late start and late finish calculations for the network diagram.

TABLE 4.2   Backward pass

Task	Late Start	Late Finish
A	0	3
B	3	5
C	7	17
D	5	20
E	17	20

Float   The final step in determining the critical path is to calculate float for each activity on the network diagram. Float is determined by subtracting the early start from the late start or the early finish from the late finish for each activity. Use the calculations from Tables 4.1 and 4.2, and start with Task A. The early finish is 3 and the late finish is 3, making the float 0. Continue through the network diagram until you have computed the float time for each activity.

Table 4.3 shows the float for each of the tasks.

TABLE 4.3   Float

Task	Early Start	Late Start	Float
A	0	0	0
B	3	3	0
C	3	7	4
D	5	5	0
E	13	17	4

You are now ready to determine the critical path. Remember we said earlier that the critical path is the path with zero float, and it also happens to be the longest full path on the project. In the example in Figure 4.4, both Tasks C and E have float, which means they are not on the critical path. A-B-D is the critical path, because each of these tasks has zero float. If any of the tasks on the critical path do not start on time or take longer than planned, the end date of the project will be impacted. Remember that you must pay particular attention to the status of your critical path tasks over the course of the project to keep your schedule on track.

There are times when you complete the network diagram, calculate the critical path, and find that the duration of the project is unacceptable to the project stakeholders. If you find yourself in that situation, you can use duration compression techniques to help shorten the schedule. We'll cover those techniques next.

Duration Compression

You have just learned how to develop a network diagram of your project tasks and create your schedule using CPM. But what happens if your calculation of the total project duration is longer than your target project completion date?

This is where *duration compression* scheduling techniques come into play. These techniques can be used during planning to shorten the planned duration of the project or during project execution to help resolve schedule slippage. The two duration compression techniques are crashing and fast tracking. We'll explain both next.

Crashing

Crashing is a technique that looks at cost and schedule trade-offs. Crashing is typically implemented by adding more resources to the critical path tasks in order to complete the project more quickly. Crashing could also be accomplished by requiring mandatory overtime for critical path tasks, by speeding up delivery times from vendors, and so on.

> One common misconception about adding resources is that if you double the resources, you can cut the duration in half. In other words, if two programmers can write the code in four weeks, then four programmers must be able to do it in two weeks. This isn't always the case. Typically, the original resources assigned to the task are less productive when you add new resources because they're busy helping the new resources come up to speed on the work.

Crashing can produce the desired results if used wisely, but you should be aware that crashing the schedule may increase risks and/or impact your budget. Be certain you've examined these impacts to the project when using this technique.

Fast Tracking

Fast tracking is performing two tasks in parallel that were previously scheduled to start sequentially.

For example, suppose you have a project where you need to build four servers that are going to interact with one another. You might have initially created four "build server" tasks that were supposed to happen one right after the other. However, when you decide to fast track the project, you schedule all four tasks to begin in parallel.

There is a great deal of risk in fast tracking. If you decide to compress your project schedule using this method, be sure you get input from the team members as to what could go wrong. In the previous example, there may not be enough resources to physically start all four of the tasks at the same time, or there could be reasons why one of the servers must be completed before another. Document all the risks, and present them to your sponsor, your client, and other key stakeholders. Many project managers make the mistake of trying to do the project faster without communicating any of the potential risks or impacts to the project. You need to make sure that everyone understands the potential consequences.

Chapter 9, "Controlling the Project," will cover what you can do if you have critical path tasks that are taking longer than planned.

Project Management Software

Project management software is a wonderful tool that can save you a lot of time. It provides you with the ability to display a number of different views of the project, which can be a great communication tool. We'll cover a couple of ways you can display your project in the next section.

Communicating the Project Schedule

The purpose of the project schedule is to determine the start and finish dates for each of the project activities. Now that you've finished that, it's time put the schedule together into a format that's easily understood by the project team and stakeholders.

You can use several methods to display the project schedule. One is the network diagram method you saw in Figure 4.4. However, you'll need to add the start and stop dates for each of the activities in the top portion of the boxes on this figure, and you'll also want to highlight the critical path.

Milestone charts are another method to display your schedule information. A milestone marks a key event in the project life cycle or the completion of a major deliverable. A milestone chart tracks the scheduled dates and actual completion dates for the major milestones. Table 4.4 shows an example milestone chart. As the project manager, you should pay close attention to milestone dates, because they are also a communication trigger. Stakeholders need to be informed when major deliverables are completed or when a project has successfully moved to a new phase. If these dates are not met, you need to communicate the current status, the plans to bring the project back on track, and the new milestone date. All the details of communications planning will be covered in Chapter 5, "Communicating the Plan."

TABLE 4.4 Milestone chart

Milestone	Scheduled Date	Actual Date
Sign-off on scope statement	9/25	9/25
Sign-off on deliverables	2/02	2/02
Sign-off on hardware test	2/02	2/06
Programming completed	4/15	
Testing completed	5/8	
Acceptance and sign-off	5/22	
Project closeout	6/3	

Gantt charts are probably one of the most commonly used methods to display the project schedule. They can show milestones, deliverables, subdeliverables, or all the activities of the project, if needed. Gantt charts typically display the tasks using a horizontal bar chart format across a timeline. Gantt charts are easy to read and can show the activity sequences, start and end dates, resource assignment, dependencies, and critical path.

Figure 4.5 shows a sample Gantt chart.

FIGURE 4.5 Gantt chart

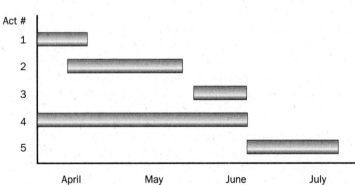

Schedule Baseline

The schedule baseline is the final, approved version of the project schedule that includes the baseline start and finish dates and resource assignments. It's important that you obtain sign-off on the project schedule from your stakeholders and functional managers who are supplying resources to the project. This assures you that they have read the schedule, understand the dates, and understand the resource commitments. Ideally, it will also keep them from reneging on commitments they've made, activity due dates by their team members, and promises of resources at specific times on the project.

The schedule baseline will be used throughout the project to monitor progress. This doesn't mean that changes can never be made to the schedule. But we encourage you to heavily consider changes that will change the project end date. We'll talk more about proper change management processes and procedures in Chapter 8, "Processing Change Requests."

Real World Scenario

Chaptal Wineries

You've created an initial project schedule with dates for each activity and have determined most of the dependencies among tasks. But something doesn't seem quite right about the dates. As you study the schedule, the reason occurs to you.

The server installation itself should go fairly smoothly. And provided WAN connectivity is set up and working, you should have few issues with the actual software installation. You'll also be setting up an intranet-based web server while you're at each location. You believe the server administrator can accomplish all the installation work in two days per location, and you're building in an additional day for any issues that might arise. The total duration for this task is three days per location.

Provisioning the WAN connectivity through the various local telcos must be accomplished before arriving on site, which makes this a predecessor task to each site visit. The administrator will have to work hand in hand with the local winery representative to provide them with the telecommunications company contact information, important documentation, and anticipated installation lead times, as well as to make sure that the contracts are signed and installation dates set. But you don't anticipate any major delivery problems and have required that the connectivity task be completed two weeks before the team arrives on the site.

You and the server administrator and trainer will be flying to each location, installing servers, implementing the new software and conducting user training, and then flying to the next location. Considering a flight from France to Australia, there's a minimum of one day on the airplane and probably a half day for jetlag recovery, plus the configuration time to get the server up and running. Then user training must be conducted. But what occurs to you is that you haven't accounted for the travel time in the schedule.

You modify the schedule and include travel time for each site visit as a task so that you can calculate an accurate project duration.

Summary

Many steps are involved in schedule planning. Activity Definition takes the work packages from your WBS and breaks them down into assignable tasks. Activity Sequencing looks at dependencies between tasks. These dependencies can be mandatory, discretionary, or external. A dependent task is either a successor or a predecessor of a linked task.

There are four types of logical relationships: finish-to-start, start-to-start, start-to-finish, and finish-to-finish. A network diagram is a pictorial representation of the task-dependency (logical) relationships.

Activity Duration estimating is obtained using analogous (also called top-down) estimating, parametric estimating, expert judgment, three-point estimates, and PERT.

The most complex schedule planning process is Schedule Development. The critical path method (CPM) creates a schedule by calculating forward and backward passes through the network diagram and then determining float. Float is the difference between the early and late start dates and the early and late finish dates. The critical path is the longest full path on the project.

Duration compression is the technique used to shorten a project schedule to meet a mandated completion date. Crashing shortens task duration by adding more resources to the project. Fast tracking is where two tasks are started in parallel that were previously scheduled to start sequentially.

A project schedule may be displayed as a milestone chart. Milestones mark major project events such as the completion of a key deliverable or project phase. Gantt charts are a common method to display schedule data as well. The completed, approved project schedule becomes the baseline for tracking and reporting project progress.

Exam Essentials

Describe the Activity Sequencing process.   Activity Sequencing is the process of identifying dependency relationships between the project activities and scheduling activities in the proper order.

Name the two major relationships between dependent tasks.   A predecessor is a task that exists on a path with another task and occurs before the task in question. A successor is a task that exists on a common path with another task and occurs after the task in question.

Name the four types of logical relationships.   The four types of logical relationships are finish-to-start, start-to-start, start-to-finish, and finish-to-finish.

Know and understand the five most commonly used techniques to estimate activity duration.   Expert judgment relies on the knowledge of someone familiar with the tasks. Analogous or top-down estimating bases the estimate on similar activities from a previous project. Parametric estimates are quantitatively based estimates that typically calculate the rate times quantity. Three-point estimates use the most likely, optimistic, and pessimistic estimates to determine an average estimate. PERT uses the same estimates as the three-point estimating technique, but it calculates an expected value or weighted average estimate.

Define the purpose of CPM.   CPM calculates the longest path in the project. This path controls the finish date of the project. Any delay to a critical path task will delay the completion date of the project.

Explain a network diagram.   A network diagram is used in Activity Sequencing to depict project activities and the interrelationships and dependencies among these activities.

Name the two most common ways project schedules are displayed.   Project schedules are typically displayed as milestone charts or Gantt charts; a Gantt chart is a type of bar chart.

Key Terms

Before you take the exam, be certain you are familiar with the following terms:

Activity Duration	fast tracking
activity list	float time
Activity Sequencing	forward pass
analogous estimating	late finish
backward pass	late start
crashing	logical relationships
critical path	mandatory dependency
critical path method (CPM)	network diagram
dependencies	parametric estimating
discretionary dependency	precedence diagramming method (PDM)
duration compression	predecessor
early finish	program evaluation and review technique (PERT)
early start	successor
expected value	three-point estimates
expert judgment	
external dependency	

Review Questions

1. Which of the following is not true for the critical path?

   A. It has zero float.

   B. It's the shortest activity sequence in the network.

   C. You can determine which tasks can start late without impacting the project end date.

   D. It controls the project finish date.

2. You are a project manager for a major movie studio. You need to schedule a shoot in Denver during ski season. This is an example of which of the following?

   A. External dependency

   B. Finish-to-start relationship

   C. Mandatory dependency

   D. Discretionary dependency

3. What is analogous estimating also referred to as?

   A. Bottom-up estimating

   B. Expert judgment

   C. Parametric estimating

   D. Top-down estimating

4. You are working on your network diagram. Activity A is a predecessor to Activity B. Activity B cannot begin until Activity A is completed. What is this telling you?

   A. There is a mandatory dependency between Activity A and Activity B.

   B. There is a finish-to-start dependency relationship between Activity A and Activity B.

   C. Activity A and Activity B are both on the critical path.

   D. Activity B is a successor to multiple tasks.

5. What is the most commonly used form of network diagramming?

   A. ADM

   B. Precedence diagramming

   C. CPM

   D. PERT

6. What are the crashing and fast track techniques used for?

   A. Duration compression

   B. Activity sequencing

   C. Precedence diagramming

   D. Activity Definition

7. Which of the following is true for float or slack time?

   A. It's calculated by adding the durations of all activities and dividing by the number of activities.

   B. It's time that you add to the project schedule to provide a buffer or contingency.

   C. It's the amount of time an activity can be delayed without delaying the project completion.

   D. It is only calculated on the longest path of the network diagram.

8. Which of the following is not a tool used to determine a project's critical path?

   A. Forward pass

   B. Mandatory dependency

   C. Float calculation

   D. Backward pass

9. Activity B on your network diagram has a most likely estimate of 8 days, a pessimistic estimate of 11 days, and an optimistic estimate of 6 days. What is the three-point estimate for this task rounded to the nearest whole number?

   A. 11 days

   B. 25 days

   C. 8 days

   D. 6 days

10. Which of the following is not true for critical path activities?

   A. The early start is always less than the late start.

   B. These activities are on the longest path on the network diagram.

   C. The float is zero.

   D. The late finish is always the same as the early finish.

11. You're working on a project in which the time to complete the project has been heavily restricted and funds are short. You have one resource working on preparing six servers for use in a balanced web array. The servers will all look basically alike. What technique can you use to slim down some of the time required to perform this task in the project?

   A. Fast tracking

   B. Crashing

   C. Reducing the number of servers

   D. Purchasing a server that runs a number of virtual machines simultaneously

12. Your task requires 4 miles of paving, and it will take 30 hours to complete a mile. On a past project similar to this one, it took 150 hours to complete. Which of the following is true regarding this estimate?

   A. The total estimate for this task is 120 hours, which was derived using expert judgment.

   B. The total estimate for this task is 120 hours, which was derived using parametric estimating.

   C. The total estimate for this task is 150 hours, which was derived using analogous estimating.

   D. The total estimate for this task is 150 hours, which was derived using expert judgment.

13. Suppose that you're working on a project in which you've established this milestone: "Database servers built and functional." The following tasks are needed to complete this milestone:

   Task 1: Build three database servers.

   Task 2: Install database software on each server.

   Task 3: Validate that software is running correctly.

   Task 4: Install database schemas from development environment.

   Task 5: Test that it's 100 percent successful.

   Which of these tasks would represent the acceptance criteria for this milestone?

   A. Task 1

   B. Task 2

   C. Task 3

   D. Task 4

   E. Task 5

14. You're working on a project that you and your team have estimated takes 15 business days to complete. Your team does not work on Saturday, Sunday, or holidays. Given the work calendar shown here and a start date of Tuesday, November 1, what is the scheduled completion date for this task?

Sun	Mon	Tue	Wed	Thu	Fri	Sat
		1	2	3	4	5
6	7	8	9	10	11 Holiday	12
13	14	15	16	17	18	19
20	21	22	23	24 Holiday	25	26
27	28	29	30			

   A. 21

   B. 15

   C. 22

   D. 23

15. All of the following are true regarding milestone charts except for which one?

    A. Milestone charts list the major deliverables or phases of a project.

    B. Milestone charts show the scheduled completion dates.

    C. Milestone charts show the actual completion dates.

    D. Milestone charts are commonly displayed in bar chart format.

16. You're in the process of developing a project schedule for a new project for which you've just completed the WBS. What would be the smart next step in figuring out what tasks go into the project schedule?

    A. Develop an activity list.

    B. Determine the critical path tasks.

    C. Develop a network diagram.

    D. Estimate activity duration.

17. You've defined a task in a project schedule in which your team members will develop an XML application that uses a MySQL back end. Although the data base administrator (DBA) has plenty of experience with Oracle and Microsoft SQL Server, he has never been exposed to MySQL. Which of the following elements will most likely be affected?

    A. Resource allocation

    B. Task estimation

    C. Activity definitions

    D. Determining critical path tasks

18. Which is the most commonly used logical relationship?

    A. Finish-to-start

    B. Start-to-finish

    C. Start-to-start

    D. Finish-to-finish

19. How long is the critical path in days in the graphic shown here?

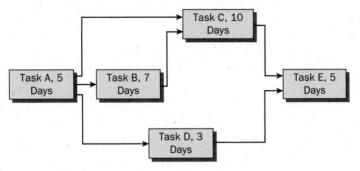

- **A.** 13 days
- **B.** 20 days
- **C.** 27 days
- **D.** 30 days

20. The following exhibit shows a series of steps in a network diagram. Which path represents the critical path?

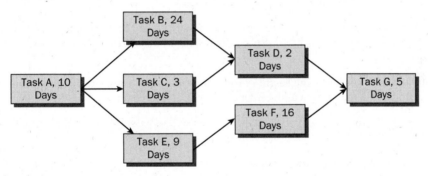

- **A.** A-E-F-G
- **B.** A-C-D-G
- **C.** A-B-D-G
- **D.** A-B-D-F-G

Answers to Review Questions

1. B. The critical path is the longest activity sequence in the network. It has zero float or slack time, and it controls the project end date. Using critical path, you can determine which tasks can start late or go longer than planned without impacting the project end date.

2. A. A requirement such as weather conditions or a specific season that drives the scheduling of a task is an example of an external dependency.

3. D. Analogous estimating is also called top-down estimating. It is used early in the project, when there is not enough detail to do a detailed estimate.

4. B. There is a finish-to-start dependency relationship between Activity A and Activity B. You do not have enough information to determine whether the dependency between the two activities is mandatory, discretionary, or external or if they are critical path activities.

5. B. Precedence diagramming is the most commonly used diagramming method. The arrow diagramming method (ADM) is a less-used diagramming method that uses arrows to represent the tasks. CPM is a schedule development technique. PERT is a schedule development technique that uses weighted averages.

6. A. Duration compression involves either crashing the schedule by adding more resources or by creating a fast track by working activities in parallel that would normally be done in sequence.

7. C. Float or slack time is the length of time a task may be started late or the additional duration a task may take without impacting project completion.

8. B. The tools used to calculate critical path are forward pass, backward pass, and float calculation.

9. C. The three-point estimate is calculated by averaging all three estimates. 8 + 11 + 6 = 25. 25/3 = 8.3.

10. A. Float is always zero for the critical path activities, so early start and late start are the same date.

11. A. You have only one resource and funds are limited, so crashing the project isn't the solution. The fast tracking option allows you to start more than one task at the same time. Previously, each server was scheduled to start and complete sequentially. You could start two or three servers at once, thereby fast tracking the schedule.

12. B. If you didn't know the quantity and rate, option C or D would be acceptable. In this case, you'd use the parametric estimating technique because you do know the quantity and rate; 30 hours times 4 miles is a total duration of 120 hours.

13. E. Building the servers, installing software on them, validating that the software works, and bringing up the schemas represents work toward the milestone but does not adequately represent that you've reached the milestone. Task 5, which says that you've successfully tested the database servers, indicates that you've reached your goal.

14. C. Starting with November 1 and counting it as the first full workday, the completion date for this task is November 22.

15. D. Milestone charts list the major deliverables, key events, or project phases and show the scheduled and actual completion dates of each milestone. They may include other information, but that information would not be displayed as bar charts.

16. A. After the WBS is developed, the next step involves creating an activity list that describes the activities required to complete each work package on the WBS.

17. B. Since the question states this DBA is unfamiliar with MySQL, the task estimation process is the most likely affected by all the options. You should use a three-point estimate or have another expert verify the estimate for this task since the DBA doesn't know this software well.

18. A. Finish-to-start is the most commonly used logical relationship in network and schedule diagrams.

19. C. The critical path is longest path through the network diagram, which is path A-B-C-E.

20. C. Tasks A, B, D, and G represent the longest dependent path through the network diagram at 41 days.

Chapter

5

Communicating the Plan

THE COMPTIA PROJECT+ EXAM TOPICS COVERED IN THIS CHAPTER INCLUDE

✓ **2.7 Identify components of an internal/external communications plan**

- Frequency

- Format (formal, informal, written and verbal)

- Method of distribution

- Distribution list

✓ **2.9 Identify roles and resource requirements based on WBS and resource availability**

- Identify existing resource availability

- Identify training needs / outsourcing requirements

- Assign resources to scheduled tasks

✓ **2.12 Explain the procurement process in a given situation**

- Project needs assessment / gap analysis

- Make or buy decisions

- RFI, RFQ, RFP (Request for: Information, Quote, Proposal)

- Request seller response

- Evaluate seller response

- Vendor selection

- Contract development

Planning can be the most time-consuming process on a project. There are many aspects to planning, so we're taking five chapters to discuss all the processes involved. Communications Planning will lead the charge in this chapter. It's always a good idea to document your communications plan early in the process so that you're getting the right information to the right stakeholders at the right time.

Once the scope statement and the WBS are developed, your next step in the planning phase is to determine the resource requirements for the project. In the previous chapter, we discussed the WBS and jumped right to the project schedule because they are so closely linked. It's sometimes easier to understand how the WBS and schedule work together when discussed at the same time. In reality, after developing the WBS, you might work on resource estimates before beginning the project schedule. There's no precise order to the way project planning occurs, and many times you'll decide which planning process occurs next based on the information available at the time.

When it comes to Resource Planning, you'll need to determine what resources are required, along with the quantity of resources. You'll also use this information to perform cost estimates. (We'll cover that topic in the next chapter.) From there, you'll define the human resource makeup of the project and then understand the procurement needs. Once you have this information, along with your scope and schedule, cost estimating will be easier.

Not all processes are required for every project. For example, in this chapter one of the topics we'll cover is procurement. If you are not purchasing any goods or services from outside the organization, you don't need to complete this process. However, the first three processes we'll cover in this chapter—Communications Planning, Resource Planning, and Human Resources Planning—are processes you will always want to perform for any project, small or large. So, let's get started with the most important aspect of any project: communications.

Communications Planning

Good communication is the key to project success. Granted, you need a solid plan including the scope statement, schedule, and budget. But if you aren't able to communicate the plan or keep stakeholder expectations in line with the project goals, you could end up with an unsuccessful project on your hands in spite of having a great plan.

Good communication involves far more than just setting up distribution lists and talking with your stakeholders at the watercooler. You need a plan to determine what gets communicated to whom and when. *Communications Planning* is the process of identifying what people or groups need to receive information regarding your project, what information each group needs, and how the information will be distributed. The communication system should monitor the project status and satisfy the diverse communication needs of the project's stakeholders.

The need for good communication starts from the day the project charter is issued and you are formally named project manager (perhaps even earlier if you've been filling the project manager role informally). As you've already seen, the project charter is the first of many project documents that needs to be reviewed with your stakeholders. The scope statement, project schedule, budget, and final project plan are all documents that should be discussed, reviewed, and approved by your stakeholders. But the communication can't stop with reviews and approvals. They'll want to know the status of the schedule and budget, and it will be your job to inform them of potential risk events, changes, and issues that may impact the project. To do that, you need a plan.

We'll start by reviewing some of the general principles of exchanging information.

How Much Time?

According to PMI, project managers should spend as much as 90 percent of their time communicating.

Exchanging Information

The act of communicating is part of your daily life. Every aspect of your job as a project manager involves communicating with others. Communication is the process of exchanging information, which involves these three elements:

Sender   The sender is the person responsible for putting the information together in a clear and concise manner and communicating it to the receiver. The information should be complete and presented in a way that the receiver will be able to correctly understand it. Make your messages relevant to the receiver. Junk mail is annoying, and information that doesn't pertain in any way whatsoever to the receiver is nothing more than that.

Message   The message is the information that is being sent and received. Messages can take many forms, including written, verbal, nonverbal, formal, informal, internal, external, horizontal, and vertical. Horizontal communications are messages sent and received between peers. Vertical communications are messages sent and received between subordinates and executive management.

The message should be appropriate and relevant to the receiver. Information that isn't needed or isn't pertinent to the intended audience is considered noise and will likely be discarded before it's read or heard.

Receiver   The receiver is the person for whom the message is intended. They are responsible for understanding the information correctly and making sure they've received all the information.

Keep in mind that receivers filter the information they receive through their knowledge of the subject, culture influences, language, emotions, attitudes, and geographic locations. The sender should take these filters into consideration when sending messages so that the receiver will clearly understand the message that was sent.

The sender-message-receiver model, also known as the *basic communication model*, is how all communication exchange occurs, no matter what format it takes. The sender encodes the information (typically in written or verbal format) and transmits it, via a message, to the receiver. The receiver decodes the message by reading it, listening to the speaker, and so on. Both the sender and the receiver have responsibility in this process. The sender must make sure the message is clear and understandable and in a format that the receiver can use. The receiver must make certain they understand what was communicated and ask for clarification where needed.

Project communication always involves more than one person. Communication network models are a way to explain the relationship between the number of people engaged in communicating and the actual number of interactions taking place between participants. For example, if you have five people in a meeting exchanging ideas, there are actually ten lines of communication among all the participants. Figure 5.1 shows a network model showing the *lines of communication* among the members.

FIGURE 5.1   Network communication model

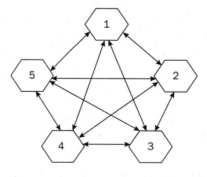

The nodes are the participants, and the lines show the connection between them all. The formula for calculating the lines of communication looks like this:

(Number of participants × (Number of participants −1)) ÷ 2

Here's the calculation in mathematical terms:

$n(n - 1) \div 2$

Figure 5.1 shows five participants, so let's plug that into the formula to determine the lines of communication:

$5(5 - 1) \div 2 = 10$

Effective vs. Efficient Communication

Keep in mind there is a difference between effective and efficient communication. *Effective* communication concerns providing the right information in the right format for the intended audience at the right time. *Efficient* communication refers to providing the appropriate level and amount information at the right time; that is, only the information that's needed at the time.

In the sender-message-receiver model, there's one critical communication skill that we all need to possess as a receiver, and that is the art of listening. Listening isn't the part where you plan out what you're going to say because someone else is speaking. It's the part where you actively engage with the sender and ask clarifying questions to make sure you're understanding the message correctly. Making eye contact with the speaker, nodding, and restating in your own words what the speaker has said are all effective listening techniques.

The primary forms of communication exchange include verbal and written formats. Verbal communication is easier and less complicated than written, and it's usually faster. The risk with verbal communication is that misunderstandings can take place and there's no record of what was said other than everyone's memories. Written communications are good for detailed instructions or complex messages that people may need to review. The risk with written communication is that stakeholders are inundated with emails, memos, documents, and other information, and your project information could get lost in the sea of information overload.

Deciding whether your information should be verbal or written is an important decision. Most formal project information, such as the project charter, scope statement, budget, and project plan, should be written. You'll most likely have meetings to discuss the contents of these documents, which means the verbal format will be used as well. It's always good practice to think about what you're communicating beforehand and how it will be communicated. Planning your communications before you speak or write is even more critical if your message is sensitive or controversial. Things will go much easier if you send the right message to begin with, rather than apologizing or retracting it later.

The next questions are, who should get the information, what format should it be in, and when should they get it? We'll look at these topics next.

The Communications Plan

The communication plan can be very simple, and you can easily construct a template using a spreadsheet or table format.

You can document an overall communications plan by doing the following:

- Defining who needs information on your project
- Defining the types of information each person or group needs
- Identifying the communications format and method of transmission
- Assigning accountability for delivering the communication
- Determining when the communications will occur and how often

Table 5.1 shows a simple way to display this information.

TABLE 5.1   Example communication plan

Stakeholder Name	Communication Type	Format of Communication	Method	Responsible Person	Frequency
Kelley Hart	Project plan, project status reports	Written	SharePoint—document requires digital signature approval	Project manager	At completion of planning process
Brett Maas	Project status reports	Written and oral (meetings)	Email notification/ SharePoint repository	Project manager	Weekly

You may also choose to include information in this plan on how to gather and store information, how to obtain information between communications, and how to update the communications plan.

Although you can use the template from this example to create an overall communications plan for all stakeholder groups, there are some additional considerations when it comes to communicating with your project team that we'll cover next.

Communicating with Project Team Members

One of your most important jobs as a project manager is communicating with your project team members. It is your responsibility to make sure all the team members understand the project goals and objectives and how their contribution fits into the big picture. Unfortunately, this is an area that is frequently overlooked in Communications Planning.

Your interactions with your project team will involve both formal and informal communications. *Formal communications* include project kickoff meetings, team status meetings, written status reports, team building sessions, or other planned sessions that you hold with the team. *Informal communications* include phone calls and emails to and from your team members, conversations in the hallway, and impromptu meetings.

The challenge that project managers face is matching their communication style with that of each team member. Getting input from your team members will help you better communicate with them. If you are scheduling a kickoff meeting or other team-building session, ask for suggestions on agenda items or areas that require team discussion. Team members may have suggestions for the structure and frequency of the team meetings or format for status reporting, based on their previous project experience. The project manager may not be able to accommodate all suggestions, but taking the time to consider input and reviewing the final format will go a long way toward building a cohesive team.

How Much Is Too Much?

Once, one of us was a team member on a project where the project manager created distribution lists for both email and paper documents and sent everything she received that even remotely involved the project to everyone on the lists. She thought she was doing an excellent job of communicating with the team, but the team was going crazy. We were buried with data, and much of it was not relevant to our role on the project. It got to the point where most of the team members were so overwhelmed we stopped reading everything. That, of course, led us to missing information we did need. The project manager did not understand why there was so much confusion on the team. She had not put any planning into her communications process.

Everyone has a communications method they are most comfortable with. Some of your team members may prefer email, while others prefer phone calls or voice mail. Some may prefer to drop in on you and share a piece of information they have or get an update from you. For these informal one-on-one types of communications, try to accommodate what is most comfortable for each team member whenever possible.

Some of your stakeholders may not understand how they are involved with the project. Extra steps are required to properly engage them, and we'll cover this next.

Engaging Stakeholders

In Chapter 2, "Project Process Groups and the Project Charter," we identified some of the typical project stakeholders: project sponsor, functional managers, customers, and end users. Remember that a stakeholder is anyone who has a vested interest in the outcome of a project.

On large projects that cross multiple functional areas, you may have stakeholders who are not actively participating in the project or do not fully understand their role. This can occur when large systems are being implemented or new products are being deployed across several geographic regions. For example, if the customer services director does not understand how his team is involved or what the total impact on his group will be, you need to get him connected to what's happening.

It may be useful to develop a stakeholder engagement plan that describes the key points you need to get across:

- Identify which aspects of the project plan to communicate.
- List any known or probable benefits or concerns from the stakeholder.
- Determine key message to convey to each stakeholder.

Figure 5.2 shows an example of a stakeholder engagement plan using the customer operations scenario for a new product deployment.

FIGURE 5.2   Stakeholder engagement plan

Communications Plan Stakeholder Engagement Example

Project:_____   Stakeholder Group: <u>Customer Operations</u>

	HIGH LEVEL OVERVIEW (5 minutes)	KEY POINTS (30 minutes)	SUPPORTING DETAIL (1-2 hours)
WHY (are we doing this project?)	Expand product offering	Increase customer base and projected revenue	Market research
WHAT (does this mean to the stakeholder?)	All sales channels will require training	Product functionality highlights Training expectations	Product functionality detail Product demos
HOW (will the project goal be achieved?)	Launch product in selected channels on March 7	Channel sales goals Channel training dates	Sales channel product proficiency
WHEN (will the stakeholder be involved?)	Supply Core Team lead starting November 9	Development of training Delivery of training	Interface with Human Factors team Interface with Customer Care

This particular example uses three scenarios based on the amount of time you are spending with the stakeholder. This approach has two key benefits:

- You have carefully thought out what you need to say.
- You are ready for the next meeting or to extend your current meeting if the stakeholder wants more detail.

The communications plan should be reviewed with your sponsor. If your project requires communication to executive team members, the sponsor can help you by identifying what information the group needs and how and when communication will take place.

Next we'll cover the resources required to complete the project.

> **Process Order**
>
> Although we discuss several processes in each chapter and take you step-by-step through each one, remember that in many cases you'll find you can work through several processes at the same time or in very quick successions, particularly on small projects.

Resource Planning

Resource Planning is the process of determining the resources you'll need for the project, including human, equipment, and material resources. This process will also determine the quantity of each resource required to complete the work for your project (for example, two servers, four person-hours, and so on).

Before you start the Resource Planning process, it's a good idea to review your scope statement and WBS and investigate whether you can obtain historical resource information from similar projects. Understanding the resources from a similar project may help you get started in the right direction. It is also a good idea to review any specific corporate policies regarding the allocation of resources to projects. For example, corporate policy may require you to obtain formal department-head approval before utilizing more than 40 hours of time from an employee who is not in your department.

 One of the benefits of a project management office (PMO) is that much of the information you need regarding policies, past project information, and subject matter experts is available through the PMO.

Although the project team members may get the most attention during Resource Planning, there is more to Resource Planning than just the staffing requirements. We will take you through the three types of project resources you need to identify before you can start the cost estimating process (which we'll discuss in Chapter 6, "Defining the Cost, Quality, and Risk Plans").

Types of Resources

When we mention project resources, the first thought that probably comes to mind is the people required to complete the project activities. Although people are certainly an important component and perhaps the one you'll pay the most attention to, Resource Planning involves far more than just the project team. Focusing on just the people can cause major disruptions down the road when you find you do not have the workstations you need or there is no power supply in your training room. It turns out that it's the little things that bite you. You must plan for three different and equally important types of resources: human resources, equipment, and material.

Human Resources

Once you've identified the tasks on the project, you'll identify the skill set required to perform each activity. *Human resources* are the people who have the experience and skills needed to complete those activities. When identifying the staff members needed for each task, it's important that you involve functional managers or team members who are knowledgeable in the work required to perform a given task. For example, who better to tell you who is the best choice for a web programming project than the manager of the applications development department?

Equipment

Equipment includes anything from specialized test tools to new servers to earthmovers and more. Equipment needs are specific to the type of project you're working on. Using historical information from past projects of similar size and scope can help you understand the types of equipment you'll need for the current project. Remember that some types of equipment have long lead times when ordering, so your up-front planning needs to be very thorough.

Materials

Materials is kind of a catchall category that includes utility requirements such as software, electricity, or water; any supplies you will need for the project; or other consumable goods.

Failure to think through and plan for materials can lead to major issues. For example, if your project requires a special training room, you will probably identify the need for PCs when you plan your equipment needs. What you may not think about are the connections for power for each of the PCs or the need to have them connect to a corporate local area network. This same scenario could apply to any specialized workspace required to complete the project work.

You should understand the types of materials needed for the project and the ordinary supplies you can obtain from the organization. For example, you may not have to identify paper, pens, and file folders as materials for the project, but if you want key team members to have a copy of Microsoft Project, it probably needs to be included as part of the project resource requirements. If there is any question, check out your departmental policy—do not assume all materials are covered under the functional budget.

Now that you understand the types of resources you need to be concerned with, you can start assigning resources to your project tasks.

Documenting Resource Requirements

Armed with an understanding of the three types of project resources, your scope statement, and your WBS, you are ready to start defining the specific resources needed to complete your project. You will document this information in a resource requirements document. This document contains a description of each of the resources needed—human, equipment, and material—for each of the work packages on the WBS.

During the Resource Planning process, you do not need to be concerned with identifying the names of people who will complete the work. What you need to identify in the resource requirements document is a resource based on job title or job description, that is, "web programmer" or "server administrator." We will discuss how you actually go about naming the human resources in the "Human Resources Planning" section later in this chapter.

Equipment and Material Descriptions

The resource requirements document should detail the types of materials and equipment the project is expected to acquire to complete the work of the project. It should also include the equipment you'll need to provide to the team members to perform their jobs. This information will be useful when planning the procurement process for the project. We'll discuss this topic later in this chapter in the section "Procurement Planning."

Job Descriptions and Titles

A tool that can be very useful for developing the human resource requirements is a *resource pool description*. This is a list of all the job titles within your company. If you work in a very large corporation, you may want only those job titles associated with a specific department. This list provides a brief description of the job and may identify the number of people currently employed in each job title. Check with your human resources representative to see whether this type of information is tracked in your organization and whether it can be made available to you for Resource Planning purposes. If this type of data is not available or if it is confidential, you could look at resource information from similar projects as a guide to the various job functions you may need to identify. Corporate organizational charts are also a source of information on job titles, although they do not usually include job descriptions.

Responsibility Assignment Matrix (RAM)

A well-known tool used in project management circles for defining and documenting the human resource requirements is a *responsibility assignment matrix (RAM)*. A RAM is a chart that matches your WBS elements with the required resources. Table 5.2 shows a sample portion of a RAM for an IT development project. It lists the WBS identifier, the type of resource required, and the number of resources needed for each skill set.

TABLE 5.2   Sample project responsibility assignment matrix

WBS Identifier	Programmer	Tester	Marketing	Tech Writer	Server
10-1-1-1				1	
10-1-1-2	2				
10-1-1-3		3			1
10-1-1-4	4				
10-1-1-5			1		

We haven't identified individuals to perform these tasks, or individuals with the skills yet. However, we want to make you aware of another form of RAM called an *RACI chart* while we're discussing resource charts. An RACI chart identifies the task to be performed, the individual or organization assigned to the task, and what level of responsibility or involvement they have for this task. Their level of involvement or responsibility is designated by the letters R-A-C-I, which stand for the following:

R = Responsible, the one who performs the work

A = Accountable, the one who is responsible for producing the deliverable or work package and approves or signs off on the work

C = Consult, someone who has input to the work or decisions

I = Inform, someone who must be informed of the decisions or results

Table 5.3 shows a sample RACI chart.

TABLE 5.3   Sample RACI chart

Task	Jeff	Harley	Kelley	Dara
Programming	R	A	C	C
Testing	I	R	C	A
Technical writing	C	I	R	A

Real World Scenario

The Equipment Was There, but the Electricity Wasn't!

Jill is a project manager for a large corporation based in the Pacific Northwest. The corporate managers decided to build a new building to house all the departments in one place. The company planned to save money by reducing lease contracts while increasing the level of efficiency because co-workers would be in closer proximity to one another. Jill was put in charge of a project to move all the people into the new building. The project would take about six months, and she would be required to move 1,000 people in "move waves," with a total of six waves.

Shortly after she received the project, Jill met with the building's contractor to discuss the location of the different departments and the data centers for the servers, as well as the power, and to determine lighting diagrams for the cubicles throughout the building and the data center. The contractor told Jill that, in the interest of saving money, the corporate engineers had opted to reduce the number of electrical cables—called *whips*—in the data center, though he assured her he had planned for enough connections.

Jill discovered that even though the company had a central IT shop, seven separate mini-IT shops, along with the central IT department, needed to place server equipment in the data center. Going on the word of the contractor, she thought there would be plenty of electricity to meet the needs of the various IT stakeholders.

During the first-wave move, some, but not all, of the servers that were going into the data center were delivered, and the various administrators showed up to hook them up. Jill was shocked to find out that all the electrical connections were used up in the first wave! Even though there were more servers to come, she had nowhere for them to hook up to power. The assurance that the contractor gave her was suddenly out the window.

Jill went back and inventoried the electrical requirements for the remaining servers and discovered some had regular 15-amp requirements, others needed 20-amp circuits, and still others required a specialized 277/480-amp circuit. When she informed the contractor of this discovery, she found that he had only installed 15-amp circuits and wasn't aware of the other power requirements.

Jill assessed the number of circuits she needed for each of the remaining servers and their power requirements, and the total came to seventeen 15-amp, ten 20-amp, and two 277/480-amp circuits. Next she went back to the contractor to get an estimate of the cost for the 31 new circuits. That estimate came in at $17,500!

Finally, with much trepidation, she went to the project sponsor, explaining that she had overlooked the power requirements and that additional monies were required to complete the project.

In retrospect, Jill realized she should have used subject matter experts to help determine the server-move and circuit requirements.

You can use other tools besides a RAM to identify resource requirements. If the project is small in scope, you could note the resources on the WBS. Resource requirements can also be documented using project management software and are often noted on the project schedule. You could also use resource templates from previous projects.

The specifics of how you identify resources are not as important as making sure that you capture all the resources that are needed.

Next we'll cover the human resources aspect of project planning.

Human Resources Planning

Human Resources Planning involves defining team member roles and responsibilities, establishing an appropriate structure for team reporting, acquiring the right team members, and bringing them on the project as needed for the appropriate length of time. This process starts out with organizational planning, which includes defining the human resources needed for the project. After the resources are defined, we need to acquire them, which requires a strong set of negotiation skills. We'll start out by talking about organizational planning.

Organizational Planning

Managing a group of people to complete a unique project within a limited time frame can be very challenging. Each team member needs to have a clear picture of their role on the team and what they are accountable for.

Additionally, team members and the other project stakeholders need to understand how the team will be organized. If you have a small 8-person team all located in the same building, the team reporting structure will look very different than if you have a team of 150 people who are spread across 6 different organizations in 4 cities.

Organizational planning is the process of addressing various factors that may impact how you manage your project team, define roles and responsibilities for project team members, identify how your project team will be organized, and document your staffing management plan.

Human Resources Planning Constraints

You should consider several potential constraints when performing organizational planning. These include labor-union agreements, organizational structure, and economic conditions:

Labor-union agreements   Labor-union agreements are a contractual obligation of the organization to the employees. They may require specialized reporting relationships, working conditions, holidays, and so on, that you'll need to consider when planning your team.

Organizational structure   Organizational structure can be a constraint to your project and team members. For example, if you work in a functional organization, you'll have to work closely with functional managers to secure resources and negotiate for their time.

Economic conditions   Economic conditions can constrain the team because of limits put on the project budget for things such as team training, additional staff or consultants, and travel. If the budget is limited or there are no funds available for these needs, it could impact the project scope or schedule.

Real World Scenario

The Geographically Dispersed Team

Recently one of us took a college class in organizing technical projects. The instructor for that class was a senior systems analyst for a large aerospace contracting firm during the day. We'll call him Jim.

Jim's entire premise for the class was that it's very difficult to put together a group of people—especially highly specialized aerospace engineers, some of whom live in California, others overseas, still others in Colorado, and so forth—to design, build, assemble, and deploy a rocket. His points were limited but salient:

- You have to understand the project thoroughly. All team members have to be clear about what it is you're building. There can be no question about vision.

- With big projects, you use the "eat an elephant one bite at a time" principle, breaking the project into manageable chunks and grouping together the team members who pertain to the chunk you're interested in talking about today.

- There is a center point to all projects. You can't, for example, design the fuselage first and *then* design an engine to fit in it. All components of a rocket project center on the engine. Thus, the engine is a well-known, well-understood quantity—the rest of the parts are designed around it. We believe this is probably true for the vast majority of IT projects.

- In the case of geographically dispersed teams, you simply don't have the funding to fly everyone around the country so they can get together to work on the project (though this happened for Jim's teams at very critical junctures in a project's stage). Jim and his teams rely heavily on online collaboration, using software and video technology to bring people together over the Internet in order to discuss drawings, design characteristics, and other components of the project.

- You don't necessarily need to be afraid of geographic boundaries when assembling people with the skills you need. A little thinking outside the box might lead to a well-formed albeit nonlocal team. That being said, you, the project manager, are the final arbiter of what will and what will not work for a given project.

Moreover, the primary take-away from the class was that projects—IT or otherwise—of massive proportions are being worked on every day. The power of the Internet has greatly impacted the speed with which team members can communicate and bring their projects to fruition.

Environmental Factors

You need to consider various environmental factors as part of your organizational planning as well, because they may impact both the selection of project team members and how the team is managed. In this case, environmental factors include elements such as organizational policies regarding personnel, location and logistics of personnel, and so on. We've listed a few of the environmental factors you should take into consideration when planning your team:

Organizational factors   Organizational factors are the relationships that must be managed when a project spans multiple departments. The way you structure your team meetings, how you provide feedback to team members, and how you communicate status are a few of the areas that may be managed differently if you are managing a cross-functional project.

Technical factors   Technical factors drive how the technical work of the project is completed. You should consider the specialized skills needed to complete the work of the project, such as knowledge of programming languages, engineering skills, specialized industry knowledge, and so on.

Personnel policies   Make certain you have an understanding of the personnel policies in the organization regarding hiring, firing, and tasking employees. Other considerations include holiday schedules, leave-time policies, and so on.

Location and logistics   Consider where the project team is located and whether they are all located together or at separate facilities (or cities or countries).

Interpersonal factors   Interpersonal factors are the reporting relationships between the people working on the project. In an ideal world, everyone gets along, with no conflicts or disputes; in the real world, a project manager needs to be prepared to deal with differences between team members. Knowledge of previous conflicts may even impact the team member selection process.

Roles and Responsibilities

A roles and responsibilities document lists each group or individual team member on the project and their responsibilities. But roles and responsibilities of project team members are more than just the assigned tasks. There are standards and methodologies to be adhered to, documentation to be completed, and time-reporting responsibilities, to name a few. So in addition to assigning people to tasks, it is a good idea to develop a template to document roles and responsibilities beyond just the task assignment. The more clarity around who is responsible for what, the better.

🌐 Real World Scenario

Roles and Responsibilities Example

Every team member should have clearly documented roles and responsibilities. That includes the project manager, so let's take a look at how you might define the roles and responsibilities for the project manager on the Voice Activated Dialing project first introduced in Chapter 3.

Title   Project manager

Role   Lead the project management activities associated with the launch of voice-activated dialing.

Primary responsibilities   The project manager may perform some or all of the following:

- Identify any departmental project management standards.
- Lead team in all aspects of project planning.
- Manage project team in the execution of the project work.
- Develop schedule and maintain updates on a weekly basis.
- Run weekly project team status meeting.
- Track, assign, and report progress on any project issues.
- Track implementation of contingency or mitigation plans.
- Provide weekly status of critical issues to project sponsor and key stakeholders.
- Prepare and present formal monthly project status for the stakeholders.

Similar documentation should be developed for each project team member. This document not only clarifies for each team member what they will be held accountable for but can also be used to communicate team member accountabilities with the sponsor, functional managers, or other stakeholders.

Many teams often include the project sponsor in the roles and responsibilities documentation. This can be a good way of confirming joint understanding between the sponsor and the project manager as to when and how the sponsor will be involved in the project work.

Whatever format you choose, the intent is to be as clear and precise as possible in defining the key areas of accountability for each team member.

Roles and responsibilities may change over the course of the project, so be sure to update this document as needed.

The development of project roles and responsibilities is a good time to clarify the project manager's authority with the project sponsor, especially if the project charter was vague or did not include this information. The project manager's authority can be formally documented in the roles and responsibilities, or it may be an informal agreement where the sponsor delegates some of his or her authority to the project manager. Any authority surrounding hiring and firing decisions or the spending of the project budget should be documented.

Roles and responsibilities can be documented in a variety of ways—bulleted lists, tables, paragraph format, and so on. Check for any templates available in your organization, or use the format that seems most appropriate for your team.

Project Organization Chart

It is always a good idea to develop a project organization chart; not only does it provide a snapshot of who is working on the project, but it also shows the reporting structure. Depending on the complexity of your project and the number of people involved, there may be multiple reporting levels.

In a small centrally located project team, all team members may report directly to the project manager. However, for an 85-person team working on a large application development project spanning multiple departments, the structure will typically have many team members report to someone other than the project manager. Large, complex projects often establish project team lead positions. The project team lead is accountable for either the people assigned to a particular phase such as development or testing or for the team members from a specific department such as sales, training, IT, or accounting. Figure 5.3 shows a sample project organization chart using the team lead concept.

FIGURE 5.3 Project organization chart

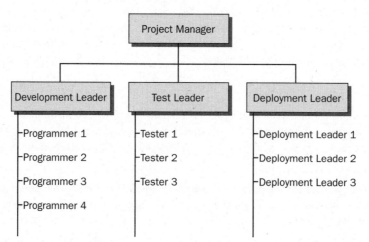

Staffing Management Plan

The staffing management plan is a document where you pull all your staffing data together. The *staffing management plan* documents when and how human resources will be added to and released from the project team and what they will be working on while they are part of the team. Adding and releasing resources may be an informal or a formal process, depending on your organization. Make sure you are familiar with any corporate human resources policies that may impact how you release team members from the project. This is particularly important if any of your team members are covered by a collective bargaining agreement. Very specific rules regarding both advance notification and the specific process may be used to move these people on and off a project.

If your project involves complex factors, be they organizational, technical, or interpersonal, document how you plan to manage these factors in the staffing management plan. If certain work components must be assigned to a specific work group, this requirement should be documented as well. If your team spans multiple cities or crosses multiple departments, you need to document the plans to manage these circumstances. Training requirements and employee rewards are also documented in the staffing management plan.

The team member roles and responsibilities and the project organization chart also become part of the staffing management plan to make this a cohesive, comprehensive document covering all aspects of managing your team.

 Your staffing management plan is the blueprint you need to manage the human resources assigned to your project.

Now that you have a plan for managing the staff, it is time to staff your project.

Staff Acquisition

In the *staff acquisition process*, you'll choose the team members (or organizations) who will work on the project. You'll need to use some of the general management skills we discussed in Chapter 1 for this process.

How the project manager actually goes about obtaining project team members and the amount of project manager involvement in the decision-making process for staff assignments varies across organizations. In the best-case scenario, the project manager interviews candidates for project team positions and has full authority to select the team members; however, in many organizations, project managers must negotiate with the functional managers providing the resources.

Interviewing Potential Team Members

The control a project manager has in the team member selection process varies with the type of organizational structure and the policies associated with project staffing. If you're in a strong matrix or projectized organization, you'll likely have the authority to decide who will be included on the team. Be prepared for the interview process with the questions you'll ask and the factors you'll use to make your decision ahead of time. When preparing for an interview, you should make sure to cover several areas.

Skill Level

- Does the person have the training and experience to complete the tasks?
- Does the experience level of the candidate match what is required to complete the tasks?

Project Experience

- Does the person have previous experience working on a project team?
- What types of projects has the candidate worked on?
- What were the candidate's previous project responsibilities?

Interpersonal Skills

- Does the person demonstrate the ability to be a team player?
- Does the candidate have strong written and oral communication skills?
- What are the candidate's strengths and weaknesses?

This is a starting point. Based on the specifics of your project, you should add other areas to this list.

The purpose of an interview is to determine the best person for the job. Preparation is the key to conducting a successful interview. Have a list of written questions that you want to ask each candidate and take notes as you conduct each interview. There are laws governing the personal information that can be requested from job applicants. If you do not have experience interviewing job candidates, you should find a mentor to assist you or obtain a template or checklist from your human resources department.

Negotiating with Functional Managers

In a more traditional organizational structure, you'll need to negotiate with functional managers to obtain your project staff. You may or may not have an opportunity to interview potential candidates, depending on how staffing is handled within your organization. Even if you interview candidates, you will need to work through the functional manager to finalize project-staffing decisions.

The functional manager will determine whether resources are available on a full-time or part-time basis. If you are acquiring people who are assigned to additional projects or other work, you must establish a clear understanding as to the number of hours each person is dedicated to your project.

In a matrix organization, where the project team members will have multiple bosses (the functional manager and at least one project manager), it is essential to clarify and obtain agreement on the team member accountability. A team member should only be accountable to one person for a given result.

Performance assessment is another topic that should be discussed at the time resources are obtained. Your organization may have a formal policy that includes input from the project manager as part of the process, or you may need to reach an agreement with each functional manager as to how you will provide feedback into the performance appraisal process.

As the project manager, you should initiate a meeting with each impacted functional manager to discuss your staffing needs and come to an agreement on who will be assigned to your project. Functional managers often have very large teams and are constantly fielding requests to provide staffing resources to project teams. You need to come into the meeting prepared to identify your needs and have a game plan to negotiate with the functional manager. Here are some suggestions to help make this process smoother:

Schedule a separate meeting with each functional manager.   Unless your organization has a formal staff allocation process involving all project managers and all impacted functional managers, meet individually with each functional manager so that you can focus on the project needs from that specific area and make the best use of the functional manager's time. When scheduling a meeting, be clear on the purpose, allow adequate time to work through any issues, and hold the meeting in a workroom or private office. Do not try to complete the staff negotiation process in the hall or on the elevator.

Identify who would be part of your "dream team."   Do your homework and become familiar with the people who report to each functional manager. Use your staffing management plan, your roles and responsibilities matrix, any documented information regarding the experience and qualification of available resources, and previous work experience with potential team members to draft a list of who you would bring to the team if the decision were in your hands.

Plan who you will request from each functional manager.   If you want specific people on your team or you require people with a specific experience level, explain to the functional manager who you want and the reason behind your request. Let's face it: every project manager wants the best people, so you'll need to make your case and go head-to-head with the competition. Be prepared to provide a brief overview of your project, its strategic importance, and the importance of the resources coming from this functional area. Have a backup plan if you cannot obtain the resources you want, and be prepared to negotiate.

Request your most critical resources first.   It is very unlikely that you will get everyone you ask for. Certain people may already be committed to other projects, or the timing of your request may conflict with critical functional activities. You need to prioritize your staffing needs. Understand which activities are the most complex, are on the critical path, and have the highest risk potential. These activities are the areas where you want to make sure you have the best people. Work at getting these areas assigned first. You have more flexibility to agree to a different resource or accept the person assigned by the functional manager for activities that are less complex or aren't on the critical path.

Following these steps may not always get you the team members you want, but it will help establish your credibility with the functional managers if you handle your requests in a professional manner. Whatever the outcome of a particular meeting, maintain a good business relationship with the functional managers because you'll be back to see them again for future projects.

 You may find yourself on a project where at least part of the staff is preassigned before the project begins. If that's the case, remember to document this in the project charter.

Other Staffing Scenarios

In some situations, you may not be able to negotiate for staff. Only one person may be available with the skill set required. The project sponsor may assign some of the project team members, or the client or other executive stakeholder may request certain team members. Assignments made without your input may be good choices or bad choices. If you choose to challenge one of these assignments, make sure you're doing so based on hard facts, such as the lack of the required technical skills. Unless the person simply is not qualified to do the work, you will probably have to live with this decision and make the best of it.

One last staffing scenario involves procuring resources from an outside supplier. Contract workers may be brought in if no internal resources are available for a time-critical project or if internal resources do not have the required skill sets. Staffing augmentation is planned for in the procurement planning process, which we'll discuss next.

Procurement Planning

Procurement planning is the process of identifying the goods and services required for your project that will be purchased from outside the organization. If your project doesn't require any external resources, you don't need a procurement plan.

One of the first techniques you should use when thinking about the procurement planning process is whether you should make or buy the goods and services needed for the project. *Make-or-buy analysis* determines whether it's more cost-effective to produce the needed resources in-house or whether it's more cost-effective to procure them from outside the organization. You should include both direct costs and indirect costs when using the make-or-buy analysis technique. Direct costs are those that are directly attributed to the project, such as costs needed to produce the resource. Indirect costs are those costs associated with overhead, management, and ongoing maintenance costs. You can also use make-or-buy analysis when deciding whether it's more cost-effective to buy equipment or to lease it. Other considerations to take into account in make-or-buy analysis include capacity, skill sets, availability, and company trade secrets.

The procurement process is very complex and often involves the legal department. Many organizations have a procurement department that manages all aspects of the process. If that's the case in your organization, you'll want to make certain you understand the forms and processes you're required to follow, or you may end up with some significant schedule delays. Most procurement departments are highly process-driven, and if you miss something along the way, the procurement folks may or may not choose to show mercy and lend a hand in getting the forms through.

Do not underestimate the power your procurement department possesses. We have been involved on projects that were delayed for months because we forgot to start a procurement process on time or missed one of the myriads of forms they require to complete the transaction. Make certain you know and understand your procurement department's rules and processes so that you don't bring about unnecessary time delays on your project.

As the project manager, you're the buyer of goods and services for your project so we'll cover the procurement process from the buyer's perspective. The organization selling the goods or services is referred to as a vendor, a seller, a supplier, a consultant, or a contractor.

The typical areas where you may need to procure goods or services are discussed next:

Equipment   For some projects, the equipment needs may be fairly simple to determine. If you are developing a new application that requires new hardware, you'll need to obtain the hardware from outside your company. If you're working on a project that requires equipment your organization routinely has available, you'll want to reserve the equipment for the tasks and time frames needed for the project.

Staff augmentation   Staff augmentation may come about for several reasons. Perhaps your organization lacks the expertise needed in certain areas. Or, there may be other critical projects that have reserved the same resources you need for your project. Time-critical projects may also require more resources than are currently available. Contract resources can help fill this gap.

Staff augmentation may range from contracting with a vendor to run the entire project to contracting for specific resources to perform certain tasks. In our experience, staff augmentation is often needed for large, complex projects.

Other goods and services   Goods and services that your organization typically does not produce or keep on hand are good candidates for procurement. You may also find that some of the project deliverables are best met by procuring them from outside the organization.

Procurement planning starts with the decision to procure goods or services outside the organization. Once that decision has been made, you need to determine what type of procurement vehicle is best for the purchase you need to make. A simple purchase order may suffice, or you may need a contract. For contract work, a statement of work (SOW) is developed to define exactly what work the vendor is being asked to deliver. The SOW is incorporated in a solicitation document that's distributed to the vendors who will be bidding on the work. We'll look at that process right after we talk more about the SOW.

Statement of Work

If you're working with vendors to perform some or all of the work of the project, it's critical that they know exactly what you are asking them to do. The *statement of work (SOW)* details the goods or services you want to procure. In many respects it's similar to the project scope statement, except that it focuses on the work being procured. It contains the project description, major deliverables, success criteria, assumptions, and constraints. The project scope statement is a good starting point for documenting the SOW.

The project manager should be involved in the process of creating the SOW to ensure accuracy of the project requirements. Vendors use the SOW to determine whether they are capable of producing the deliverables and to determine their interest in bidding on your project work. The SOW must be very clear and precise. Anything in the SOW that is ambiguous could lead to a less-than-satisfactory deliverable.

Many organizations have templates for creating a SOW. This ensures that all required items are covered, and it provides consistent information to vendors. Once the SOW is complete, you're ready to ask for vendors to bid on the work.

Vendor Solicitation

Solicitation planning is the process of identifying the requirements of the product and identifying potential sources. *Solicitation* refers to obtaining responses from vendors to complete the project work as documented in the SOW. Typically, a procurement document is prepared to notify prospective sellers of upcoming work. You can prepare the solicitation notice in several ways. The most common are as follows:

- Request for Information (RFI)
- Request for Proposal (RFP)
- Request for Quotation (RFQ)
- Request for Bid (RFB) or Invitation for Bid (IFB)

These terms are often used interchangeably and may have different meanings in different organizations. Regardless of what these documents are called, they should include your SOW, information regarding how responses are to be formatted and delivered, and a date by which responses must be submitted. Potential vendors may also be required to make a formal presentation, or they may be asked to submit a bid.

Most procurement processes allow for a meeting with prospective vendors prior to their completing the RFP; this is called a *bidder conference*. This meeting usually occurs right after the RFP is published, and all prospective vendors are invited to the meeting in order to ask questions and clarify issues they may have identified with the RFP. The bidder conference helps assure that vendors prepare responses that address the project requirements.

At the time the procurement documents are distributed (or earlier), you need to develop the criteria the selection committee will use to evaluate the bids, quotes, or proposals you receive.

Vendor Selection Criteria

Most organizations have a procurement department that will assist you with vendor solicitation and selection. They will advise you regarding the information you need to provide and will usually assign a member of their team to manage the vendor selection process and the contract for your project. Some organizations have approved vendor lists made up of vendors that have already met the basic criteria the company requires for them to do business with them. If that's the case, your solicitation and selection process will be easier because you'll be working with preapproved vendors that have already crossed several of the procurement hurdles required to proceed.

If you're responsible for vendor selection, you'll need to develop criteria to use when evaluating vendor bids or proposals. It helps to decide up front with the sponsor and other key stakeholders who will be involved in the review and selection of vendor proposals. This group should develop the selection criteria as a team and reach agreement ahead of time regarding the weighting of the criteria. These are some of the criteria you should consider when evaluating bids and proposals:

- The vendor's understanding of the needs and requirements of the project
- Vendor costs, including warranty
- Technical ability of the vendor to perform the work of the project
- References
- Vendor's experience on projects of similar size and scope
- Vendor's project management approach
- Financial stability of the vendor's company
- Intellectual property rights and proprietary rights

You can use several techniques to evaluate the proposals, including weighted scoring systems, screening systems, seller rating systems, independent estimates, and more. One of the most common methods is using a weighted scoring model or system. The idea is that each of the criteria you're using to evaluate the vendor is assigned a weight. Each vendor is then given a score for each of the evaluation elements, and the weight is multiplied by the score to give an overall score. Table 5.4 shows a sample weighted scoring model using some of the evaluation criteria shown earlier. The scores are assigned a value of 1 to 5, with 5 being the highest score a vendor can earn. You multiply the weight by the score for each element and then sum the totals to come up with an overall score for each vendor. You would almost always choose the vendor with the highest score using this selection method.

TABLE 5.4   Weighted scoring model

Criteria	Weight	Vendor A Score	Vendor A Total	Vendor B Score	Vendor B Total
Understand requirements	5	2	**10**	4	**20**
Cost	3	3	**9**	4	**12**
Experience	4	1	**4**	2	**8**
Financial stability	3	4	**12**	3	**9**
Final weighted score			**35**		**49**

In this example, vendor B has the highest score and is the vendor you should choose.

Sole-Source Documentation

Sometimes you'll have a procurement situation where you can use only one vendor to fulfill your needs. For example, suppose you have a computer system that is unique to your line of business. You've used that software for several years and are ready for an upgrade. You don't want to go through the headache of installing a new system—you simply want to update the one you already have. This situation calls for a sole-source procurement because there's only one vendor that can meet your requirements.

Types of Contracts

A *contract* is a legal document that describes the goods or services that will be provided, the costs of the goods or services, and any penalties for noncompliance. Most contracts fall into one of the following categories: fixed-price contracts, cost-reimbursable contracts, and time and materials contracts. Let's take a closer look at each of these:

Fixed-price contract   A *fixed-price contract* states a fixed fee or price for the goods or services provided. This type of contract works best when the product is very well defined and the statement of work is clear and concise. Using a fixed-price contract for a product or service that is not well defined or has never been done before is risky for both the buyer and the seller. This type of contract is the riskiest for the seller. If problems arise during the course of the project and it takes longer to complete a task than anticipated, or the goods they were to supply can't be obtained in a timely manner, the seller bears the burden of paying the additional wages needed to complete the task or paying the penalty for not delivering the goods on time.

Cost-reimbursable contract   A *cost-reimbursable contract* reimburses the seller for all the allowable costs associated with producing the goods or services outlined in the contract. This type of contract is riskiest for the buyer because the total costs are unknown until the project is completed. The advantage in this type of contract is that the buyer can easily change scope.

Time and materials contract   A *time and materials contract* is a cross between fixed-price and cost-reimbursable contracts. The buyer and the seller agree on a unit rate, such as the hourly rate for a programmer, but the total cost is unknown and will depend on the amount of time spent to produce the product or service. This type of contract is often used for staff augmentation, where contract workers are brought on to perform specific tasks on the project.

Real World Scenario

Chaptal Wineries

The Chaptal project plan is coming together. You've developed a roles and responsibilities worksheet, communication plan, and procurement plan for the project. Let's look at each.

Roles and responsibilities and team member designations

Title   Yourself—project manager for Chaptal

Role   Project manager

Primary responsibilities   The responsibilities are as follows:

- Manage the work of the project and assure its adherence to the project plan.
- Acquire project hardware and software, as well as WAN telecommunications connections.
- Manage vendor contracts and maintenance agreements.
- Manage contractors and other winery employees in bringing about the deliverables.
- Work with the day-to-day project team and resolve issues.

Title   Guillaume, Mariano, and Jason—IT project team members

Role   Work with contract vendor on IT tasks for the project

Primary responsibilities   Responsible for WAN connectivity issues, testing, and server deployment at the various winery sites

Communications plan

Kate Cox, the project sponsor, needs weekly updates on project progress. She says she doesn't expect a point-by-point synopsis; she'd just like to know any standout issues or problems that you've run into. She'd also like a quick update on schedule progress and budget.

The IT project team needs to receive project-status updates, and updates on any procurement issues that may arise.

When the various contractors at each site begin working, you'll need daily status updates on their deliverables progress. The following table shows a partial communication plan for the Chaptal project:

Stakeholder Name	Communication Type	Format of Communication	Method	Responsible Person	Frequency
Kate Cox	Project plan, project status reports, issues, risk events	Written and verbal	In person, email, or phone	Project manager	Weekly
IT project team	Project plan, project status reports	Written and verbal	Team meetings, in person	Project manager, IT team members	Weekly
IT contractors	SOW, deliverables, acceptance criteria	Written and verbal	In person, email, or phone	Project manager, contractors	Daily

Procurement plan

Servers   Will use a purchase order to procure hardware from existing vendor. Servers must be shipped to respective sites to avoid additional shipping charges.

Telecommunications equipment   Provided by respective telecommunications providers at each site upon contract signing.

IT contractors   RFPs will be placed on the website, and the project manager will work with each location to notify potential vendors of the contracting opportunity.

Summary

Most project managers spend the majority of their project management time in the act of communicating. Communication is performed using the sender-message-receiver model. Communications Planning is a process where you determine who needs what types of communication, when, and in what format, and how that communication will be disseminated. The network communication model shows the lines of communication that exist between any number of project participants.

Resource Planning involves determining all the materials, goods, equipment, and human resources you'll need to perform the work of the project. You can depict the roles and responsibilities of human resources graphically in a RAM or an RACI chart.

Human Resource Planning identifies the specific resources that will be assigned to your project as well as how and when they will join the project team and be returned to their functional department. You'll document the resources needed in the human resource management plan. Be aware of constraints that may impact the human resource management plan, such as labor union agreements, organizational structure, and economic conditions.

Staff acquisition is where you choose the team members (or organizations) who will work on the project. You should be prepared to negotiate with functional managers for resources and also be prepared to interview potential team members to determine experience levels, skill, and overall fit on the team.

Procurement planning is performed when goods or services for the project will be provided outside the organization. Procurement planning involves a make-or-buy analysis, SOW preparation, vendor solicitation, and vendor selection criteria. The typical solicitation vehicles for contracting include an RFQ, RFP, and RFI or IFB.

Exam Essentials

Describe the importance of Communications Planning.   Communications Planning is the key to project success. It involves determining who needs information, when, and in what format, and the frequency of the communication.

Describe Resource Planning.   Resource Planning determines what resources are needed for the project, including human, equipment, and material.

Describe a RAM.   A RAM is a resource assignment matrix that shows the WBS identifier, the type of resource required, and the number of resources for each skill set. An RACI chart is a type of RAM that describes the resources and their level of responsibility, including responsible, accountable, consult, or inform.

Describe the two components of Human Resources Planning.   The two components are organizational planning and staff acquisition.

Be able to describe make-or-buy analysis.   Make-or-buy analysis is performed in order to determine the cost-effectiveness of either making or buying the goods and services you need for the project.

Be able to name the types of contracts.   The contract types include fixed-price, cost-reimbursable, and time and materials.

Key Terms

Before you take the exam, be certain you are familiar with the following terms:

bidder conference	materials
Communications Planning	organizational planning
contract	procurement planning
cost-reimbursable contract	RACI chart
equipment	Resource Planning
fixed-price contract	resource pool description
formal communications	responsibility assignment matrix (RAM)
human resources	solicitation planning
Human Resources Planning	staff acquisition process
informal communications	staffing management plan
lines of communication	statement of work (SOW)
make-or-buy analysis	time and materials contract

Review Questions

1. Why should you spend time developing a solid communications plan? Choose three.

    A. To set stakeholder expectations

    B. To set aside time for your own needs

    C. To keep vendors informed

    D. To understand where the blame lies when something goes wrong

    E. To keep stakeholders updated on your progress

    F. To keep team members informed of project progress

2. This person is responsible for understanding the information correctly and making certain they've received all the information.

    A. Sender

    B. Messenger

    C. Project manager

    D. Receiver

3. There are four participants in your upcoming meeting. How many lines of communication are there?

    A. 6

    B. 4

    C. 8

    D. 16

4. This process involves determining the human, equipment, and material resources needed for the project.

    A. Human Resources Planning

    B. Organizational Planning

    C. Resource Planning

    D. Procurement Planning

5. This type of chart depicts the WBS identifier, the type of resource required, and the number of resources required.

    A. RACI

    B. RAM

    C. RAMI

    D. RAC

6. What are the processes that you use for Human Resources Planning? Choose two.
   A. Performance reporting
   B. Contract administration
   C. Organizational planning
   D. Staff acquisition

7. You have been assigned as project manager for a major software development project. Andy is the functional manager who will be providing the resources for your development team. Andy is being asked to supply resources to several projects concurrently. You have a list of the people you want assigned to your team, but you fear other project managers may want these same people. How should you approach Andy regarding the assignment of his people to the project?
   A. Schedule a meeting with Andy to discuss resources. Explain your project deliverables and the skill sets you need. Negotiate with Andy for your most critical resources first.
   B. Send Andy a memo listing the resources you need and the start date for each resource.
   C. Catch up with Andy just before a meeting both of you need to attend so that he will not have time to think up reasons to turn down part of your request.
   D. Meet with Andy's boss to let her know that your project is critical, and provide her with the list of resources you need from Andy.

8. Communications Planning is the process of which of the following?
   A. Scheduling a regular meeting for the project team
   B. Developing a distribution list for the stakeholders
   C. Identifying the people or groups that need information on your project
   D. Creating a template to report project status

9. You are the project manager for a new software application that will provide online help to sales consultants regarding the features of the products they sell. You are putting together your human resources plan and realize that all but which of the following is a Human Resources Planning constraint?
   A. Labor-union agreements
   B. Legal requirements
   C. Organizational structure
   D. Economic conditions

10. What is the technique of looking at the trade-offs between producing goods or services internally vs. procuring it from outside the organization?
    A. Cost estimating
    B. Vendor selection criteria
    C. Staff augmentation
    D. Make-or-buy analysis

11. You are a project manager for a telecommunications company assigned to a project to deploy a new wireless network using a technology that does not have a proven track record. You have requested vendor bids for portions of the development that will include researching various scenarios. What type of contract is most likely in this situation?

    A. Fixed-price contract

    B. Time and materials contract

    C. Cost-reimbursable contract

    D. A procurement method other than a contract

12. This plan documents when and how human resources will be added to and released from the project.

    A. Staff acquisition plan

    B. Staffing management plan

    C. Communications plan

    D. Human resources plan

13. This process performed within the Human Resources Planning process addresses various factors that may impact how you manage your project team, how you'll define roles and responsibilities for team members, and how the team will be organized; it also documents your staffing management plan.

    A. Organizational planning

    B. Staff acquisition

    C. Staff management planning

    D. Environmental factors planning

14. During this process, you'll interview prospective team members, negotiate with functional managers, and assign staff to the project.

    A. Resource Planning

    B. Staff augmentation

    C. Human Resource Planning

    D. Staff acquisition

15. This document describes the goods or services you want to procure from outside the organization.

    A. Scope statement

    B. RFP

    C. RFI

    D. SOW

16. This process involves obtaining responses from vendors to complete the work of the project as documented in the SOW.

   A. Procurement planning

   B. Bidder conference

   C. Solicitation

   D. Vendor selection

17. You have just posted an RFP and have invited the vendors to participate in a meeting to ask questions about the work of the project. What is this meeting called?

   A. RFP conference

   B. Bidders conference

   C. Procurement communication conference

   D. Sellers conference

18. This vendor selection method weighs various criteria from the RFP and SOW, scores each vendor on each of the criteria, and determines an overall score for each vendor.

   A. Weighted scoring model

   B. Screening system

   C. Seller rating system

   D. Independent estimates

19. This type of contract is the riskiest for the buyer.

   A. Time and materials

   B. Fixed price

   C. Fixed price plus incentive

   D. Cost reimbursable

20. This type of contract assigns a unit rate for work or goods, but the total cost is unknown.

   A. Time and materials

   B. Fixed price

   C. Fixed price plus incentive

   D. Cost reimbursable

Answers to Review Questions

1. C, E, F. A communication plan is developed to determine who needs communication, when, and in what format, and the frequency of the communications. Once the plan is developed, it's used to update stakeholders, team members, vendors, and others who need information on the project.

2. D. In the sender-message-receiver model, the receiver is responsible for understanding the information correctly and making certain they've received all the information.

3. A. There are four participants in the meeting, and six lines of communication. The formula for this is $4(4 - 1) \div 2 = 6$.

4. C. Resource Planning involves determining all the resources needed for the project, including human, material, and equipment needs.

5. B. A responsibility assignment matrix (RAM) chart depicts the WBS identifier, types of resources needed, and number of resources for the task.

6. C, D. Organizational planning is the process used to define roles and responsibilities for project team members and the plan to manage the project team. Staff acquisition is the actual acquisition of people and assignment of those people to the project team.

7. A. Obtaining the right resources for your project requires good planning and skillful negotiation. An individual meeting with each functional manager who will be providing resources is the best approach. Although you identify all the ideal resources you need, do not expect that you will get everyone you want. Negotiate for your most critical resources first, and be willing to compromise. An assumption that the functional manager just needs your list or an attempt to obtain resources by circumventing the functional manager provides a perception that you do not value the functional manager, and can create a poor working relationship.

8. C. Communications Planning is the process of identifying who needs to receive information on the project, what information they need, and how they will get that information. Scheduling a project team meeting, developing distribution lists, and creating a project status template are all activities that might be a result of the communications plan.

9. B. The three constraints associated with Human Resources Planning include labor-union agreements, organizational structure, and economic conditions.

10. D. Make-or-buy analysis is the technique of determining the cost-effectiveness of procuring goods or services outside the organization.

11. C. A cost-reimbursable contract is often the only option if you do not have a well-defined product or if the vendor is being asked to provide something that has not been done before.

12. B. The staffing management plan documents when and how human resources will be added to and released from the project.

13. A. Organizational planning addresses various factors that may impact how you manage your project team, how you'll define roles and responsibilities for team members, and how the team will be organized; it also documents the staffing management plan. Environmental factors are one of the considerations you'll take into account when performing organizational planning.

14. D. The staff acquisition process is part of the Human Resources Planning process, and it involves interviewing prospective team members, negotiating with functional managers, and assigning staff to the project.

15. D. The statement of work (SOW) describes in detail the goods or services you are purchasing from outside the organization.

16. C. Solicitation is the process of obtaining responses from vendors on the work of the project.

17. B. Bidders conferences are usually set up shortly after the RFP is posted and allow vendors the opportunity to ask questions about the project.

18. A. Weighted scoring models weigh various criteria from the RFP and SOW, which allows you to score each vendor on each of the criteria and determine an overall score for each vendor.

19. D. Cost-reimbursable contracts are the riskiest for buyers, since the buyer is responsible for reimbursing the seller on the costs of producing the goods or services.

20. A. Time and materials contracts are a cross between fixed-price and cost-reimbursable contracts. They assign a unit rate for work, but the total cost isn't known until the work is complete.

Chapter

6

Defining the Cost, Quality, and Risk Plans

THE COMPTIA PROJECT+ EXAM TOPICS COVERED IN THIS CHAPTER INCLUDE

✓ **2.3 Outline a process for managing changes to the project**

- Approvals required
- Forms needed
- Turnaround times
- Document routing
- Communication flow

✓ **2.8 Outline the components of a risk management plan**

- Initial risk assessment
- Risk matrix
- Risk register
- Risk response strategies
- Stakeholder risk tolerances

✓ **2.10 Identify the components of a quality management plan**

- Quality metrics, control limits, and frequency of measurement
- Quality assurance processes
- Quality control processes
- Quality baseline

✓ **2.11 Identify components of a cost management plan**

- Control limits

- Assign costs

- Chart of accounts

- Project budget

- Cost estimates (bottom up, top down, parametric, expert judgment, analogous)

- Cost baseline

✓ **2.13 Explain the purpose and common components of a transition plan**

- Ownership

- Transition dates

- Training

- Extended support

- Warranties

This chapter will wrap up the remaining planning processes. We'll discuss Cost Estimating and Cost Budgeting, Risk Management Planning, and the components of a solid quality management plan.

To many project managers, the most important components of a project plan are the scope statement, schedule, and budget. As you probably recall, these also happen to constitute the classic definition of the triple constraints. This doesn't mean that other components of the plan aren't important. The communication plan and the risk management plan, for example, are also important on any project.

Together, all the plans and documents you've developed, including the ones we'll discuss in this chapter, comprise the project management plan. We'll finish this chapter with a discussion of project plan approvals, sign-off, and transition.

Cost Estimating

Once you've documented the project resource requirements, you're ready to begin *Cost Estimating*, which is the process of estimating what you will spend on all your project resources. The cost estimates are the input for developing the project budget.

Cost estimates will be communicated to the project stakeholders. The project manager needs to be very clear about the potential accuracy of an estimate, especially those estimates made early in the planning process. Stakeholders have a way of casting both cost and schedule estimates in stone, so make certain they are aware that these are estimates and that more information will be known about total cost as the project progresses.

If multiple estimates are made during the course of project planning, always communicate the new estimate to the stakeholders, and explain how it differs from the previous estimate in terms of both content and accuracy. Let them know any new information that has come to light since you made the first estimate so they can understand your basis for the new estimate.

You can use a number of techniques in Cost Estimating. We'll cover three in this chapter, including analogous (also known as *top-down*), parametric, and bottom-up. We'll also provide some tips to help you work through the estimating process. Don't forget that you can also use three-point estimates in Cost Estimating. We talked about three-point estimates in Chapter 4, "Schedule Planning."

Cost-Estimating Techniques

You can use several techniques to estimate project costs; you may use some or all of these methods at various stages of project planning, or you may use one type of estimating for certain types of activities and another method for the rest.

The methods have varying degrees of accuracy, and each method can produce different results, so it is important to communicate which method you are using when you provide cost estimates. We'll now cover each of these estimating methods in more detail and discuss how they work.

Analogous Estimating (aka Top-Down Estimating)

We talked about analogous estimating when we discussed schedule planning in Chapter 4. For cost-estimating purposes, an analogous estimate approximates the cost of the project at a high level by using a similar past project as a basis for the estimate. (You may also hear this technique referred to as *top-down estimating* or as making an *order-of-magnitude* estimate.) This type of estimate is typically done as part of the business case development or during the early stages of scope planning when there isn't a lot of detail on the project. Analogous estimating uses historical data from past projects along with expert judgment to create a big-picture estimate. Remember that expert judgment relies on people who have experience working on projects of similar size and complexity or who have expertise in a certain area. An analogous estimate may be done for the project as a whole or for selected phases or deliverables. It is not typically used to estimate individual work packages.

 Analogous estimates are the least accurate of all the estimating techniques but also the least costly. Analogous estimates rely on expert judgment.

Analogous estimating will likely be the best technique to use at the early stage of the project because you'll have very little detail to go on. The key here is to make sure that everyone involved understands how imprecise this estimate is.

Parametric Estimating

We discussed parametric estimating in Chapter 4. You'll recall that this technique uses a mathematical model to compute costs, and it most often uses the quantity of work multiplied by the rate. Also, commercial parametric modeling packages are available for complex projects or those performed within specialized industries.

Parametric estimating is dependent on the accuracy of the data used to create the model. If your organization uses parametric modeling, spend some time learning about the specific models that are available and whether this technique is appropriate for your specific project.

Bottom-Up Estimating

The most precise Cost Estimating technique is called the *bottom-up estimate*, which assigns a cost estimate to each work package on the project. The WBS and the project resource requirements are critical inputs for a bottom-up estimate. The idea is that you start at the work package level of the WBS and calculate the cost of each activity assigned to that work package. The sum of all the work package estimates provides the estimate of the total project cost.

Bottom-up estimates are the most accurate of all the estimating techniques, but they're also the most time-consuming to perform.

When we discussed schedule planning in Chapter 4, we talked about calculating duration estimates for each task to determine the length of time your project will take. When you are calculating cost estimates, you need to base the estimate on *work effort*, which is the total time it will take for a person to complete the task if they do nothing else from the time they start until the task is complete. A work effort estimate is also referred to as a *person-hour estimate*. For example, assume a task to perform technical writing has an activity duration estimate of four days. When you perform cost planning, you need to know the actual number of hours spent performing the task. So, let's say the technical writer is allocating 5 hours a day to the project over the course of 4 days. The work effort estimate is 5 hours a day multiplied by 4 days, which equals 20 hours.

The duration estimates that you complete in schedule planning help you define how long the project will take to complete. The work effort estimates that you obtain in cost planning are used to define how much the project will cost.

The final piece of data you need for a bottom-up estimate is the rate for each resource. Rates for labor and leased equipment are typically calculated on an hourly or daily rate, while the purchase of materials or equipment will generally have a fixed price.

Deciding the correct rate to use for Cost Estimating can be tricky. For materials or equipment, the current cost of a similar item is probably as accurate as you can get. The largest overall cost for many projects is the human resource or labor cost, and this cost is often the most difficult to estimate. The actual rate that someone will be paid to perform work, even within the same job title, can fluctuate based on education and experience level. If you're procuring contract resources, you'll get a rate sheet that describes the rates for a given job title and the resource's travel rates if they're coming from out of town.

Table 6.1 shows the work effort and rate assigned for each of the resources in a sample project.

TABLE 6.1 Sample project resource rates

Task	Resource	Work Effort	Rate
4.1.1	Tech writer	20 hours	$30/hr
4.1.2	Programmer	100 hours	$50/hr
4.1.3	Server	Fixed rate	$100,000
4.1.4	Testers	60 hours	$30/hr
4.1.5	Programmer	200 hours	$50/hr
4.1.6	Marketing	30 hours	$60/hr

Now that you have the resource requirements, the work effort estimates, and the rate for each task, you can complete the cost estimate by adding a Total Cost column to the table. The cost of each task is calculated by multiplying the work effort for each resource by the rate for that resource. This will give you the total project cost estimate. Table 6.2 shows a completed cost estimate for the tasks in the sample project.

TABLE 6.2 Sample project cost estimate

Task	Resource	Work Effort	Rate	Total Cost
4.1.1	Tech writer	20 hours	$30/hr	$600
4.1.2	Programmers	100 hours	$50/hr	$5,000
4.1.3	Server	Fixed rate	$100,000	$100,000
4.1.4	Testers	60 hours	$30/hr	$1,800
4.1.5	Programmer	200 hours	$50/hr	$10,000
4.1.6	Marketing	30 hours	$60/hr	$1,800
Total				$119,200

Estimating Tips

Cost Estimating can be very complex, and cost estimates often turn into the official cost of the project before you have the proper level of detail. You will probably never have all the information that you'd like when calculating cost estimates, but that's the nature of project management. Here are some thoughts to keep in mind as you work through the estimating process:

Brainstorm with your project team.   Work with your team and other subject matter experts to make certain you've accounted for cost estimates that may not be so obvious. For example, do any of your project team members require special training in order to perform their duties on the project? Are there travel costs involved for team members or consultants? Getting the team together to talk about other possible costs is a good way to catch these items.

Communicate the type of estimate you are providing.   Make certain your stakeholders are aware of the types of estimates you're using and the level of accuracy they provide. If you're preparing an analogous estimate based on a similar project, be up front regarding the possibility of this estimate deviating from the actual cost of the project.

In addition to emphasizing the potential inaccuracies of an analogous estimate, provide stakeholders with a timeline for a definitive estimate. A project sponsor is more willing to accept that your current estimate may be much lower than the actual cost of the project if they understand why the current estimate is vague and what is being done to provide a more accurate estimate.

Make use of any available templates.   Many companies have cost-estimating templates or worksheets that you can use to make this job easier. They will also help you in identifying hidden costs you may not have thought of and may list the rates from the vendor agreements the organization has entered into.

Templates may also be a good source of rate estimates for internal resources. The salary of the people on your project will vary based on both their job title and specific experience. Your organization may require you use a loaded rate, which is typically a percentage of the employee's salary to cover benefits such as medical, disability, or pension plans. Individual corporate policies will determine whether loaded rates should be used for project cost estimates.

Get estimates from the people doing the work.   The reason that a bottom-up estimate is the most accurate is that work effort estimates are provided for each activity and then rolled up into an overall estimate for the deliverable or the project. The person performing the activities should be the one to develop the estimate. If your project includes tasks new to your team or uses an untested methodology, you may need to look outside for assistance with work effort estimates. You could consult published industry standards or hire a consultant to assist with the estimating process.

Document any assumptions you have made.   Make certain to document any assumptions you've made when performing cost estimates. For example, you may need to note that the rate sheet you're using to determine contractor costs will still be valid once the work of the project begins.

The cost estimates will be used to create the project budget, which we'll cover next.

Cost Budgeting

When you have the cost estimates completed, it's time to prepare the budget. *Cost Budgeting* is the process of aggregating all the cost estimates and establishing a cost baseline for the project. The *cost baseline* is the total expected cost for the project. Once approved, it's used throughout the remainder of the project to measure the overall cost performance.

The project budget is used to track the actual expenses incurred against the estimates. You can use several calculations to determine the performance of the budget to date for the project. We'll talk more about this topic in Chapter 9, "Controlling the Project."

Before learning about the mechanics of the budget itself, you should make sure you have an understanding of the processes within your organization regarding budgets, authority levels, how expenses are approved, and more. Here are a few questions you can use to help get you started:

- Are all project expenses submitted to the project manager for approval?

- What spending authority or approval levels does the project manager have regarding project expenses?

- Does the project manager approve timesheets for project team members?

- Are there categories of cost or dollar amounts that require approval from the project sponsor or customer?

Getting the answers to these questions before spending the money will eliminate problems and confusion later in the project.

Tracking project expenses as they're incurred is not always the responsibility of the project manager. Once the cost estimates have been provided and the project budget is established, the actual tracking of expenses may be performed by the accounting or finance department. Some organizations use their program management office (PMO) to oversee project budgets, approve expenses, track all the project budgets, and so on. Make certain you know who is responsible for what actions regarding the budget.

No matter who actually tracks the budget expenditures, as the project manager, you're the person accountable for how the money is spent and for completing the work of the project within budget. You'll want to monitor the budget reports regularly so you can identify any significant overruns and take corrective action to get the budget back on track.

Set up a routine meeting with all the budget analysts from the various departments providing project funding so that everyone is aware of the status of the project budget at any point in the project.

Now we'll cover how to create the project budget.

Creating the Project Budget

Project budgets are usually broken down by specific cost categories that are defined by the accounting department. A few examples of common cost categories include salary, hardware, software, travel, training, and materials. Make certain to obtain a copy of your organization's cost categories so that you understand how each of your resources should be tracked and classified.

 Check with your PMO or accounting department to see whether there are standard budget templates that you can use for the project.

Project budgets are as varied as projects themselves. Although the format for budgets may be similar from project to project, the expenses, budget amounts, and categories you use will change for each project.

Most budgets are typically created in a spreadsheet format and may be divided into monthly or quarterly increments or more depending on the size and length of the project. If you don't have a template available to start your budget, contact your accounting department to get the chart of accounts information needed to construct the budget. The chart of accounts lists the account number and description for each category of expense you'll use on the budget. You may remember that we used the chart of accounts codes earlier in the book for the work package level of the WBS as well.

To begin creating the budget, list categories such as salaries, contract expenses, materials, license fees, travel, training, and others, and record the cost estimates you derived for each. Add a column for actual expenditures to date. We'll use this information later in the Monitoring and Controlling process to determine the financial health of the project. Table 6.3 shows a high-level sample budget.

TABLE 6.3 Sample project cost estimate

Account Code	Category	Estimate for This Period	Actual Cost at Reporting Date	Variance
1001	Contract labor	$50,000	$48,500	$1,500
1003	Materials	$2,500	$2,500	$0
1005	Hardware	$22,700	$24,500	$(1,800)
1010	Training	$7,000	$5,000	$2,000
Total Variance This Period				**$1,700**

You may want to include two additional types of expenses in the project budget: contingency reserves and management reserves. Make certain you check with your organization regarding the policies that dictate the allocation of these funds and the approvals needed to spend them.

Contingency reserve   A *contingency reserve* is a certain amount of money set aside to cover costs resulting from possible adverse events on the project. These costs may come about for many reasons, including scope creep, risks, change requests, variances in estimates, cost overruns, and so on. There is no set rule for defining the amount you should put in a contingency fund, but most organizations that use this allocation often set the contingency fund amount as a percentage of the total project cost.

Be aware that stakeholders may misunderstand the meaning of a contingency reserve and see it as a source of funding for project enhancements or additional functionality they didn't plan into the project. Make certain they understand the purpose of this fund is to cover possible adverse events. With the exception of very small projects, our experience has been there are always expenses that come up later during the project that we didn't plan for up front. The contingency fund is designed to cover these types of expenses.

Management reserve   A *management reserve* is an amount set aside by upper management to cover future situations that can't be predicted. As with the contingency reserve, the amount of a management reserve is typically based on a percentage of the total project cost.

What makes the management reserve different from the contingency reserve is the spending authority and the fact that it covers unforeseen costs. The contingency fund is usually under the discretion of the project manager, who controls how these funds are spent. The management fund is usually controlled by upper management, and the project manager can't spend money out of this fund without approval from upper management. Management reserves are not included as part of the project budget or cost baseline.

The terms *contingency reserve* and *management reserve* may be considered interchangeable in some organizations.

The project budget is used to create the cost baseline, which is a tool used during project execution and during the Monitoring and Controlling process.

Cost Baseline

The key members of the project team should review the draft budget. It may be appropriate to have a representative from the accounting department or the PMO review the draft as well. The project team needs to understand the critical link between the schedule and the budget. Any questions about budget categories or how the dollars are spread across the project timeline should be addressed at this time.

Once the budget review with the project team is complete, it is time to get the project sponsor's approval and then create a *cost baseline*. The cost baseline is the total approved expected cost for the project. This should be set before any work begins. All future expenditures and variances will be measured against this baseline.

The cost baseline is used during project execution to track the actual cost of the project against the estimated or planned numbers. It is also used to predict future costs based on what's been spent to date and to calculate the projected cost of the remaining work.

The project manager should communicate the cost baseline to the project stakeholders. Some stakeholders may want a copy of the total project budget, while others may only be interested in the budget for specific phases of the project. You should note each stakeholder's needs regarding budget information in the communication plan.

Quality Planning

Quality Planning is the process of identifying quality standards that are applicable to your project and determining how your project will meet these standards.

Numerous articles and books have been written on the subject of quality. You may be familiar with the work of one of the quality movement gurus such as Philip B. Crosby, Joseph M. Juran, or W. Edwards Deming. Although each of these men defined a specific approach to quality, one common thread in their philosophies is that quality must be planned.

Quality management programs such as total quality management (TQM) and Six Sigma strive for consistent quality modifications that result in nearly 100 percent throughput in terms of high quality. Do an Internet search for *TQM, Six Sigma,* and *ISO 9000,* and you'll get plenty of hits for more thorough reading on this subject.

A key component of Quality Planning is the corporate quality policy. You need to determine whether such a document exists in your organization and, if so, review the quality standards and determine how you'll apply them to your project. If you are referencing a corporate quality policy, make certain you review that policy with your project team and the stakeholders to assure that everyone is familiar with the standards.

It would be impractical to quality-check every single task on the project plan. Several tools and techniques are available to assist you in determining what to measure and how to measure. The decisions regarding quality measurement are documented in the quality management plan. We'll discuss this document in the section "Quality Management Plan" later in this chapter.

Quality Planning Tools and Techniques

Your first plan of action is to determine those areas of the project that will most likely have quality issues that could impact the success of the project. The corporate quality plan may include useful ideas on determining where to focus your quality efforts and may also include suggested tools and techniques to help in performing Quality Planning.

Another area to consider in regard to quality is industry standards or government regulations. In particular, if you are producing a product that is regulated, you must be certain that it meets the criteria defined in the regulations. Failure to meet the provisions of a regulation could result in fines or jail terms. Regulations may also exist for safety reasons to protect workers and consumers.

Even if you do not have a corporate quality process and are working on a project with no predefined standards or regulations, you can use several techniques to determine what quality aspects of your project to measure. We will look at four of the most commonly used quality tools and techniques: cost-benefit analysis, benchmarking, flowcharting, and assessing cost of quality.

Cost-Benefit Analysis

We discussed cost-benefit analysis in Chapter 2 in terms of a project selection tool. This technique is also useful in planning quality management because you'll use it to consider the trade-offs of the cost of quality. For example, it's much cheaper to prevent defects in the first place than to have to fix them after they've found their way into the final product. The benefits of meeting quality requirements include the following:

- Increased stakeholder and customer satisfaction
- Less rework
- Higher productivity among workers
- Lower costs

Benchmarking

Benchmarking is a technique that uses similar activities as a means of comparison. It's a very useful technique if you're changing or upgrading the way you currently do business. If you're changing the work environment, you want results equal to if not better than the current environment. Benchmarking works by comparing the before and after results or comparing previous similar activities for the current project to past projects.

Flowcharting

Flowcharting uses diagrams that depict the relationship of various elements in the project. Developing a flowchart can help you anticipate where and when a problem may occur. You can build in checkpoints to assess the quality of a particular activity before the next step is started. Data flow diagrams (DFDs) are used to help programmers break down a system into its various components, and they're similar to flowcharts. Figure 6.1 shows a sample flowchart and DFD for the process of a customer interacting with a company through a customer service website.

FIGURE 6.1   A comparison between a flowchart and a DFD

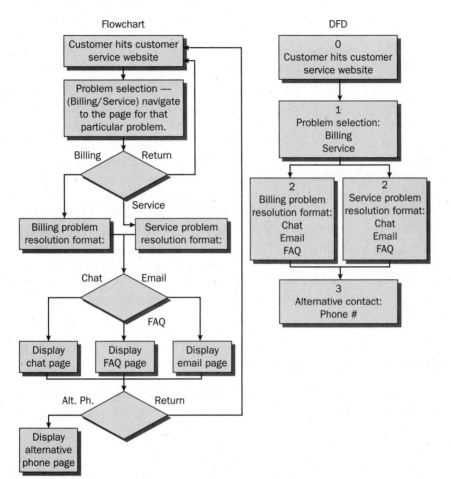

At first glance, the flowchart looks more difficult to interpret than the DFD. However, the flowchart describes the flow from start to finish. DFDs start with what's called a *context zero* diagram (note the 0 in the upper center of the starting box) and drill down into diagram levels 1, 2, and so on. The idea is that as you drill down, you get more and more information about a specific context. At some point, you've finally fleshed out the context so much that you have a solid place from which to begin coding.

Cost of Quality

Cost of quality is the total cost of all the work required to assure the project meets the quality standards. These costs include all the work required, planned and unplanned, to meet these standards, as well as the cost of nonconformance, rework, and quality assessments. The three types of costs associated with quality are prevention, appraisal, and failure:

Prevention   *Prevention costs* are the costs of keeping defects out of the hands of the customers. These costs include quality planning, training, design review, contractor or supplier costs, and any product or process testing you may perform.

Appraisal   *Appraisal costs* include the activities performed to examine the product or process and make certain the quality requirements are being met. Appraisal costs include inspection, testing, and formal quality audits.

Failure   *Failure costs* include the cost of activities needed if the product fails. Failure costs are also known as the cost of poor quality. There are two categories of failure costs: internal and external. Internal failure costs result when the customer requirements are not satisfied but the product is still in the control of the organization. Some examples of internal failure costs include corrective action, rework, scrapping, and downtime.

External failure costs occur when the product has reached the customer and they determine it doesn't meet their requirements. Example external failure costs include inspections at the customer site, returns, and customer service costs.

The specific quality techniques you'll use on the project should be documented in the quality management plan. We'll cover that next.

Quality Management Plan

The *quality management plan* describes how the project team will carry out the quality policy. It documents the outputs from the quality activities that were performed, the procedures used to complete the quality activities, and the resources required. This plan will be the basis for performing quality control when you are in project execution.

The procedures section of the plan includes more detailed information regarding the expected results from quality activities and the steps used to determine whether the quality standards are being met. The quality standards and the method used to measure these standards should be clearly defined.

You can use several methods when measuring whether quality standards have been met, including metrics, checklists, and exit criteria:

Quality metrics   A *quality metric* is a standard of measurement that specifically defines what will be measured and how it will be measured. You can define metrics for any area of the project. We'll use a web sales application as an example. If you're going to measure quality of the checkout process, your metric might state that when the customer implements the checkout process, the system will multiply the price of each item by the quantity of items ordered and compute the applicable sales tax and shipping charges 100 percent of the time. This metric would be part of the test scenarios used in the user acceptance test.

Quality checklists   A quality checklist is a tool that lists a series of steps that must be taken to complete an activity or process. As each step is completed, it is marked off the list. This provides documentation that the steps were completed and can also be used to track when the step was taken and who performed the work.

Exit criteria   Your project may include exit criteria that must be met at the completion of the project. Or, if you're using milestones to mark the end of one project phase and the beginning of the next phase, the milestones between phases may include quality exit criteria. In this case, your quality plan should document the criteria that must be met at each phase to consider that phase complete. Software development projects frequently use a series of tests to confirm the quality of the major deliverables for each phase. These tests can be established as exit criteria.

The quality management plan should also address how the results of the quality activities will be reviewed with the project sponsor and other stakeholders. Identification of any quality activities requiring formal sign-off are also documented in the plan.

Risk Planning

Risk is something that we deal with in our everyday lives. Some people seek out jobs or leisure activities that are considered high risk. They may get a thrill or a feeling of great accomplishment from taking on the challenge of skydiving or mountain climbing or from working as a lineman on high-voltage electrical lines.

A *risk* is a potential future event that can have either negative or positive impacts on the project. However, if you mention the word *risk* in association with a project, the majority of people will immediately think of something negative. In our experience managing projects, the vast majority of the time that a risk event occurs, it has negative consequences. But risks are not always negative. There is the potential for positive consequences as a result of a risk occurrence.

Risk Planning deals with how you manage the areas of uncertainty in your project; it has three major components: identifying the potential risks to your project, analyzing the potential impact of each risk, and developing an appropriate response for those risks with the greatest probability and impact. We'll cover each of these next.

Risk Identification

All projects have risks. *Risk Identification* is the process of determining and documenting the potential risks that could occur on your project.

You can view risks both by looking at the project as a whole, from the global level, and by analyzing the individual tasks in the project schedule. Global risks can include such items as the level of funding committed to the project, the overall experience level of the core project team, the use of project management practices, or the strategic significance of the project. Risks may also be associated with particular phases of the project or with certain key tasks.

You should include stakeholders, core team members, and any other subject matter experts who may have experience or knowledge of this project in your Risk Identification and analysis process. You can use several techniques to help define the initial risk list, including brainstorming, interviews, and facilitated workshops.

One way to get a jump start on a brainstorming session is to review a list of common potential risks:

- Budgets or funding
- Schedules
- Scope or requirements changes
- Contracts
- Hardware
- Political concerns
- Management risks
- Legal risks
- Technical issues

In addition, you could also devise a set of questions to pose to the group. Examples of Risk Identification questions include the following:

- Is the task on the critical path?
- Is this a complex task?
- Does the task involve a new or unfamiliar technology?
- Does the task have multiple dependencies?
- Have we had problems with similar tasks in previous projects?
- Is this task controlled by outside influences (permits, county hearings, and so on)?
- Are there inexperienced resources assigned to this task?
- Are there adequate resources assigned to the task?
- Are we unfamiliar with the hardware or software we're going to use for the tasks?

You can conduct the brainstorming meeting in a couple of ways. You can provide everyone with a marker and a sticky-note pad and ask them to write one risk per sticky note as they review the risk types and the questions. You can post the risks to a whiteboard and begin to categorize them. You can also invite someone to attend the meeting and take notes. No matter which method you use to identify the risks, at the conclusion of the meeting you should have a completed *risk list*. This is essentially a list of risks that you can record in a simple spreadsheet that includes an identification number, risk name, risk description, and risk owner. The risk owner is the person responsible for monitoring the project to determine whether the potential for this risk event is high and then implementing the risk response plan should it occur.

Once you have identified all the possible risks to the project, you need to analyze the risks to determine the potential for the risk event to occur and the impact it will have on the project if it does occur. A good place to start your risk analysis is by referring to the sample questions we posed in the brainstorming session and determine whether any of these questions have "yes" responses. For those questions, you may want to ask a further set of questions to help you begin defining the risk probability and impact:

- What issues or problems might occur?
- What problems occurred with similar tasks in the past?
- What could cause this problem?

We'll cover risk probability, impact, and analysis next.

What Could Possibly Go Wrong?

Another brainstorming technique you can use to identify risks is to hand out sticky notes and ask the risk team to answer one question: what could go wrong?

By letting people freely think and blurt out all the possibilities that occur to them, you may get some input that proves to be valuable in the Risk Identification process.

Risk Analysis

Risk analysis is the process of identifying those risks that have the greatest possibility of occurring and the greatest impact to the project if they do occur. Before you begin the analysis process, it's important to understand your stakeholder's risk tolerance levels. This may be partially based on the type of industry you work in, corporate culture, departmental culture, or individual preferences of stakeholders. For example, research and development industries tend to have a high risk tolerance, while the banking industry leans toward a very low risk tolerance. Make certain you understand the risk tolerances of your stakeholders before assigning probability and impacts to the risk events.

You can approach risk analysis from a qualitative or quantitative perspective. *Qualitative Risk Analysis* uses a subjective approach to determine the likelihood that a risk will actually occur and the impact to the project if it does occur. This process also involves prioritizing the risks according to their effect on the project. *Quantitative Risk Analysis* uses a more complex mathematical approach to numerically analyze the probability that a risk will occur, its effect on the project goals, and the consequences to the overall project. A detailed discussion of quantitative risk analysis methodologies is beyond the scope of this book, but you should be aware of some of the terms you may see. The more advanced techniques for computing quantitative risk analysis include sensitivity analysis, decision tree analysis, simulation using the Monte Carlo technique, and interviewing. Organizations that use these techniques as part of risk management typically have in-house experts to complete the assessment or assist project teams in doing so. We'll focus our attention on Qualitative Risk Analysis in the remainder of this section.

The first step after identifying the risks in the risk list is to determine their probability and impact:

Risk probability   *Probability* is the likelihood that a risk event will occur. For example, if you a flip a coin, there's a .50 probability the coin will come up heads. Probability is expressed as a number from 0.0 to 1.0, with 1.0 being an absolute certainty the risk event will occur.

So, the next step after identifying the risk is to ask the project team to assign a probability for each risk on the list. The safest way to determine probability is by using expert judgment. This typically comes from knowledgeable project team members or subject matter experts who have experience on similar projects. You could also review historical data from past projects that are similar to the current project to rate the probability of risk occurrence.

Risk impact   *Impact* is the amount of damage (or opportunity) the risk poses to the project if it occurs. Some risks have impacts that are very low and won't impact the overall success of the project, while others could have impacts that cause a delay in the project completion or cause a significant budget overrun. Again, rely on the expert knowledge and judgment of the team members and on historical data to rate the severity of the each risk. You can use a simple rating like the following to rate risk impact:

- High
- Medium
- Low

Next, you'll convert the high, medium, and low scores to a number between 0.0 and 1.0, with a score of 1.0 having the highest impact to the project, so that you can plug the scores into the probability and impact matrix (we'll discuss this next). For example, a high impact may have a score of 1.0, a medium impact may have a score of 0.5, and a low impact may have a score of 0.1.

   Check with your PMO to determine whether any templates are available that have predefined ratings for risk impacts.

Next you'll construct a probability impact matrix to calculate a final risk score for each of the risks on your list. The final score is determined by multiplying the probability by the impact. Table 6.4 shows a basic probability and impact matrix using the risk impact scores from earlier.

NOTE　Make certain you understand the risk tolerances of your stakeholders before assigning probability and impacts to the risk events. If your stakeholders are primarily risk-averse but the team is assigning probability and impact scores that are allowing for a higher tolerance toward risks, when a risk event occurs, your stakeholders may react in a way you didn't expect. For example, if they perceive a certain risk as high and the team rated it as medium and the risk event comes about, you may have stakeholders recommending canceling the project because of their unwillingness to deal with the risk event. Stakeholder reactions may bring about unintended consequences on the project, so be certain you're in tune with their comfort level regarding risk.

TABLE 6.4　Probability and impact matrix

Risk	Probability	Impact	Risk Score
Risk A	1.0	1.0	1.0
Risk B	0.3	0.5	0.15
Risk C	0.8	0.1	0.08
Risk D	0.5	0.5	0.25

The closer the risk score is to 1.0, the more likely the risk will occur and have a significant impact on the project. In Table 6.4, risk A has a high probability of occurring and has a significant impact. Risk C has a high probability of occurring but a low impact if it does occur.

The last step in the risk process is to create an appropriate course of action for those risks with the highest scores.

Risk Response

Risk Response Planning is the process of reviewing the risk analysis and determining what, if any, action should be taken to reduce negative impacts and take advantage of opportunities as a result of a risk event occurring.

Your organization may have a predetermined formula for identifying risks that require a response plan. For example, they may require that all risks with a total risk score greater than 0.6 must have a response plan.

You'll use several strategies when determining both negative risks and opportunities and formulating your response plans. The strategies to deal with negative risks include the following:

- *Avoid*: Avoiding the risk altogether or eliminating the cause of the risk event
- *Transfer*: Moving the liability for the risk to a third party by purchasing insurance, performance bonds, and so on

- *Mitigate*: Reducing the impact or the probability of the risk
- *Accept*: Choosing to accept the consequences of the risk

The strategies associated with positive risks or opportunities include the following:

- *Exploit*: Looking for opportunities to take advantage of positive impacts
- *Share*: Assigning the risk to a third party who is best able to bring about the opportunity
- *Enhance*: Monitoring the probability or impact of the risk event to assure benefits are realized

The last technique for determining risk responses is *contingency planning.* Contingency planning involves planning alternatives to deal with risks should they occur. This is different from accepting the risk, because acceptance doesn't involve a plan. It's different than mitigation because mitigation is concerned with reducing negative impacts. For example, if there's a risk totally outside the control of the project team (such as pending legislation or a possible work stoppage), a contingency plan is developed to identify the most likely impacts to the project and the strategy to deal with the impacts.

As you perform risk analysis, assign owners, and determine whether response plans are needed, you should record this information in the risk register. The risk register looks somewhat like the risk list but includes more information. On small projects, we generally add columns to the risk list to accommodate the types of information found in the risk register. Table 6.5 shows a sample risk register.

TABLE 6.5 Risk register

Risk	Risk Description	Probability	Impact	Risk Score	Response Plan	Risk Owner
Risk A	Bad weather	1.0	1.0	1.0	Y	Peterson
Risk B	Vendor delays	0.3	0.5	0.15	N	Hernandez
Risk C	Budget overrun	0.8	0.1	0.8	Y	Whatley
Risk D	Technical issues	0.5	0.5	0.25	N	White

The risk owner is responsible for monitoring the risks assigned to them and watching for risk triggers. *Risk triggers* are a sign or a precursor signaling that a risk event is about to occur. If the risk requires a response plan, the owner should be prepared to put the response plan into action once a trigger has surfaced.

Use the risk register to communicate the project risks and action plans to other stakeholders.

Project Management Plan Sign-off and Transition

The project management plan is the final, approved documented plan that you'll use throughout the remainder of the project to measure project progress and, ultimately, project success. The project management plan consists of all the documents you've produced in these last few chapters.

The key components of the project management plan include the following documents:

- Scope statement
- Project schedule
- Communications plan
- Resource plan
- Procurement plan
- Project budget
- Quality management plan
- Risk management plan

This completed plan serves as the baseline for project progress. You'll use this plan during the Executing and Monitoring and Controlling phases of the project to determine whether the project is on track or whether you need to take action to get the work in alignment with the plan.

The project management plan is also used as a communication tool for the sponsor, stakeholders, and members of the management team to review and gauge progress throughout the project. As such, it's a good idea to obtain sign-off from the sponsor and key stakeholders on the final project plan. This helps assure a common understanding of the objectives for the project, the budget, and the timeline and will ideally prevent misunderstandings once the work of the project begins.

Real World Scenario

After-the-Fact Plan

We can remember being on a project with a very large project plan that was updated on a weekly basis during project execution because most of the sections were created as the project work was being done.

This method of developing the comprehensive project plan created a scenario where the project manager, the project team members, and other stakeholders did not have a plan to guide execution of the project. What we received instead was a history of what was decided after the fact.

> As you can imagine, confusion was rampant, and to no one's surprise, the project was quickly off track.
>
> This is definitely not the way you want to transition into project execution. A project plan isn't a reflection of what has been done but what has been planned to be done.

Updating the Plan

Even after you've completed the initial project management plan document, reviewed it with all the stakeholders, and obtained formal approval from the sponsor and key stakeholders, your project plan may still change as you move into the project execution phase.

Updating the project management plan is an iterative process. As key components of the plan change throughout the course of the project, the corresponding sections of the project management plan will require updates. For example, the scope may change, a new stakeholder may become involved, an additional major deliverable may be added, or a deliverable may be deferred to another phase. The challenge of maintaining a project management plan is keeping the plan current and communicating updates to the project team, the sponsor, and other key stakeholders. Plans that are updated haphazardly will quickly become inaccurate and lose their usefulness as a road map for project execution.

To help alleviate these difficulties, you need a documented change control process. The change control process outlines the forms project members will need to fill out in order to request a change, the approval process for the changes, turnaround times, how the changes and documents describing the changes will be distributed, and the communication process for notifying the sponsor and key stakeholders of the changes. We'll talk at length about the change control process in Chapter 8, "Processing Change Requests."

To keep the sponsor and key stakeholders informed, schedule regular meetings with them to update them on project progress and change requests.

Transition

The completion of the comprehensive project plan signals the transition from the planning phase to the Executing process group. There's one more plan you'll want to create at this point, called the *transition plan*. This plan describes how the transition of the final product or service of the project will be transitioned to the organization.

In Chapter 1 we talked about ongoing operations. The ending of some types of projects signifies a turnover to the operations group. For example, if you're working on a project to implement a new software program, once the project itself is completed and implemented, someone has to pick up the ongoing duty of maintaining the system and applying patches and upgrades, and so on. That's where the transition plan comes into play. It includes a description of each of the following elements:

- Who the owner of the product or service of the project is once it's transitioned
- When the product will be transitioned
- Training needs and schedules
- Extended support schedules
- Warranties that may be applicable

The transition plan isn't part of the project management plan, but you should take the time before beginning the work of the project to document this plan. Once you do, schedule a meeting with the new owner of the completed project to make certain they are aware of the dates the product will be turned over and any training their staff members may need to attend before transitioning the final product.

Closing Out the Planning Process Group

At various stages throughout the project, and particularly when you come to the end of a process group, you'll assess whether the project should move forward. Holding a meeting to close out the planning process is an excellent opportunity to obtain stakeholder concurrence regarding the viability of the project business case and finalized project plan. If there have been any substantial changes in the business need that initially drove the approval of the project, now is the time, before the project work begins, to evaluate whether the project should move forward.

This review session should bring closure to any outstanding issues from the planning process as well. Ideally, any issues that were raised previously have been addressed and resolved throughout the planning phase. But don't assume that issues do not exist just because you're not made aware of them. Be sure to ask the stakeholders directly if anything regarding the planning phase is unresolved in their minds. It is much easier to resolve disputes before the project work begins.

It might be helpful to remember that as the project manager, in some people's eyes you're in a position of power. They may be reluctant to reveal a problem to you because they don't want to appear as non-team players or as troublemakers. It's important to try to foster open, honest, straightforward communication that supports a sense of security for people to be able to speak their minds about issues they see. Yes, there are people who will freely speak their minds no matter what. But you know who those people are. It's up to you to try to get the information out of those who know but won't tell.

Another key focus area of the planning review is to assure that stakeholder expectations of the project are aligned with what's detailed in the plan. It's your responsibility as the project manager to make sure that everyone involved in the project understands and supports not only the end result of the project but also the plan to reach that end result.

A successful transition from planning into execution should leave everyone clear about their individual role on the project and generate excitement about moving forward.

Real World Scenario

Chaptal Wineries

You have your list of resources, you've obtained some quotes from the vendors you'll be working with at each site, and you have determined the materials you'll need to complete the work, so now it's time to create the project budget. The quotes provided by the vendor are based on parametric estimating techniques. Each vendor provided a rate of pay and the estimated number of hours they thought it would take to complete the work. The internal team obtained quotes for the hardware and network equipment needed for the project. All of the costs were then summed to come up with a total budget estimate.

The following table shows a partial budget for this project. (All estimates have been converted to U.S. dollars.) Once the work of the project has started, we'll add an Actual Cost and Variance column to this spreadsheet to track budget expenditures.

Description	Work Effort	Rate	Estimated Cost
Hardware			$78,900
Network equipment			$37,200
Intranet developers	112 hrs	$125	$14,000
French contractor	40 hrs	$142	$5,680
Australian contractor	40 hrs	$165	$6,600
Chilean contractor	40 hrs	$94	$3,760
Californian contractor	40 hrs	$180	$7,200
Travel costs			$8,000
Training development	120 hrs	$85	$10,200
Total Estimate			$171,540

Quality Plan

We've determined the quality plan consists of three elements:

- It includes server hardware and software testing and validation. The project manager will be responsible for verifying that all server software has been correctly installed, that all service packs and necessary security patches have been applied, and that all hardware is functional and operating correctly with the software.

- The telecommunications contractors will be responsible for testing and validating that the telecommunications circuits are operational, fully functional, and error-free. Telecommunications companies will provide a warranty of error-free operation and an operational-level agreement (OLA) that specifies how they will perform if any problems occur.

- There will be significant unit, system, and user acceptance testing on the intranet pages. There will also be user acceptance testing on the email system.

Risk Assessment

After performing a risk assessment analysis with the project team, the following potential risk events were identified:

WAN circuits   There is a marginal (20 percent) probability that the minimum speed of the circuit could introduce bottlenecking at peak information load times. Risk mitigation involves either waiting out the peak or purchasing a higher-load circuit. Chaptal management thinks that the best approach is to monitor the circuits for load at deployment time and to accept any minor bottlenecks that might occur. Load testing will identify more significant load factors than anticipated as of this writing.

Hardware failure   There is a slight probability that the hardware will fail upon initial power-up and short-term operation or that it will be delivered in a nonfunctional state. The vendor contract calls for a next-day air shipment on all defective parts that cannot be replaced by in-the-field warranty personnel. Otherwise, there is a three-hour turnaround time on warranty work for hardware. Thus, risk response will include utilizing vendor warranty services, which is a transference risk strategy.

Internetworking equipment failure   There is minimal chance of a failure on all new router and switch gear that's deployed in the field—regardless of international location. Risk mitigation involves warranty replacement (a three-hour window) by contract field personnel.

Programming errors   The vendor has previous experience using the development protocols on the same platforms we're using on this project. Testing will occur throughout the various phases of code development as well. There is a warranty stipulation in the SOW that details the test and validation plans that will be used on the project. It also states that all systems must be working as advertised before the last scheduled payment from Chaptal is made to the vendor.

Sign-off and Transition Meeting

After documenting the last of the project plans, you call a meeting with the sponsor, Kate, and the key stakeholders on the project to review the plan, ask for sign-off, and ask whether there are any outstanding questions or issues that should be resolved before moving into the Executing processes. You also let everyone know that you'll be meeting with the head of the information technology area separately to discuss the transition plan.

Summary

The Cost Estimating process is performed after the resources for the project have been determined. You can use several techniques to create project estimates. Analogous or top-down estimates use expert judgment and historical data to provide a high-level estimate for the entire project, a phase of the project, or a deliverable. Parametric estimating uses a mathematical model to create the estimates and, in its simplest form, multiplies the duration of the project task by the resource rate to determine an estimate. The bottom-up method creates the project estimate by adding up the individual estimates from each work package.

Cost estimates are used to make up the project budget. The project budget is established by using the organization's chart of accounts and then documenting work effort, duration, equipment and material costs, and any other costs that may be incurred during the course of the project. The cost baseline is the total approved expected cost for the project and is used for forecasting and tracking expenditures throughout the project.

Quality Planning identifies the quality standards that are applicable to the project and determines how the project will meet those standards. Some of the most common tools used in Quality Planning include cost-benefit analysis, benchmarking, flowcharting, and cost of quality. Cost of quality is the total cost of all the work required to assure the project meets the quality standards. There are three types of quality costs: prevention, appraisal, and failure costs.

Risk Planning involves identifying potential risk events that could occur during the project, determining their probability of occurrence, and determining their impact to the project. Probability is always expressed as a number between 0.0 and 1.0. Risk response plans should be developed for those risks that have a high probability of occurrence, have a significant impact to the project if they occur, or have an overall risk score that is high.

The final project management plan consists of all the documents created during the planning phase of the project. It's good practice to obtain sign-off on the project plan from the sponsor and key stakeholders before proceeding. Once approval is obtained, the project management plan becomes the baseline for the project.

Exam Essentials

Know the difference between analogous, parametric, and bottom-up estimating techniques.   Analogous, or top-down, estimates use expert judgment and historical data to provide a high-level estimate for the entire project, a phase of the project, or a deliverable. Parametric estimates use a mathematical model to create the estimates. The bottom-up method starts at the lowest level of the WBS and calculates the cost of each item within the work packages to obtain a total cost for the project or deliverable.

Name the two discretionary funding allocations a project may receive.   The two types of discretionary funding are a contingency reserve and a management reserve. Contingency reserves are monies set aside to cover the cost of possible adverse events. Management reserves are set aside by upper management and are used to cover future situations that can't be predicted during project planning.

Explain the purpose of a cost baseline.   The cost baseline is the total approved, expected cost for the project. It's used in the Executing and Monitoring and Controlling processes to monitor the performance of the project budget throughout the project.

Name the Quality Planning tools and techniques.   The Quality Planning tools and techniques are cost-benefit analysis, benchmarking, flowcharting, and cost of quality.

Name the types of costs associated with the cost of quality.   The types of costs associated with the cost of quality are prevention costs, appraisal costs, and failure costs. Failure costs include both internal and external failure costs.

Explain the three processes used to develop a risk management plan.   Risk Identification is the process of identifying and documenting the potential risk events that may occur on the project. Risk analysis evaluates the severity of the impact to the project and the probability that the risk will actually occur. Risk response planning is the process of reviewing the list of potential risks impacting the project to determine what, if any, action should be taken and then documenting it in a response plan.

Name the negative risk response strategies.   The negative risk response strategies are avoid, transfer, mitigate, and accept.

Name the positive risk response strategies.   The positive risk response strategies are exploit, share, and enhance.

Key Terms

Before you take the exam, be certain you are familiar with the following terms:

appraisal costs	Qualitative Risk Analysis
benchmarking	quality management plan
bottom-up estimating	quality metric
contingency reserve	Quality Planning
cost baseline	Quantitative Risk Analysis
Cost Budgeting	risk
Cost Estimating	risk analysis
cost of quality	Risk Identification
failure costs	risk list
impact	Risk Planning
management reserve	Risk Response Planning
prevention costs	risk triggers
probability	work effort

Review Questions

1. You are asked to prepare an estimate for a project business case to install a new group of servers at a new satellite office. There is very little detail about this project. What will you use to compute your estimate?

   A. The price the client is willing to pay

   B. A sophisticated modeling technique

   C. The estimate provided by the project sponsor

   D. The actual cost of a similar project

2. Top-down estimating is another name for which type of estimating technique?

   A. Parametric estimating

   B. Analogous estimating

   C. Three-point estimating

   D. Expert judgment

3. The total time it will take for one person to complete a task from beginning to end without taking into account holidays, time off, or other project work is known as this.

   A. Duration estimate

   B. Work effort estimate

   C. Bottom-up estimate

   D. Parametric estimate

4. A discretionary fund used by the project manager to cover the cost of possible adverse events during the project is known as which of the following?

   A. Management reserve

   B. Chart of accounts

   C. Contingency fund

   D. Cost baseline

5. You are in the process of aggregating the cost baseline. All the following are used during the creation of this baseline except for which one?

   A. Management reserves

   B. Chart of accounts

   C. Human resource cost estimates

   D. Materials and equipment estimates

6. You are developing a bottom-up estimate for the first phase of your project. Which of the following is the most important input to complete this task?

   A. Historic data from a similar project

   B. Chart of accounts

   C. The WBS

   D. The scope statement

7. What is the most accurate estimate?

   A. Analogous estimate

   B. Bottom-up estimate

   C. Estimates based on expert judgment

   D. Parametric estimate

8. You are asked to present and explain your project cost baseline. All the following are true except which one?

   A. The baseline will be used to track actual spending against the cost estimates.

   B. The baseline can be used to predict future project costs.

   C. The baseline is tied to the chart of accounts.

   D. The baseline is the total expected cost for the project.

9. You're the project manager for a large IT project. At the time you performed your cost estimates, the vendor you're working with provided you with the following estimates: Programming estimate = 320 hours at $135/hour. Project management estimate = 320 hours at $155/hour. Testing estimate = 150 hours at $85/hour. What type of estimate are these?

   A. Analogous

   B. Bottom-up

   C. Cost benefit

   D. Parametric

10. Who is responsible for approving the project budget?

    A. Project manager

    B. Project team

    C. Project sponsor

    D. CEO

11. The work effort multiplied by which of the following will bring about the total estimate for each task?

    A. Duration

    B. Rate

    C. Number of resources

    D. Number of hours

12. A quality technique that analyzes similar activities as a means of comparison is known as what?

    A. Cost-benefit analysis

    B. Cost of quality

    C. Flowcharting

    D. Benchmarking

13. The benefits of meeting quality requirements include all of the following except for which one?

    A. Increased satisfaction

    B. Less rework

    C. Higher productivity

    D. Lower costs

    E. Improved quality metrics

14. Which of the following are the types of cost of quality? Choose three.

    A. Failure costs

    B. Prevention costs

    C. Appraisal costs

    D. Equipment costs

    E. Resource costs

    F. Quality Planning costs

    G. Extended support costs

15. These costs are also known as the cost of poor quality.

    A. Appraisal costs

    B. Corrective costs

    C. Prevention costs

    D. Failure costs

16. Risk Identification is the process of which of the following?

    A. Quantifying the impact to the project of a potential risk event

    B. Determining and documenting potential risk events on the project

    C. Assigning a probability that a particular risk event will occur

    D. Defining the action to take in response to a risk event

17. This risk analysis technique uses a complex mathematical approach to numerically analyze the probability and impact of risks.

    A. Quantitative Risk Analysis

    B. Risk impact analysis

    C. Risk probability analysis

    D. Qualitative Risk Analysis

18. All of the following are strategies for dealing with negative risks, except for which one?

   A. Accept

   B. Transfer

   (C.) Share

   D. Mitigate

19. Once risks have been identified and analyzed, this tool helps you determine an overall risk score.

   (A.) Probability impact matrix

   B. Risk list

   C. Risk register

   D. Risk template

20. Which of the following describe components of a transition plan? Choose three.

   A. Resource availability

   B. Assumptions

   (C.) Ownership

   D. Transition approach

   E. Communication methods

   (F.) Training

   (G.) Warranties

Answers to Review Questions

1. D. In this situation you would use an analogous estimate, which is based on historical data from a similar project. There isn't a lot of detail about the project at this point, so a sophisticated modeling technique won't work. The price the client is willing to pay won't reflect the costs or profit margin needed for the organization, and the project sponsor is not the most likely person to know the cost estimate.

2. B. Top-down estimating is another name for analogous estimating.

3. B. A work effort estimate or person-hour estimate is used to develop the cost estimates. This is the amount of time it will take to complete the task from beginning to end without accounting for work breaks, holidays, and so on. Duration estimates account for holidays, work breaks, and so on. Bottom-up estimates are estimates for individual components of work that are rolled up into the overall estimate, and parametric estimates are usually derived by multiplying quantity times rate.

4. C. A contingency fund is an amount allocated to cover the cost of possible adverse events, and the project manager generally has the ability to use this fund. The project manager does not usually have the authority to spend money from the management reserve. The chart of accounts is a description of the accounts listed in the accounting ledger, and the cost baseline is the total expected cost for the project.

5. A. Management reserves are not part of the project cost budget or cost baseline.

6. C. Bottom-up estimates start at the work package level of the WBS. Each work package on the WBS for the first phase of the project is summed to come up with an overall estimate for this phase. Historical data would be useful if you were using the analogous estimating technique. The chart of accounts don't help at all with this exercise, and the scope statement will give you an understanding of what's detailed on the WBS, but it won't help with estimating.

7. B. Bottom-up estimates are the most accurate estimates, and analogous estimates are the least accurate. Estimates based on expert judgment are analogous estimates. Parametric estimates are only as accurate as the data you're using for the parametric model.

8. C. The chart of accounts is used in creating the cost baseline. The baseline is the total expected cost for the project, and each category of cost is tied to the chart of accounts, not the total estimate for the project.

9. D. These estimates are parametric estimates. You've been given a quantity and a rate you can use to calculate the total estimate. Analogous estimates are based on expert judgment, and bottom-up estimates are provided for each of the work packages and added together to come up with an estimate. Cost benefit is not a type of estimating technique.

10. C. The project sponsor is the one who grants the authority to expend the resources required to create the deliverables of the project. Hence, the sponsor is the one who approves the budget.

11. **B.** The rate that is established for a given resource times the work effort (usually expressed in hours) will yield the total estimate for the task.

12. **D.** Benchmarking is a technique that uses similar activities as a means of comparison. Cost-benefit analysis analyzes the costs vs. the benefits, cost of quality determines the costs to meet the quality objectives, and flowcharting is a graphical technique that maps out activities or processes.

13. **E.** Quality metrics are a standard of measurement that defines what will be measured and how it will be measured.

14. **A, B, C.** The three types of cost of quality include prevention costs, appraisal costs, and failure costs. Failure costs include internal cost and external costs.

15. **D.** Failure costs are also known as the cost of poor quality. Appraisal costs are the costs associated with examining the product for quality; prevention costs are the costs associated with keeping defects out of the hands of customers.

16. **B.** Risk Identification is the process of determining and documenting the potential risk events that could occur on the project. Quantifying the impacts and assigning a probability both occur during the risk analysis process, and risk responses are developed during the risk response process.

17. **A.** Quantitative Risk Analysis uses a complete mathematical approach to determine risk probability and impact. Qualitative Risk Analysis is subjective in nature. Risk impact analysis and risk probability analysis are performed using either Quantitative Risk Analysis or Qualitative Risk Analysis.

18. **C.** Sharing is a positive risk strategy. The negative risk strategies are avoid, transfer, mitigate, and accept.

19. **A.** A probability impact matrix multiplies the probability score by the impact score to come up with an overall risk score. The risk list is a list of potential risk events, and the risk register is similar to the risk list but includes more details about the risk events.

20. **C, F, G.** The components of a transition plan include ownership, transition dates, training, extended support, and warranties. Resource availability, assumptions, and communication methods are all part of the project management plan. Describing the transition approach is the purpose of the transition plan, not an individual component of the plan.

Chapter

7

Executing the Project

THE COMPTIA PROJECT+ EXAM TOPICS COVERED IN THIS CHAPTER INCLUDE

✓ **3.1 Coordinate human resources to maximize performance**

- Assemble and develop project team, build team cohesiveness, perform individual performance appraisals

- Identify common causes of conflict

  - Competing resource demands

  - Expert judgment

  - Varying work styles

- Detect conflict and apply conflict resolution techniques

  - Smoothing

  - Forcing

  - Compromise

  - Confronting

  - Avoiding

  - Negotiating

✓ **3.2 Explain the importance of a project kick-off meeting and outline the common activities performed during this meeting**

- Communicate stakeholder expectations, high level timeline, project goals and objectives, roles and responsibilities to the project team

✓ **3.3 Recognize the purpose and influence of organizational governance on a project's execution**

- Standards compliance

  - Local, state, federal, ISO

- Internal process compliance

  - Audit trails, retention, version control

- Decision oversight
  - Change Control Board, committee consulting
- Phase gate approval
  - Tollgate approval, project phase transition

✓ **3.4 Given a scenario, select which component(s) of a project plan is affected and select what action(s) should be taken.**

- Actions
  - Schedule meetings
  - Manage scope
  - Follow communications plan
  - Manage project quality
  - Manage risks
  - Issue management
  - Prepare performance reports
  - Receive work performance information
  - Manage costs within budget
  - Implement approved changes
- Components
  - Risk register
  - Communications plan
  - Issues log
  - Change management form
  - Quality management metrics
  - Project schedule
  - WBS
  - Budget
  - Resource requirements
  - Scope statement

Now the real work begins—project execution. Successful project execution involves developing the project team, hosting the kickoff meeting, performing according to the project plan, and recognizing the influences the organization has on the project's execution.

You'll have relationships with a number of individuals and groups during the life of the project. All of your people management skills will come into play as you negotiate with the sponsor, team members, vendors, functional managers, clients, users, and other internal organizations.

If you talk to veteran project managers about what makes them successful, many will list the project team. Understanding how to build this temporary group into a team, making sure appropriate training is provided, and implementing a meaningful rewards and recognition plan are all challenges you face in developing a cohesive team.

Once the team is assembled, you'll host a kickoff meeting and begin working on the activities that bring about the deliverables. Along the way, you'll discover some bumps in the road that will require you to determine what actions to take to get the project back on course and what components of the project plan may need updating.

We'll start this chapter by discussing how to assemble and develop the project team. Let's dive in.

Forming and Developing the Project Team

Many of the resources you'll need for the project were identified in the human resources process of the Planning phase. Depending on the length of your project-planning cycle, it could be that some of those resources are no longer available, or you may have identified additional resources because of some last-minute changes in the project plan. Now it's time to bring those resources together and officially assign them tasks.

Managing a project team differs from managing a functional work group. Project teams are temporary, and getting everyone to work together on a common goal can be a challenge, especially if your team members are specialists in a given discipline without a broad business background. As the project manager, you must mold this group into an efficient team that can work together to deliver the project on time, on budget, and within scope, all while producing quality results. This is not always an easy undertaking, especially if you factor in a combination of full- and part-time team members, technical and nontechnical people, and in some cases a team dispersed over a large geographic area.

Building and Managing a Cohesive Team

Every team progresses through a series of development stages. It's important to understand these stages because team member behaviors will change as you progress through them, and the stage they're in affects their interactions with each other.

Dr. Bruce Tuckman developed a model that describes how teams develop and mature over time. According to Tuckman, all teams progress through the following five stages of development: forming, storming, norming, performing, and adjourning. We'll take a brief look at each of these next:

Forming   *Forming* is the beginning stage of team formation, when all the members are brought together, introduced, and told the objectives of the project. This is where team members learn why they're working together. During this stage, team members tend to be formal and reserved and take on an "all-business" approach.

Storming   *Storming* is where the action begins. Team members become confrontational with each other as they're vying for position and control during this stage. They're working through who is going to be the top dog and jockeying for status.

Norming   Now things begin to calm down. Team members know each other fairly well by now. They're comfortable with their positions in the team, and they begin to deal with project problems instead of people problems. Decisions are made jointly at this stage, and team members exhibit mutual respect and familiarity with one another.

Performing   Ahh, perfection. Well, almost, anyway. *Performing* is where great teams end up. This stage is where the team is productive and effective. The level of trust among team members is high, and great things are achieved. This is the mature development stage.

Adjourning   As the name implies, *adjourning* refers to breaking up the team after the work is completed.

Different teams progress through the stages of development at different rates. When new team members are brought onto the team, the development stages start all over again. It doesn't matter where the team is in the first four phases of the development process—a new member will start the cycle all over again.

Progressing through these stages can be enhanced with the use of team-building activities. *Team building* is simply getting a diverse group of people to work together in the most efficient and effective manner possible. These activities might involve events organized by the project manager (or specialists in the area of team building) that involve the entire project team, or they may include individual actions designed to improve team performance.

We find that organized team-building activities are very effective when a team is in the forming and storming stages, especially if they don't know each other. Search the Web or ask your human resources department for team-building activities that help your new staff get to know each other better. In our experience, once the team moves into the norming stage and beyond, there may not be as much of a need for organized team activities; however, informal activities are a great benefit in this stage, especially if the team arranges them, such as lunches, pizza nights, beers after work, and so on.

Some other instances where you may find team-building activities will help is if your team is experiencing personality clashes or if there are changes to the team makeup where old members have rolled off and new members have rolled on. Organizational changes are another good reason to employ team-building activities.

Monitoring Team Performance

Managing team member performance can be a complex undertaking. A successful project manager understands that most people work at their best when they're allowed to do the work they were assigned without someone preapproving every action they take. As long as the end result is accomplished according to plan and there is no impact on scope, schedule, budget, or quality, team members should be given freedom and choices regarding how to complete their tasks.

 To build and maintain the trust of your project team members, you need to demonstrate competence, respect, honesty, integrity, and openness. You must also demonstrate that you are willing to act on performance problems.

Although you shouldn't micromanage team members, they do need feedback on how they're doing. Most team members perform well in some areas and need improvement in others. Even if your organization does not require project managers to conduct formal written appraisals, you should take the time to provide feedback and not get so caught up in managing the project issues that you neglect your team members. The following are important areas of focus as you prepare to discuss performance with your team members:

- Specifying performance expectations
- Identifying inadequate performance behaviors
- Rewarding superior performance
- Reprimanding inadequate performance
- Providing specific consequences for choices made

Performance feedback should be given in a timely fashion. It is of little value to attempt corrective action on something that happened several weeks ago. The team member may not even remember the specifics of the performance in question.

Rewards for superior performance can be given publicly, but a discussion of inadequate performance should always be done privately. Berating a team member in front of others is inappropriate and will likely make the person angry and defensive. It may also negatively impact the morale of the team members who witnessed the berating.

Developing your team and improving overall performance can also be accomplished through training. We'll discuss this next.

Training

Training involves determining your team member's skills and abilities, assessing the project needs, and providing the training necessary for the team members to perform their activities. In some industries or organizations, one of the perks associated with being assigned to a new project is the opportunity to expand a skill set or get training on new products or processes.

One of the most common types of training provided to project teams is project management training. Project management training may include a session developed by the project manager, formal training provided by an outside company, or training from an internal PMO on the standard methodologies, tools, and templates all project members are expected to use.

Conflict management is an important aspect of team building and team cohesiveness. We'll look at this topic next.

🌐 **Real World Scenario**

Project Management 101

One of the most successful experiences we have had with project management training involved a project team in an organization that was just starting to implement the project management discipline. Based on the chaos surrounding earlier attempts at running projects, it was clear that the team members needed a common understanding of what project management was all about.

We contracted with a professional project management training company to teach a beginning class in project management concepts. All project team members were required to attend this session. All of the exercises associated with the class were based on the actual project the team members were assigned to. Not only did the team members gain knowledge of the project management discipline, but they were able to contribute to the project itself while in class.

Although this took some time and money, it was well worth the effort. All the team members used common definitions of terms, and it was much easier to talk about the meeting requirements, the project baseline, scope creep, and other fundamental project management concepts. The success of this project resulted in the organization setting goals regarding project management training for the entire department.

Conflict Management

One thing is certain: you'll likely experience conflict at least once, if not many times, during the course of the project. Conflict is the incompatibility of goals. When team members are focused on different goals, it's likely they'll resist or block others from reaching their goals.

Conflict may arise on a project for one of several reasons. We'll look at three of them that CompTIA identifies as common causes of conflict:

Competing resource demands   As we've discussed in several places throughout the book, resources in most organizations are in high demand. Many team members perform more than one function within the organization, and if you're working in a functional organization, you may find your project team members are available only part-time. It's also likely that all the project managers, and certainly the functional managers, know who the star team players are, and everyone is going to want them on their project. This competition for resources can cause conflicts among the project managers, functional managers, and even project team members who may not be happy with less stellar selections for the team.

Expert judgment   Expert judgment relies on the expertise of team members, consultants, industry experts, and others familiar with the project or topic at hand. However, expert judgment can cause conflicts for the team when there are differing expert views on the topic. One expert may recommend solution X, and another may recommend solution Y. As the project manager, you'll have to determine between the two experts. You also need to know whether this is a decision within your realm of authority to make or whether it must be escalated to the project sponsor to resolve.

Varying work styles   We've all probably worked with team members whose desks were so buried in papers and books and other stuff that you couldn't see the desktop. And of course, we've seen the opposite as well—those team members without a speck of paper on the desk, only the telephone and a computer monitor. Some team members are early birds and show up for work before the sun is up but are tired and cranky by 4 p.m., while others do their best work in the afternoon and early evening hours. We could discuss hundreds of ways that work styles can vary. Obviously, differing work styles can cause conflicts on the team. You should be aware of the preferences of your team members and accommodate reasonable solutions whenever possible for as many of them as possible.

You can use several conflict-resolution techniques to address these common forms of conflict. We'll cover them next.

Managing Conflict

One of the many lessons we've learned over the course of our careers managing hundreds of projects and personnel is that conflict will not go away on its own. You can't just wish it away and hope for the best. You need to address conflict head-on before it grows and gets out of hand.

According to CompTIA, there are several ways to detect and resolve conflict. We'll look at each technique next:

Smoothing *Smoothing* is a temporary way to resolve conflict; the areas of agreement are emphasized over the areas of difference, so the real issue stays buried. This technique does not lead to a permanent solution. Smoothing can also occur when someone attempts to make the conflict appear less important than it really is. Smoothing is an example of a lose-lose conflict-resolution technique because neither side wins.

Forcing *Forcing* is just as it sounds. One person forces a solution on the other parties. Although this is a permanent solution, it isn't necessarily the best solution. People will go along with it because, well, they're forced to go along with it. It doesn't mean they agree with the solution. This isn't the best technique to use when you're trying to build a team. This is an example of a win-lose conflict-resolution technique. The forcing party wins, and the losers are those who are forced to go along with the decision.

Compromise *Compromise* is achieved when each of the parties involved in the conflict gives up something to reach a solution. Everyone involved decides what they'll give on and what they won't give on, and eventually through all the give-and-take, a solution is reached. Neither side wins or loses in this situation. As a result, neither side really buys in to the decision that was reached. If, however, both parties make firm commitments to the resolution, then the solution can become a permanent one.

Confronting *Confronting* is also called *problem solving* and is the best way to resolve conflict. One of the key actions you'll perform with this technique is to go on a fact-finding mission. The thinking here is that one right solution to a problem exists and the facts will bear out that solution. Once the facts are uncovered, they're presented to the parties, and the decision will be clear. Thus, the solution becomes a permanent one, and the conflict expires. This is the conflict-resolution approach project mangers use most often and is an example of a win-win technique.

Avoiding *Avoiding*, sometimes known as withdrawal, never results in resolution. This occurs when one of the parties gets up and leaves and refuses to discuss the conflict. It is probably the worst of all the techniques because nothing gets resolved. This is an example of a lose-lose conflict-resolution technique.

Negotiating *Negotiating* is a technique we've discussed before. However, in light of conflict resolution, negotiating usually involves a third party who acts on the behalf of one of the parties (or takes one side of the issue) and helps all parties reach an agreement. For example, negotiating is a technique often used by collective-bargaining organizations.

These conflict management styles can help you understand the behaviors you're observing and help you reach resolution. Two additional situations that require special treatment are dealing with team member disputes and handling disgruntled team members, which we'll discuss next.

Team Member Disputes

Given the diverse backgrounds and varying areas of expertise among project team members, it should come as no surprise that team members will have disagreements. Sometimes people just need to have a conversation and work though the issues, but other times disputes require the intervention of the project manager.

You may be tempted to make a snap judgment based on what you see at any given point in time, but this may only exacerbate the situation. You need to get the facts and understand what is behind the dispute. Interview each of the team members involved to get as much information as you can. If it's a minor dispute, you might consider hosting a meeting, with you as the moderator, and ask each person to explain their issues and offer potential solutions. You could turn this into a brainstorming session in order to engage everyone and place the burden of finding a solution on them.

Sometimes, the dispute is very deep or potentially involves threats or other workplace issues. Always get your human resources department involved in these issues as soon as you are made aware of the problem. Most organizations have strict policies and guidelines in place regarding disputes of this nature. They may recommend mediation, training, disciplinary action, or replacing one of the team members. Don't attempt to resolve these types of issues on your own. If you do, you may find yourself entangled in legal issues, especially if you acted outside of the company policy.

 It's always a good idea to check with your human resources department before jumping into the middle of dispute resolution. You want to make certain you are following company policies and don't end up part of the problem yourself, rather than part of the solution.

Disgruntled Team Member

Few situations can poison team morale more quickly than a disgruntled team member. This can happen at any time during the project and can involve anyone on the team.

The behavior of a discontented team member can take a variety of forms. They may become argumentative in meetings or continually make side comments putting down the project. Even worse, this unhappy person may spend time "cube hopping" in order to share these negative feelings about the project with other team members. When otherwise-satisfied team members constantly hear statements that the project is stupid, is doomed to fail, or is on the cutting block, overall team productivity will be impacted.

As the project manager, you need to spend some private time with this employee to determine the cause of the dissatisfaction. It may be that the unhappy team member doesn't fully understand the project scope or how their contribution will lead to the project success. Or, it could be this person never wanted this assignment in the first place and feels forced onto a project they don't believe in.

It is best to start by listening. Stick to the facts, and ask the person to clarify the negative comments. If the team member is repeating incorrect information, set the record straight.

If they are frustrated about some aspect of the project and feel no one is listening, find out what the issue is, and explain that going around bad-mouthing the project is not the way issues get resolved. If the person truly does not want to be part of the project team or does not want to do their assigned tasks, work quickly with the functional manager or your sponsor to get this person replaced.

It's your responsibility as the project manager to hold your team members accountable. Once you've given them an opportunity to state their case and have made a few positive changes to address their concerns, make it clear you expect their negative behavior to stop. If they don't, you'll need to get your human resources experts involved and begin disciplinary action.

Ideally, conflict resolution will not dominate your time with the team. In our experience, this is typically a one- or two-time issue on most projects, depending on the length and complexity of the project. Most likely, you'll be more involved with building and managing a cohesive team and using an effective rewards and recognition system to motivate the team. We'll look at rewards and recognition systems next.

Rewards and Recognition

Recognition and rewards are important elements of both individual and team motivation. Project teams work hard and often overcome numerous challenges to deliver a project. If your company has a functional organizational structure, the project work may not receive the appropriate recognition from the functional managers. That means it's up to you to recognize the job your team is doing and implement a recognition and reward system.

When you think of rewards, you generally think of monetary rewards. And that's great if you're lucky enough to have money for a reward system, either as a direct budget line or as part of a managerial reserve. But there are options besides money that you can use as a reward—for example, time off, movie tickets, sporting or cultural events, team dinners, trophies, and so on. We've worked in organizations where an ordinary object was designated the "trophy" for outstanding performance. Individuals were responsible for recognizing each other and passing on the trophy.

Not all project managers have the resources to reward team members either individually or collectively, but that does not mean superior performance should go unrecognized. One of the easiest things you can do that doesn't cost any money at all is simply to tell people that you are aware of their accomplishments and that you appreciate their efforts.

Another no-cost idea is a letter of recognition sent to an employee's manager, with copies to the appropriate organizational executives and the project sponsor. This can be a very powerful means of communicating your appreciation for outstanding performance.

The key is to establish a program to acknowledge the efforts of your project team members, whether it involves money, prizes, letters of commendation, or a simple thank-you. Whatever form your rewards and recognition program takes, you must make sure that it is applied consistently to all project team members and that the reward is appropriate for the level of effort expended or the results that were achieved. Inconsistent application of rewards is often construed as favoritism.

Now that you have the team established and assembled, it's time to have the project kickoff meeting.

Project Kickoff

A project kickoff meeting is the best way to formally introduce team members and stakeholders and convey the same message to everyone at the same time. You may not know all of your team members, and you may not even have had the opportunity to interview them for the positions they will fill, depending on how they were selected (or appointed) to work on the project. As we've discussed, some organizations provide team members based on the functional manager's say-so, with little input from the project manager.

The tone that you set at the project kickoff meeting can make or break your relationship with the team. An ideal project kickoff session is a combination of serious business and fun. Your goal is to get the team aligned around the project goals and to get the team members comfortable with each other. This is a great opportunity to begin the forming stage.

You may know project managers who dislike the idea of a project kickoff and consider it a waste of time and money, but our experience proves that the results of a good kickoff meeting make it well worth the effort. There are a lot of different ways to structure a kickoff meeting. Here are some of the key components you may choose to include:

Welcome   It is a good idea to start the meeting by welcoming the team members and letting them know that you are looking forward to working with them. The welcome also gives you an opportunity to set the stage for the rest of the day. Take a few minutes to run through what participants can expect out of the meeting and what activities they will be involved in.

Introductions   A typical introduction format may include the person's functional area, brief background, and role in the project. The project manager should start the process to set an example of the appropriate length and detail. Put some thought into the information you want team members to share so that the time invested is worthwhile.

Project sponsor and key stakeholders   Invite the project sponsor, the customer, and any other executive stakeholders who are key to the project. It's important that the team members know them and hear their goals and expectations for the project firsthand. These people may not be able to stay for the whole session, but do your best to get them to at least make an appearance and say a few words to the team.

You may need to do some coaching here, so spend time prior to the session communicating with the executive stakeholders regarding the message they should deliver. If your sponsor happens to be a dynamic speaker, you might want to schedule them for a little more time to get the troops excited about the project they are working on.

Project overview   You'll start out this section with the project goals and objectives. You should also summarize the key deliverables for each of the project phases, as well as the high-level schedule and budget. This overview will help team members get the big picture and understand how they fit on the project. It also helps set the foundation regarding the purpose and goals for the project.

Stakeholder expectations   This section is a natural segue from the previous section. Along with explaining the goals, schedule, and budget, it's important that the team understands the stakeholder expectations for the project. Explain the reasons for the project deadline or budget constraints if they exist. Make certain team members are aware of any quality concerns, political issues, or market announcements that are tied to this project.

Roles and responsibilities   Start this section with a description of your roles and responsibilities for the project. Many of the team members may not know you or be familiar with your management style, so this is your chance to communicate how you will be managing the project and your expectations for how the team will function.

Depending on the size of the project, you may want to review the roles and responsibilities for each key team member or skill area. Let them know your expectations regarding project management procedures, reporting and escalation of issues, team meeting schedules, what you expect in terms of individual progress reports, and how they will be asked to provide input into project progress reports.

Question and answer   One of the most important agenda items for the kickoff session is the time you allocate for team members to ask questions. This engages them on the project and is the ideal opportunity to clarify questions regarding goals, deliverables, expectations, and more.

⊕ Real World Scenario

Kickoff for Remote Team Members

For a project kickoff to work effectively, it needs to include all team members. But what do you do if part of your team is located in a different city or state?

Remote team members often feel left out, especially if the majority of the team, including the project manager, sponsor, and client, is located at corporate headquarters where all of the action is.

Getting approval to bring in remote team members is a battle worth fighting, because it's so important in making everyone feel like part of the team. When making your case with the project sponsor, make sure you explain the importance of this meeting and the benefits it will have to the project. Your sponsor will be much more receptive to the idea if they know what will be covered and can see that this exercise is far more than people getting together for a free lunch.

But with more companies tightening the belt and looking closely at travel-related expenses, bringing in remote team members may not be possible. If you can't get the budget to bring in all the team members, maybe you can do the next best thing: fly the sponsor, the project manager, and a key stakeholder or two to the place where the other team members reside, and hold a separate kickoff for them. Last but not least, there are teleconferencing, video-conferencing, and web-based meeting options that you can use to at least virtually bring everyone together during the kickoff meeting.

The kickoff meeting is an excellent opportunity to get everyone on the same page. At the time you start project execution, you will probably have a combination of people who have been involved with the project since initiation and those who are relatively new to the project. This meeting is the time to set expectations and remind everyone of their role on the project.

Organizational Governance

During the Planning processes, we talked about the importance of understanding regulations, laws, and other compliance standards that may be required in your industry or organization. During the Executing process, it's once again important to reexamine any state, local, federal, or industry-imposed regulations that may impact how the work of the project is performed. Make certain the appropriate team members are aware of these regulations as well. In fact, it's a good idea to cover these at the kickoff meeting so that everyone is aware of the requirements.

Internal processes should also be examined at the beginning of the Executing process. For example, make certain you are aware of any processes you must follow in regard to documentation that may be necessary for future audits. Many organizations also have retention requirements for documents, including project documents. Perhaps you're required to retain all project documents for a certain length of time in a certain location on the company network. Make sure you're aware of this before beginning the work of the project.

One last document-related process you should be aware of is version control and the checkin and checkout procedures associated with your documents. For example, you may require updates to the project plan after the work of the project begins. You don't want to overwrite the original scope statement. Instead, you'll note that the updated scope statement is now version two, or whatever format your organization requires for document versioning and control.

According to CompTIA, organizational governance includes each of these components: standards compliance, internal process compliance, decision oversight, and phase gate approval.

Project Oversight

It's rare to complete a project without ever having to escalate an issue or decision to the sponsor or involve some type of oversight control board. When it comes to project oversight, you'll need to understand the processes that are already established for the organization regarding change requests, issue escalation, spending-authority limits, and so on, or you may have to implement them yourself if they don't exist. For example, change requests are typically reviewed and approved or denied by a change control board. You'll need to follow all the processes required to submit the change request, calculate its impact to the project, and track its disposition. We'll talk in more detail about change control boards in Chapter 8, "Processing Change Requests."

Another process you should consider implementing for project oversight, if it isn't already in place, is a *phase gate approval* process. This involves formally reviewing the project at specific points to determine whether the project should proceed. You may have an approval committee that conducts the reviews, or the project sponsor may have sole authority to make the go/no-go decision. There is any number of ways you can set up the stages for approval, such as at the completion of each phase of the project, at the completion of major milestones, at the completion of each of the project management process groups, and so on. Check with your PMO to determine whether this process is already in place.

Once the work of the project commences, you'll also begin monitoring the results to ensure they match what's in the project plan. We'll look much more closely at monitoring and controlling techniques in the next two chapters. But before we jump into that, we'll do a quick review of some of the actions you may need to take and some of the components of the project plan you'll be monitoring next.

Project Plan Components and Actions

Executing is where the project plan is put into action and the work of the project is performed. All of the major components of the project plan should be reviewed periodically. Monitoring the work for adherence to the project plan will begin in earnest in the Monitoring and Controlling processes. When decisions are made that impact the project plan, you'll need to determine what actions are necessary to get the work back in alignment with the plan. We'll talk more about the specific actions you can take in the next two chapters.

As a refresher, the components of the project plan that you'll be following during the Executing processes include these:

- Risk register
- Communications plan
- Issues log
- Change management form
- Quality management metrics
- Project schedule
- WBS
- Budget
- Resource requirements
- Scope statement

There are several actions that will begin in the Executing processes and continue into the Monitoring and Controlling processes. Some of the actions you'll be establishing include the following:

Scheduling meetings   Several meetings will begin during the Executing processes, including but not limited to project status meetings, change control board meetings, risk update meetings, steering committee meetings, budget meetings, and so on.

Managing scope   Managing scope is one of the keys to successful project management and probably one of the most important functions of the Executing process group. During the Planning processes, scope was documented, agreed upon, and signed off by the sponsor and key stakeholders. It's good practice to periodically review the scope with the stakeholders during the Executing processes and beyond to help manage expectations and keep scope creep from getting out of hand.

Following communications plan   Communication is another key to successful project management. Make certain that you follow through on the communications plan and keep the sponsor, stakeholders, and team members informed.

Managing costs within budget   It's your responsibility as the project manager to manage the costs on the project and keep watch over the estimates vs. actual costs for the activities. You'll need to gain sponsor approval for significant variances in the budget and for any additional funds you'll need because of those variances.

The actions listed previously are only a few of the things you'll be managing throughout the project. Other actions may include the following:

- Managing project quality
- Managing risks
- Managing issues
- Preparing performance reports
- Receiving performance information
- Implementing approved changes
- Managing standards compliance

Depending on the complexity and scope of the project, there may be additional actions you'll need to take that are specific to your industry or organization.

The majority of the project budget is spent during the Executing processes because that's when the vendors are hired, the goods are delivered, and the work is performed. When you're describing the Executing process group on paper, it's a separate process group from the Monitoring and Controlling group. In reality, these two groups work hand in hand. As you perform the work, you'll monitor the results (or progress points along the way) to verify that the results meet the quality standards, the stakeholders expectations, the deliverable acceptance criteria, and so on. This is where the iterative nature of project management comes into practice. As corrective actions are taken in the Monitoring and Controlling group to get the work back on track, you'll come back through the Executing processes to implement the corrections and reperform the work. We'll spend the next two chapters talking about Monitoring and Controlling.

Real World Scenario

Chaptal Wineries

You've begun the work of the project and held a project kickoff meeting via a teleconference so that everyone could be present at the same time. The telecommunications vendors have been hired, and preliminary work at each site has begun.

At the kickoff meeting, you review the following information with the team:

Major deliverables   These are the major deliverables:

- Procurement of server and internetworking hardware

- Procurement of wide-area networking connections

- Internetworking gear installation

- Server installation

- Email-software installation

- Intranet development

- Training of users

- Unit, integration, and user acceptance testing

Budget   The total project budget is $205,000. Kate Cox has agreed to subsidize the project with a $25,000 contingency fund.

Risks   These are the risks:

- Insufficient bandwidth

- Hardware failure

- Software failure

- Internetworking equipment failure

- Programming errors

Issues   It is vital that the project be completed before the crush season. Kate Cox has made it clear that no Chaptal employees are to be doing anything else but concentrating on the harvest and crush activities in September and October.

Communication   Because the email and intranet servers are not up yet, all communications will be by phone or by free temporary Internet mail such as Hotmail. Status updates are due to you twice a week during implementation, and you will compile the official project status report for distribution to the sponsor and stakeholders.

Implementation plan   Because of the requirements of the email-software system, procurement and installation of the WAN circuits must occur first, followed by installation of the internetworking equipment. After that, server builds can take place, followed by intranet programming and testing.

At the conclusion of the kickoff meeting, you ask whether there are any questions. You also give your contact information to all team members and explain how and when you want to be notified of issues.

Summary

Project execution is an exciting time because you finally get to see results of the hard work from the Initiating and Planning processes. But just because you are executing against a well-defined plan does not mean that you can sit back and watch the project pieces fall into place. You have a lot of work to do in this phase, including assembling and motivating the project team, holding the kickoff meeting, and determining the organizational oversight needed for the project.

Staffing issues may arise with the functional managers who provided you with resources for the project. You should attempt to resolve these issues with the functional manager directly, but if a compromise can't be reached, escalation to the sponsor may be required.

Successful team development includes ongoing team building and management, training, and a meaningful rewards and recognition system. It's also a time to build and establish an open, trusting environment and to encourage the free exchange of ideas.

As the work on the project progresses, you need to collect data from team members regarding their progress on the project and prepare status reports for the sponsor and stakeholders.

It's always important to understand any rules, regulations, or internal processes that you should adhere to when executing the work of the project.

Exam Essentials

Name some of the common causes of conflict. Common causes are competing resource demands, expert judgment, and varying work styles.

Name the conflict-resolution techniques. The techniques are smoothing, forcing, compromise, confronting, avoiding, and negotiating.

Name the conflict-resolution technique most often used by project managers. This is confronting, also known as problem solving. This technique involves discovering the facts regarding the issue and letting the facts help define the solution.

State the five stages of team development. They are forming, storming, norming, performing, and adjourning.

Understand the various means to recognize or reward team members. Team member contributions can be recognized with monetary rewards or prizes, a mention in the formal project review or status meeting, a letter to executive management, a thank-you, or a team celebration.

State the purpose of a project kickoff meeting. The project kickoff meeting is a way to formally introduce all project team members, to review the goals and the deliverables for the project, to discuss roles and responsibilities, and to review stakeholder expectations.

Explain the importance of organizational governance. Organizational governance recognizes the importance of regulations, laws, and other standards that may impact the project. This also involves internal processes, version control, and checkin/checkout processes.

Key Terms

Before you take the exam, be certain you are familiar with the following terms:

Adjourning	Norming
Avoiding	Performing
Compromise	Phase gate approval
Confronting	Smoothing
Forcing	Storming
Forming	Team building
Negotiating	

Review Questions

1. Your project is underway, and some conflict has arisen among the team members. It seems they were all anticipating that Tony, a genius regarding technology issues, was going to be assigned to the team. He was retained by the functional manager on another project, and your team was given someone else who is considered a junior-level player. Which of the following causes of conflict describes this situation?

   A. This describes competing resource demands.

   B. The team members are in the norming stage of development, which is causing this conflict.

   C. This describes expert-judgment conflicts.

   D. The varying work styles of the project team are causing this conflict.

2. Which of the following responsibilities of the project manager is not part of the project Executing process group?

   A. Setting the schedule baseline

   B. Tracking issues

   C. Tracking risks

   D. Reporting project status

3. A team member has come to your office to complain that a fellow team member is never available for meetings before noon and seems to ignore her requests to follow proper processes. Which of the following does this describe? Choose two.

   A. This describes a situation where the forcing conflict technique should be used.

   B. This describes an expert judgment conflict.

   C. This describes a common cause of conflict.

   D. This describes a situation where the negotiating conflict technique should be used.

   E. This describes varying work styles.

4. All of the following are stages of team development except for which one?

   A. Adjourning

   B. Negotiating

   C. Performing

   D. Storming

5. During a review of unit test results, two of your programmers disagree on the correctness of the deliverable from one of the units of code. How should you resolve this dispute?

   A. The programmers should take the issue to the test manager.

   B. You should ask clarifying questions to determine the specific issue surrounding the deliverable. Ask the team member disputing the deliverable to reference a specific requirement that is not being met.

   C. A separate meeting should be scheduled to conduct a detailed analysis of the code in question. The programming team and the test team should both be involved in this session.

   D. The project team members should decide who is correct. This item can be added to the agenda for the next regularly scheduled team meeting.

6. This conflict-resolution technique is temporary, and one of its symptoms is emphasizing the areas of agreement and keeping the real issue buried. Which conflict-resolution technique does this describe?

    A. Avoiding

    B. Forcing

    C. Confronting

    D. Smoothing

7. Which of the following is a win-win conflict-resolution technique that is generally the best way to resolve conflict?

    A. Negotiating

    B. Smoothing

    C. Confronting

    D. Avoiding

8. Which of the following are conflict-resolution techniques? Choose three.

    A. Adjourning

    B. Negotiating

    C. Norming

    D. Avoiding

    E. Compromise

    F. Storming

9. Your system engineer has started making negative comments during your weekly team meeting. He has had a heated argument with the marketing manager, and you have heard from various team members that he has become difficult to work with. What is the best course of action for you to take?

    A. You should write a memo to the system engineer's functional manager and request a replacement as soon as possible.

    B. The system engineer is critical to the project, so you should give him some slack and wait to see whether the behavior stops.

    C. You should confront the system engineer openly at the next team meeting. Let him know that his behavior is unacceptable and that he will be replaced if there is not an immediate change.

    D. You should schedule an individual meeting with the system engineer to determine whether he has issues with the project that need to be resolved. Get his perspective on how the project is progressing and how he feels about his role.

10. You are preparing for a formal monthly project review session with your sponsor and the customer. Which of the following is the best approach for making this an effective meeting?

    A. The project manager creates an agenda giving each team member an equal amount of time to provide task status.

    B. The preparation for a formal review takes valuable time that the project manager could put to better use. Assign one of the team members the task of putting together a summary of the meeting minutes from project team meetings for the last month.

    C. The project manager, with input from the project team, prepares a formal presentation that covers the previous month's key achievements, the current month's planned deliverables, the actual spending compared to the budget estimate, the overall schedule status, and any issues that could delay the project. The team determines in advance which team member will present each aspect of the review.

    D. The project manager creates a presentation to put the project in the best possible light. Any delays, overruns, or other issues should be downplayed to avoid making the sponsor look bad in front of the customer.

11. All of the following are true regarding rewards and recognition except for which one?

    A. Functional managers may not recognize the work of individual team members.

    B. Rewards and recognition are a form of motivation.

    C. Rewards and recognition should be applied consistently to all project team members.

    D. Rewards and recognition almost always involve money.

12. You're the project manager for a large IT project that's going to take a year to complete and requires input from many different IT technicians. Recently you've discovered that some fighting is going on between the person who's developing and implementing your security policies and a senior developer. You've found both to be highly credible, valuable players on your team. What's the best way to handle this situation?

    A. Call both to a meeting. Specify exactly what you're seeing happening between them. Ask for a plan from both to work out the differences. Stress the importance each of them contributes to the project.

    B. Ask the HR office to put together a meeting between you and the two fighting team members. Ask HR to work out the differences between the team members. Stress the importance each of them contributes to the project.

    C. Call both to a meeting with you and the project sponsor. Specify to the sponsor exactly what you're seeing happening between the two. Allow the sponsor to lead the group toward an amicable solution. Stress the importance each of them contributes to the project.

    D. Replace the security specialist with someone else.

13. This meeting, held during the Executing process group, formally introduces the team members and stakeholders.

    A. Project status meeting

    B. Kickoff meeting

    C. Project introductory meeting

    D. Steering-committee meeting

14. All of the following describe organizational governance considerations or processes you should take into account on the project, except for which one?

   A. Standards compliance

   B. Phase gate approval

   C. Sponsor approvals

   D. Decision oversight

   E. Internal process compliance

15. All the following describe a kickoff meeting except for which one?

   A. The roles and responsibilities overview describes how each team member will be interacting on the project, and the project manager will describe their role on the project at the first team meeting rather than the kickoff meeting.

   B. It's ideal if the project sponsor can attend the meeting and describe their goals and expectations first hand.

   C. The project overview includes a review of the project goals and objectives, a summary of key deliverables for each phase, a high-level schedule, and a high-level budget.

   D. Questions and answers help clarify the project objectives and expectations of the stakeholders and are a good opportunity to engage team members on the project.

16. Of the situations listed, which would team-building efforts have the greatest impact? Choose three.

   A. Schedule changes

   B. Low morale

   C. Personality clashes

   D. Budget changes

   E. Staff changes

   F. Organizational changes

   G. Project phase completion

17. All the following are elements of the project kickoff meeting except for which one?

   A. Introductions

   B. Overview of goals and objectives

   C. High-level budget overview

   D. Roles and responsibilities overview

   E. WBS overview

   F. Stakeholder expectations

18. You have a project that will be completed in multiple phases and have set up formal reviews at the completion of each phase to determine whether the project should progress. What is this review process called?

   A. Conversion

   B. Transition

   C. Hand-off

   D. Phase gate

19. Several actions occur during the Executing processes, such as managing project quality, managing risks, preparing performance reports and information, and more. All of the following describe other actions that start in earnest during the Executing process group except which one?

- **A.** Scheduling meetings
- **B.** Approving corrective actions
- **C.** Managing costs within the budget
- **D.** Following communications plan

20. One of your senior network engineers, Marty, is absolutely insistent that the vendor who's supplying your routers is "all wet" when it comes to a facet of a router that he's been tasked to install. However, when you consult with the systems engineers who work for the vendor, they tell you that Marty has misunderstood the way the product works and that it works the way they've advertised it. How do you handle this problem?

- **A.** Call the vendor and Marty to a meeting. Sit back and watch them hash it out.
- **B.** Call the vendor and Marty to a meeting. Act as arbitrator in an effort to get at the root of what the problem might be.
- **C.** Arrange to have some of the vendor's engineers meet Marty on-site to work through a sample configuration on one of the routers. That way, if he's right, they can see what he's talking about; if he's wrong, he'll see why.
- **D.** Tell Marty to listen to what the vendor has to say—after all, they invented it.

Answers to Review Questions

1. A. Competing resource demands are a common cause of conflict, and it's the one this question describes. The team thought they were getting an expert and instead got a junior team member, which caused conflict. Norming stages of development don't typically have conflicts; expert judgment and varying work styles are causes of conflict but don't describe this situation.

2. A. The schedule baseline is set during the project Planning process group. Issue tracking, risk tracking, and reporting project status are all Executing tasks.

3. C, E. This situation describes varying work styles, which are a common cause of conflict. The forcing and negotiating conflict-resolution techniques are not appropriate in this situation.

4. B. The stages of team development are forming, storming, norming, performing, and adjourning. Negotiating is a conflict-resolution technique.

5. B. Disputes over project deliverables should always be resolved by referring to the project plan. If a deliverable does not meet the documented project requirements, you have an issue that needs resolution. If you are dealing with a matter of personal preference, the person or group responsible for delivery chooses how to complete the tasks.

6. D. Smoothing is the conflict-resolution technique that is temporary in nature because it emphasizes the areas of agreement while keeping the real issues under the surface.

7. C. Confronting, also known as problem solving, is the best way to resolve conflict. It's a win-win conflict-resolution technique.

8. B, D, E. The conflict-resolutions techniques are smoothing, forcing, compromise, avoiding, and negotiating. Adjourning, norming, and storming are stages of team development.

9. D. To address the issue, you need to understand what is behind the system engineer's current behavior. He may have been given additional work that you are not aware of, or he may misunderstand the project goals, to name just a couple of possibilities. The situation cannot be ignored, no matter how valuable the person is, and it should be handled in private.

10. C. The purpose of a formal project review is to communicate to the sponsor the current progress, planned progress, and any roadblocks the project may be facing. This is the person who can make the hard decisions as to what the priority is between your constraints.

11. D. Rewards and recognition do not have to involve money, and many times may include rewards such as a thank-you, a letter to the functional manager, a public mention of the accomplishment at a team meeting, and so on.

12. A. Your primary goal is to bring the two team members together to try to air the differences in a way that's constructive. If possible, don't meet with them in your office; instead, choose a place that's neutral to all of you. Point out that you notice some friction going on and that you're wondering what the elements of that friction might be, because it's having an effect on the outcome of the project. Stress how valuable each of them are to the project. Ask questions that don't give either person an opportunity to blame the other. Try to find creative solutions to the problems. If this fails, the next step might be to consider asking HR to take a more active role.

13. B. The kickoff meeting is where the project team members and stakeholders are introduced to each other, and it's held at the beginning of the Executing process group.

14. C. According to CompTIA, the organizational governance components include standards compliance, internal process compliance, decision oversight, and phase gate approval.

15. A. The project manager should start the roles and responsibilities overview by describing their role on the project. It wouldn't hurt to review this and team member roles and responsibilities again at the first team meeting, but it should be covered in the kickoff meeting as well.

16. C, E, F. Personality clashes and staff changes are situations where team-building activities can assist in solving problems. Organizational changes require immediate communication from the project manager. As a rule, most people are generally sensitive to change and are asking, "What does this mean for me?" This has a tendency to disrupt working patterns and decrease efficiencies, and it requires that you act as a change agent—getting people through the change while continuing the work of your project. Additionally, it's quite possible that an organizational change may directly affect your project, in which case you, too, need to ask, "What does this mean for the project?"

17. E. The WBS is too detailed to review at a project kickoff meeting and is better handled during a meeting with project team members only.

18. D. This process is known as a *phase gate approval process* and involves formally reviewing project progress to determine whether the project should progress.

19. B. Corrective actions are approved during the Monitoring and Controlling phase but are implemented in Executing. This describes the iterative nature of project management because actions may be approved in one process group but actually get implemented in another.

20. C. This is similar to team member disputes only it involves a vendor in this scenario. Getting the vendor experts in a room with your engineer and letting them work through a sample configuration is the best way to handle this situation. You don't have enough information to know who is right. If the vendor is wrong, you'll be able to address it.

Chapter

8

Processing Change Requests

THE COMPTIA PROJECT+ EXAM TOPICS COVERED IN THIS CHAPTER INCLUDE

✓ **4.1 Given a scenario, implement proper change management procedures**

- Identify change

- Document using the appropriate change control forms

- Perform impact analysis

- Coordinate with the appropriate stakeholders to select the course of action

- Update the appropriate project plan components based on the approved change request

✓ **4.2 Evaluate the impact of potential changes to the triple constraints**

- Time/schedule

- Cost/resources

- Quality

- Scope

✓ **4.3 Using the risk management plan determine an appropriate response to potential risk/opportunity events**

- Perform qualitative and quantitative risk analysis

- Opportunities

  - Sharing

  - Exploiting

  - Enhancing

- Threats
  - Avoidance
  - Acceptance
  - Mitigation
- Update risk register with appropriate changes

✓ 4.4 Given a scenario, execute appropriate resource leveling techniques

- Fast tracking
- Crashing
- Delaying
- Optimizing
  - Use of tools as necessary

In the course of performing the work of the project, you will continually monitor the results of the work to make certain they meet the specifications of the project plan. Deviations from the project plan can be warnings that changes may be required, or have already occurred, to the original project plan. Requests for new requirements or changes to the deliverables or scope will surface during the course of the project. A sound change control process will help you and the team effectively deal with these requests.

Integrated change control looks at the overall impact of change and manages updates across all elements of the project plan. Scope change control includes understanding the impact of a scope change, taking appropriate action, and managing a process to review and approve or reject requests for scope changes.

Schedule control entails determining that a change to the schedule is needed, taking the appropriate action to deal with the schedule change, and updating the schedule based on changes in other areas of the project plan.

Risk control implements the risk prevention strategies or contingency plans developed in your risk response plan, monitors the results of preventative actions, and assesses new risks to the project.

We'll discuss the processes and techniques for these types of changes in this chapter. You'll learn about quality and cost controls in the next chapter.

Implementing Change Control Systems

Changes come about for many reasons, and most projects experience change during the project life cycle. Factors that might cause change include stakeholder requests, team member recommendations, vendor issues, risks, project constraints, and many others. You'll want to understand the factors that bring about change, such as those listed here, and how a proposed change might impact the project if it's implemented.

The types of changes others may ask for are limitless and could include requests for new features, functionality, requirements, and more. In addition, change requests may also take the form of *corrective actions*, *preventive actions*, or *defect repairs*. These usually come about from monitoring the actual project work results. Let's take a look at a brief description of each of these:

Corrective actions Corrective actions bring the work of the project into alignment with the project plan.

Preventive actions Preventive actions are implemented to help reduce the probability of a negative risk event.

Defect repairs Defect repairs either correct or replace components that are substandard or are malfunctioning.

The most important aspect of change in terms of project management is having a robust change control system in place to deal with the requests. Change control systems are documented procedures that describe how the deliverables of the project are controlled, changed, and approved. They also describe and manage the documentation required to request and track the changes and the updates to the project plan.

The key to avoiding chaos is to manage change in an organized fashion with an *integrated change control* system that looks at the impact of any change across all aspects of the project plan. Changes, no matter how small, have an impact on the triple constraints (time, cost, or quality), and they may also impact scope or any combination of these factors. Not having a process to analyze the impact of the change and determine whether it's worth the extra time, money, and so on, to implement is a recipe for project failure.

 In our experience, the three biggest project killers are lack of adequate planning, poor risk planning, and inadequate change control processes.

There are several aspects to an effective change management system. We'll look at each of these elements throughout this section. The change management process includes the following:

- Change request forms (and other documentation)
- Change request log
- Analysis of the impacts of change
- Change control board (CCB)
- Coordination and communication with appropriate stakeholders
- Updating the affected project-planning documents

Change Request Documentation

After the project management plan is approved, all change requests must be submitted through the change control system. The processes and procedures for change control should be documented and easily accessible to stakeholders and team members. The process should describe where to obtain a form for a change request, where and who change requests are submitted to for consideration, and a communication process for keeping the requestor apprised of the status.

Change requests should always be in writing. This means you'll need to devise a form for stakeholders and others to document the change request, the reason the change is needed, and what will happen if the change is not made. You could include a place for other information on the form that you think will help the review committee determine whether the change should be made. For example, other information could include potential for additional profits, increased marketability, improved efficiencies, improved productivity, social awareness or benefits, greening potential, and so on.

Beware! Stakeholders are notorious for asking for changes verbally even though there is a change control process in place. Spend time at the kickoff meeting explaining to everyone where to find the forms and how to follow the process. Make it a point that only change requests that come in via the process will be considered. Verbal requests and drive-bys to the project team will not be accepted.

Change Request Log

A number of things should happen once the change request is submitted. First, it should be assigned an identifying number for tracking purposes. Then, it should be recorded in the change request log. This log is easy to construct in a spreadsheet file. Table 8.1 shows a sample change request log.

TABLE 8.1   Change Request Log

ID	Date	Description	Requestor	Status	Disposition	Implementation or Close Date
01	11/11	Add a drop-down box on the entry screen	Nora Smith	Submitted to review committee	Approved	11/13
02	11/14	Implement virtual tape library for backups	Brett Whatley	For review on 11/25		

You could add other columns to this spreadsheet for tracking purposes, depending on the needs of your project. For example, you might want to add the date of the committee's decision, implementation status, and columns to track costs and hours expended to implement the change.

After the change request is recorded in the tracking log, the next step is an analysis of the change request.

Analyzing Change

The changes are typically analyzed by the subject matter experts working on the area of the project that the change impacts, along with input from the project manager. The following questions are a good place to start the analysis process:

- Should the change be implemented?

- What's the cost to the project in terms of project constraints: cost, time, scope, and quality?

- Will the benefits gained by making the change increase or decrease the chances of project completion?

- What is the value and effectiveness of this change?

- Is there a potential for increased or decreased risk as a result of this change?

After answering these basic questions, the expert should then analyze the specific elements of the change request, such as additional equipment needs, resource hours, costs, skills or expertise needed to work on the change, quality impacts, and so on. You can use some of the same cost- and resource-estimating techniques we discussed in previous chapters to determine estimates for change requests.

The project manager will also analyze the schedule, the budget, and the resource allocation to determine what impacts will occur as a result of the change. This information is documented (a template comes in handy here as well) and then presented to the review committee, usually called a *change control board*, for approval or rejection.

Keep in mind there is always an opportunity cost involved when analyzing change. When you ask your subject matter expert to stop working on their tasks in order to examine the impacts of the change request, their work on the project comes to a stop. This trade-off can be difficult to balance sometimes. There isn't a hard and fast rule that we can offer you about this, unfortunately. You'll have to keep an eye on the progress of the project work and the number of requests coming in. We sometimes track the number of hours spent by the team on change request analysis and report this to the stakeholders during our project status meetings. It helps them to be aware of the potential impact to the project if the change requests get out of hand, and if you have a savvy stakeholder group, they'll begin to self-discipline themselves and curtail frivolous requests.

Change Control Board

In many organizations, a *change control board* (CCB) is established to review all change requests. CCB members might include stakeholders, managers, project team members, and others who might not have any connection to the project at hand. Some organizations have permanent CCBs that are staffed by full-time employees dedicated to managing change for the entire organization, not just project change. You might want to consider establishing a CCB for your project if the organization does not have one.

Typically, the board meets at regularly scheduled intervals. Change requests and the impact analysis are given to the board for review, and they have the authority to approve, deny, or delay the requests. You should note their decision on the change request log shown in Table 8.1.

It's important to establish separate procedures for emergency changes. This should include a description and definition of an emergency, the authority level of the project manager in this situation, and the process for reporting the change after it's implemented. That way, when emergencies arise, the preestablished procedures allow the project manager to implement the change on the spot. This always requires follow-up with the CCB and completion of a formal change request, even though it's after the fact.

In many organizations, the project sponsor is required to approve changes that impact scope, budget, time, or quality if estimates surpass a certain limit. It's always good practice to inform your sponsor of major changes to scope, budget, time, or quality or any change that has the potential to increase risk. Check with your organization to understand the process for approvals.

Updating Stakeholders and Plans

Project status meetings are generally kicked off during the Executing processes to keep stakeholders apprised of progress. Change requests should be a regular agenda item at these meetings. The change request log should also be reviewed to discuss changes that were implemented during the last reporting period and those scheduled for implementation in the next period.

Changes to the project will require updates to the affected project documents, including but not limited to the project scope statement, budget, schedule, and quality plans. We'll cover more specifics regarding these updates throughout the remainder of this chapter and the next chapter.

Other Plan Changes

Scope, schedule, cost, and quality are the most frequently mentioned targets of change control, but these are not the only components of the project plan that may change. (We'll talk about cost and quality control in Chapter 9, "Controlling the Project.") Let's take a brief look at four other elements of change: resource changes, requirements changes, infrastructure changes, and configuration changes.

Resource changes Whenever a project team member is added or leaves, it is important to document the reason for the change, the name of the replacement, the person requesting the change, and any impact the change will have on the project.

Requirements changes   This can be a tricky area to manage. As detail is added to a requirement or it is updated to clarify expectations, you need to be taking a look at these changes to make sure they do not involve a scope change. Any new requirement should always go through the change control process.

Infrastructure changes   Infrastructure is the element of a project that will remain permanently after the project is completed. As an example, a team member may have planned for a Sun server running UNIX for your database, but as the project moves forward, the network team requests that you change this operating environment to Windows Enterprise Server. Infrastructure components that may change include the following:

- Computing systems
- Software development environments
- Server operating system platforms
- Networking infrastructures
- Delivery methodologies

Infrastructure changes can have a major impact on your overall project plan, particularly if your project includes equipment orders that were based on different infrastructure assumptions.

Configuration changes   Frequently, the design team will make a decision about a software or hardware configuration only to find out as the software is installed that another configuration would work better for the requirements or that the suggested configuration won't work with another system in an integrated system environment. One of the most frequent examples of a configuration change is when the database design team determines that a given set of indexes is required for the database being designed. But as the programmers begin to write code that calls the database, they may decide that another type of index would be useful and effective as well. So, a configuration change is required to add the new proposed index.

Configuration changes can be very simple or quite complex—it just depends on the nature of the configuration and what is expected of the software or hardware. However, generally speaking, most configuration changes don't require a lot of time, so they're typically not project showstoppers. Keep in mind that some configuration changes will require a reboot of the equipment and thus may not be able to be put into effect until after hours.

As your project moves forward and major deliverables are produced, you'll need to monitor the work results and take actions to get the project back in line with the plan. We'll discuss this in more detail in the next section.

Monitoring and Controlling Project Work

Managing and reporting on the work of the project is the primary focus of the Monitoring and Controlling process group. Monitoring and Controlling may require changes to the project or corrective or preventive actions to get the work in alignment with the plan. We'll discuss Scope Control, Schedule Control, and Risk Monitoring and Control in this section.

Controlling and Verifying Scope

Scope Control involves monitoring the status of the project scope, monitoring changes to the project scope, and monitoring work results to ensure that they match expected outcomes. Any modification to the agreed-upon WBS is considered a scope change. This means that adding, deleting, or modifying activities on the WBS constitutes a project scope change.

The scope baseline consists of the scope statement, the WBS, and the WBS dictionary. When a scope change has occurred, you'll need to update the appropriate baseline documents. Scope changes may require you to repeat some of the Planning processes as well.

When scope changes are requested, all areas of the project should be investigated to determine the impacts of the change. Remember that schedule revisions are always needed as a result of a scope change. If you're adding scope, you'll likely need to add time to the schedule. If you're postponing or eliminating scope, you may be able to reduce schedule time.

 If your project involves producing an actual product, you should note that changes to the product scope will require changes to the project scope, and vice versa.

Scope Verification involves stakeholders formally accepting completed deliverables and obtaining sign-off indicating the deliverables are satisfactory and meet stakeholders' expectations. You'll see in Chapter 9, "Controlling the Project," that quality controls involve techniques for checking for correct results. Verifying scope is where the acceptance of the work formally occurs.

Controlling the Schedule

Schedule Control involves determining the status of the project schedule, determining whether changes have occurred or should occur, and influencing and managing schedule changes. As you review progress reports from project team members, your goal is to confirm that activities are on track and that any changes have been analyzed for impact to the critical path.

 Changes to project scope always require changes to the project schedule.

Project management software is a useful tool for schedule control. Software systems can show the planned start and finish dates compared to actual dates, as well as forecast the impact of any changes to the critical path and the project end date. You can also perform what-if scenarios to show the impact on a particular phase or even the project end date if task duration is changed or new tasks are added because of an approved scope change.

The key to managing schedules is to focus on the critical path tasks. Remember that the critical path tasks are on the longest path of your network diagram and drive the end date of the project, so any delay to one of these tasks may lengthen the total project time.

The primary Schedule Control results include schedule updates and schedule compression techniques. Let's look at each of these topics:

Schedule updates   A *schedule update* is any change made to the project schedule as part of the ongoing work involved with managing the project. Schedules are typically updated weekly based on the team member progress reports to provide a current view of schedule progress and a comparison of status of the completed project work to the schedule baseline. Schedules are also updated to reflect new activities.

You may hear two terms in relation to schedule updates. A *revision* is an update to the approved start or end date of the schedule baseline. Revisions are typically a result of approved scope changes. If a schedule change is substantial and impacts dates for multiple milestones or major deliverables, *rebaselining* may be required to provide a new means of measuring performance. Rebaselining should not be done lightly, because it distorts the accuracy of your original plan.

Schedule compression techniques   Schedule compression techniques are a type of corrective action. Fast-tracking, you may recall, is starting two tasks in parallel that were scheduled to start sequentially. Crashing is a technique where you add resources to critical path tasks in order to shorten the project duration.

A number of factors come into play when considering whether corrective action is required as part of schedule control. Activity duration estimates are not expected to be perfect, so you won't need to take action every time the actual time required to complete a task is different than the estimate. For example, if an activity with float time has a delayed start or is taking longer than expected, you don't need to take any action as long as the activity does not use up more than the allotted float time. Your emphasis on corrective action should focus on critical path tasks or those that have used up all their float time.

Risk Monitoring and Control

Risk Monitoring and Control is the process of implementing the risk response plan, tracking and monitoring identified risks, and identifying and responding to new risks as they occur. Many activities are involved with this process, including the following:

Evaluating risk response plans that are put into action as a result of risk events   You'll want to document the effectiveness of the response plans for future projects. Some of the questions you can ask to help determine their effectiveness include the following: Was the response plan effective? Did it accomplish the goal and mitigate, transfer, exploit, share, or accept the risk appropriately? Did it cost more in time, resources, or contingency reserves than originally planned? How could it have been more effective?

Monitoring the project for risk triggers   Risk triggers are like the twitch that precedes a sneeze. They are symptoms that a risk event is about to occur. The risk owners assigned during the Risk Planning process are responsible for monitoring assigned risk events for triggers.

Reexamining existing risks to determine whether they have changed or should be closed out   This is also the responsibility of the risk owner. Once a risk has occurred or the opportunity has passed, the risk should be evaluated and closed out. The risk owner should also monitor low-priority risks for changes in status.

Monitoring residual risks   Residual risks are risks that are left over, so to speak, from the risk occurrence itself or left over after the risk responses have been planned.

Monitoring secondary risks   Secondary risks are risks that occur as a result of the original risk event or as a direct result of implementing a risk response. The risk owner is responsible for monitoring the project for secondary risks.

Reassessing project assumptions and determining validity   During the Monitoring and Controlling processes, you should review project assumptions to determine whether they are still valid. Assumptions that change throughout the course of the project may lead to unplanned risk events.

Ensuring that policies and procedures are followed   Like all of the processes we've discussed so far, Risk Monitoring and Control should have an established process for reporting risk occurrence; monitoring and reporting new risks, residual risks, and secondary risks; performing risk reassessments; implementing response plans; and reporting outcomes to the stakeholders.

Ensuring that risk response plans and contingency plans are put into action appropriately and are effective   Once a risk event occurs, the risk owner should notify the project manager and implement the response plan or contingency plan that was developed for the risk.

Ensuring that contingency reserves (for schedule and cost) are updated according to the updated risk assessment   Risks will occur on the project, and unplanned responses, or workarounds, may need to be implemented. Contingency reserves (both schedule and cost) will likely be needed to implement unplanned responses, and their appropriate documents should be updated to reflect the use of contingency reserves.

Evaluating the overall effectiveness of the risk processes   At the conclusion of the project, spend some time evaluating the overall effectiveness of your risk processes. Examine questions such as the following: Were risk planning and risk identification adequate? Were the risk scores and risk rankings accurate? Did the risk owners fulfill their duties? Were the risk responses implemented, and if so, were they effective?

Next we'll cover how to evaluate risk response plans and how to monitor the project for triggers.

Evaluating Risk Response Results

During Risk Planning, you identified risks to the project and prioritized those risks based on the probability of occurrence and the impact to the project if the risk occurred. The risk response plan includes a planned response for each of your high-priority risks, including actions to enhance opportunities and actions to lessen threats. Contingency plans were also developed during these processes.

Some questions to help you get started with evaluating the effectiveness of the risk responses are shown here:

- Have the response plans you identified to prevent the risk or mitigate the impact been implemented?
- Is the result what was expected?
- What was the cost of implementing the response?
- Did secondary risks occur as a result of implementing the response plan?
- Were resources diverted from other project activities to work on risk responses? If so, what was the impact to the project?
- For those risks that you could not control, did you implement a contingency plan to deal with the risk?
- How effective was the contingency plan?
- What was the cost of the contingency plan?

🌐 Real World Scenario

Keeping Your Eye on the Trigger

One of us worked on a project that involved extensive user training in multiple locations as part of the deployment of a new system. The training had to take place before the new application was deployed at each location, which drove the development of a complex dependency between the training and deployment schedules.

Just when we thought we had the schedule planned to perfection, we discovered that the end users were in the midst of negotiating a new labor-union contract. Talks were not going well, and it was possible for a labor strike to start in the middle of our deployment. No one associated with the project could do anything to help the outcome of the labor negotiations, so we had to develop a contingency plan.

We discussed several options, one being to tighten up the deployment schedule to complete all locations prior to the end of the current contract. That plan would have required additional resources to both train the end users and deploy the system, which we did not have. We opted to keep the existing training plan and develop an alternate plan for those offices that would not be trained before the strike date. The contingency plan called for the training to start two weeks after the end of the strike and to keep the same sequence and time between training as existed in the current schedule. All deployments scheduled prior to the strike date would continue as planned. No training or deployments would be canceled until after a strike was declared.

The customer approved this plan, a team member was assigned to monitor the progress of negotiations, and we established two triggers. The first was a vote by the union members to authorize a strike. When this occurred, a conference call was established with the managers of all offices impacted by the contingency plan. We reviewed the plan and made sure everyone understood the formula for calculating the new training date. It was agreed that a project team member would contact each office manager to confirm the training dates if we had to implement the contingency plan.

Our second trigger was the official start of the strike, which came at 12:01 a.m. on a Sunday. When the strike was declared, a message was sent to all training and deployment managers to cancel travel plans for that coming week.

Although the work stoppage delayed the overall deployment schedule by six weeks, the contingency was implemented smoothly, and the remaining offices were deployed in an orderly fashion with no disruption to customer service.

The keys to successfully implementing a contingency plan are identifying your triggers and good communication.

Identifying New Risks

The risk process evolves throughout the project life cycle. Some risks identified during planning may not materialize, and new risks may arise that were not previously included on the risk list. In addition to monitoring the existing risk list, you should also be on the lookout for new risks.

A new risk may have a greater probability and a more severe impact than previously identified risks, and the new risk may impact the overall risk ranking as a result. Approved changes to the project plan may also change the risk score or rank of a previously identified risk. For example, perhaps you identified a risk early in the Planning process and assigned it a Medium priority because the possibility for this risk occurring existed only within a certain time frame. Later in the project, a change in scope brought about a change to the critical path, which increased the probability of this risk occurring. That means the risk score changes to High, and a response plan needs to be developed and implemented.

NOTE Any change to the project scope has a potential to add risk to the project. Because the new activities associated with the scope change frequently lengthen the project schedule, they may change the critical path as well. A scope change should always include a risk analysis and review.

As you modify a response to an existing risk or identify a new risk, the action proposed to deal with the risk may itself result in a change to the project plan. The response may involve a change to the project scope, a change to the schedule, or a change to the budget. In this case, your risk response should go through the appropriate change control procedures, like any other change.

Establishing Performance Measures

The Monitoring and Controlling process group concentrates on monitoring and measuring project performance to identify variances from the project plan. *Reporting Performance* is the process where the collection of baseline data occurs and is documented and reported. It involves collecting information regarding project progress and project accomplishments and reporting it to the stakeholders. This information might also be reported to project team members, the management team, and other interested parties. The data you'll report on might include information concerning project quality, costs, scope, project schedules, procurement, and risk, and it can be presented in the form of status reports, progress measurements, or forecasts.

The project management plan contains the project management baseline data (typically cost, schedule, scope, and quality elements), which you'll use to monitor and compare results against. Deviations from this data are reported to the stakeholders. Performance measures are taken primarily during the Cost Control, Schedule Control, and Quality Control processes. In Chapter 9, we'll discuss the specifics of calculating and analyzing performance measures.

Performance Reporting

Performance reports may range from simply stated status reports to highly detailed reports. Dashboards are an example of a simple report that uses indicators like red-yellow-green to show the status of each area of the project at a glance. Red means the item being reported is in trouble or behind schedule, yellow means it's in danger and corrective action should be taken, and green means all is well.

More detailed reports may include some of the following elements:

- Previous period performance results
- Work completed in the current reporting period
- Work expected to be completed during the next reporting period

- Changes approved in the current reporting period
- Risk and issue status
- Schedule and cost actuals and forecasts
- Other information stakeholders want or need to know

Status meetings should occur regularly during the Monitoring and Controlling process. The purpose of the status meeting is to exchange information and provide updated information regarding the progress of the project. We've worked on projects where it's not unusual to have three or four status meetings conducted for different audiences. They can occur between the project team and project manager, between the project manager and stakeholders, between the project manager and users or customers, between the project manager and the management team, and so on.

> **NOTE** Notice that the project manager is always included in status review meetings. Take care that you don't overburden yourself with meetings that aren't necessary or meetings that could be combined with other meetings. Having more than three or four status meetings per month is unwieldy.

The project manager is the facilitator of the status meeting. As such, you should notify the status meeting attendees in writing of the meeting time and place. Publish an agenda prior to the meeting, and stick to the agenda during the meeting. Every so often, summarize what has been discussed during the meeting. Don't let side discussions lead you down rabbit trails, and keep irrelevant conversations to a minimum. It's also good to publish status meeting notes at the conclusion of the meeting, especially if any action items resulted from the meeting. This gives you a document trail and serves as a reminder to the meeting participants of what actions need to be resolved and who is responsible for each action item.

Monitoring Issue Resolution

Reporting issue status should be an ongoing agenda item at your project status meetings. Monitoring the progress of issue resolution is very similar to monitoring risks. Issues should be tracked in an issues log along with their status and resolution. Be aware that an issues log that is not carefully managed can turn into an unwieldy monster, with new issues added weekly and nothing getting resolved.

As you review your issues log with the project team, you want to be sure the person who has been assigned to resolve the issue is working toward closure. Sometimes project issues will remain open for weeks or even months, especially if you consider "we are still working on this one" an acceptable progress report. The status should always include both a plan for resolution and a target date to resolve the issue. If no progress is made, perhaps the responsible party needs assistance or does not really understand the issue. It may also require escalation to the sponsor to overcome roadblocks.

Although the goal is to assign all issues and resolve them as quickly as possible, in some instances you need to prioritize issues and have them worked on in sequence. If multiple issues require the same team member or group, review the impact of each issue on the outcome of the project, and establish a priority list.

Stakeholder Actions

The performance results you present at the status meeting could mean further action is necessary to get the work of the project back on track. Stakeholders should help make decisions regarding the steps needed to improve performance. For issues to be resolved, corrective actions may need to be put into place, or changes to scope or budget may be required to keep the project on track.

At this point, the stakeholders, particularly the sponsor, need to be informed of the impacts so that they can help make the decisions needed regarding the fate of the project. The project manager is responsible for communicating not only the nature of the deviations from the project plan but also the impact of these deviations and recommendations for moving forward.

A Project in Jeopardy

What starts out as a simple issue or change request can sometimes escalate into a situation that can jeopardize project completion. If the actions you have taken aren't having the desired impact or if you are identifying new issues and risks that you can't control, it is time to get with the project sponsor to determine the appropriate course of action.

Escalation to the project sponsor is a delicate balancing act. You don't want to get the reputation that you panic every time something goes off course or that you can't handle tough decisions. On the other hand, if you have done everything you can, do not delay involving the sponsor on the faint hope that things will change. If you don't raise a red flag until the project is in serious trouble, it may be too late for the sponsor to do anything.

When you meet with the project sponsor, be prepared to clearly communicate the situation, the actions you have taken so far, and the impact to the project if nothing changes. You should also be prepared to request specific actions on the part of the sponsor to help resolve the problem. If you are having issues with another department that requires a decision at the executive level, let the sponsor know who is involved and what action you need to get the project on track.

Managing Trade-Offs

All projects share common constraints: scope, time, cost, and quality. If any one of these changes during the course of a project, it impacts at least one of the other three. As project manager, you need to communicate the trade-offs to the stakeholders if there is a change to one of the constraints. You should have an idea regarding the importance of the constraints from your planning meetings with the customer so that you can present the trade-offs based on the constraint the customer does not want to change.

Trade-offs work much the same for all the constraints. Adding other features (a scope change), for example, could mean higher costs, delays in the schedule, or decreased quality. Changes to the schedule could mean higher costs, decreased quality, or changes to scope, and so on.

🌐 Real World Scenario

A Phased Delay

One of our early project experiences involved a new system application that was being developed for customer care representatives from two recently merged companies. Although the requirements and all of the major deliverables referenced one system, each company had separate back-end systems that needed to interface with the new customer care system. Unfortunately, this piece of information was not discovered until the work of the project started. So, the development team had twice the application interface work to do than was originally planned.

Everyone on the team knew there was no way that the project would be completed as scheduled. The development team provided a revised estimate that showed project completion six months later than the original schedule. Both the development manager and the project manager were afraid to go to the sponsor with this news, so they reported at the next project status meeting there would be a two-week delay and hoped for a miracle. Unfortunately, a miracle didn't occur, so they reported there'd be another two-week delay. At this point, the sponsor started asking a lot of questions, and the project manager had to admit that the best estimates of the additional work indicated a six-month delay. The sponsor was furious that she had not been told the truth from the beginning, and it ruined the credibility of the project manager. In fact, a new project manager was named shortly after this incident.

No one likes bad news, but you'll be much better off if you take one big hit and present all the facts as soon as you know them. Too many project managers try to sugarcoat project problems and convince themselves that the project will turn around—that rarely happens.

Sometimes negotiating a trade-off may not be the best solution, and it seems nothing can be done to change the situation. Perhaps a new regulation has invalidated key project assumptions, or new corporate leadership has implemented a strategy that nullifies the justification for your project. If this is the case, your request to the sponsor may be a recommendation to kill the project. In most organizations, only the project sponsor (or the executives the sponsor reports to) has the authority to kill a project.

Canceling a Project

In some cases, the best solution for dealing with project variance may be canceling the project. It's better to cancel a project that can't be adequately funded or staffed because significant changes have occurred than to let it continue and fail. Inadequate planning, ever-changing requirements, stakeholder expectations that are not based on reality, changes to business strategy, and so on, may mean the project is no longer viable.

Recommending project cancellation does not necessarily mean that the project manager failed; it means they're forcing the sponsor and other stakeholders to reassess the original objectives and determine whether the project still makes good business sense or whether it's time for the organization to cut their losses and move on.

🌐 Real World Scenario

Chaptal Wineries

You've implemented a change control process and established a CCB. There haven't been any major change requests submitted to date. So far, only two minor change requests were submitted. One change request was for one additional contract resource to help with preparing training materials, and another request was for a change in format for the user acceptance testing. Both changes were submitted to the CCB and approved. Neither change had an impact on scope or quality, but the additional training contractor added $3,400 to the overall budget. This additional expense was covered using the contingency fund.

You have also been monitoring the project for results related to scope, schedule, and risk and reported the following to the stakeholders at the project status meeting:

Scope and deliverables The installation at the French site is complete. The server and the router have been installed, baselined, tested, and certified 100 percent functional. Email was installed and validated. Training and user acceptance testing are completed.

Schedule A slight schedule slippage has occurred with the Chilean telecommunications contractor. The first resource they sent was not knowledgeable enough to resolve some issues that occurred at the site. This caused an overall two-day delay in the schedule. Since the installation in Chile is on the critical path, the overall project will be delayed by two days. You decide to make a corrective action and implement crashing to deal with the two-day delay. Originally, the California server installation was scheduled to start after the Chile installation was completed. You keep the original California schedule intact and ask a nonproject team member from the California location to oversee the server work by the vendor for the two days, plus one travel day, that you must remain in Chile to complete the work at this site.

Risk There have been no occurrences of risks with an overall ranking of High. The team is continuing to monitor the risk list and risk triggers for potential events.

Issues list You review the current issues list and update the stakeholders on their status. Currently, there are no showstopper issues, and resolution is progressing for those that are still outstanding.

Summary

As we discussed earlier in the chapter, things change. Changes come about for many reasons and may take the form of corrective actions, preventive actions, and defect repairs. An integrated change control system manages change requests, determines the global impacts of a change, and updates all impacted portions of the project plan when a change is made. Typically, a change control board is established to review and either approve, deny, or delay change requests.

Scope Control involves reviewing and analyzing requests for scope changes, and updating the scope baseline documents if a scope change occurs. The scope baseline consists of the scope statement, WBS, and WBS dictionary.

Scope Verification is the process of formally accepting the deliverables of the project and obtaining sign-off from the stakeholders that they're complete and acceptable.

Schedule Control involves determining the status of the project schedule, determining whether changes have occurred or should occur, and influencing and managing schedule changes. Particular emphasis should be placed on monitoring critical path tasks. Schedule updates may be required as a result of a schedule change. Schedule compression techniques (fast-tracking and crashing) can be used to help manage schedule changes.

Risk Monitoring and Control is when the risk response plans identified during planning are implemented if needed. Other activities that occur in this process include identifying and prioritizing new risks, implementing contingency plans based on a trigger event, and evaluating the effectiveness of response plans.

Reporting Performance is the process that involves collecting information regarding project progress and project accomplishments and reporting it to the stakeholders. Any project element that goes outside predefined limits requires action on the part of the stakeholder team. Trade-offs between quality, scope, schedule, and cost are presented by the project manager. Cancellation of the project is also an action for consideration if the project is no longer viable.

Exam Essentials

Name and describe the three types of change requests.   Corrective actions bring the work of the project into alignment with the project plan, preventive actions are implemented to help reduce the probability of a negative risk event, and defect repairs correct or replace components that are substandard or malfunctioning.

Describe the possible impacts to check for when evaluating a major change to the project scope.   A major change to the project scope may impact the critical path, schedule end date, budget, and resources, as well as introduce new risks.

Describe the elements of a change management process.   The elements of a change management process include change request forms, a change request log, analysis of changes, the CCB, coordination and communication with stakeholders, and updating the affected project planning documents.

Explain the purpose of a CCB. The change control board reviews, approves, denies, or delays change requests.

Describe the purpose for the Scope Control process. Scope Control involves monitoring the status of the project scope, monitoring changes to the project scope, and monitoring work results to ensure that they match expected outcomes.

Describe the purpose for the Scope Verification process. Scope Verification involves formally accepting completed deliverables and obtaining sign-off from the stakeholders indicating the deliverables are satisfactory and meet the stakeholders' expectations.

Describe the purpose for the Schedule Control process. Schedule Control involves determining the status of the project schedule, determining whether changes have occurred or should occur, and influencing and managing schedule changes.

Describe the Risk Monitoring and Control Process. Risk Monitoring and Control is the process of implementing the risk response plan, tracking and monitoring identified risks, and identifying and responding to new risks as they occur.

Key Terms

Before you take the exam, be certain you are familiar with the following terms:

change control board	Risk Monitoring and Control
corrective actions	Schedule Control
defect repairs	schedule update
integrated change control	scope
performance reporting	Scope Control
preventive actions	Scope Verification
rebaselining	
revision	

Review Questions

1. You are a project manager for a new software application. You have just learned that one of your programmers is adding several new features to one of the deliverables. What is the best action to take?

    A.   Make any needed adjustments to the schedule and cost baseline, and tell the programmer that any future changes must be approved by you.

    B.   Request that the programmer remove the coding for the new features, because he is outside the boundaries of the original scope statement.

    C.   Contact the appropriate functional manager, and request a replacement for this programmer.

    D.   Determine the source of the request for the new features, and run this change through the scope change process to determine the impact of the changes and obtain formal approval to change the scope.

2. You have just received the latest status updates from the team. Based on the progress to date, system testing is projected to take three weeks longer than planned. If this happens, user acceptance testing will have to start three weeks late, and the project will not complete on the planned finish date. The customer scheduled the user acceptance testing participants weeks in advance. What is the best course of action?

    A.   Explain to the test team that system test will end on the scheduled date, and they are accountable for the accuracy of the testing results.

    B.   Meet with the test team to determine the cause of the delay. If you determine that there are not enough testers to complete all of the scenarios in the time allotted, work with the sponsor to secure additional testers to complete the system test as planned.

    C.   Write a memo to the customer stating that you have a new date when the project will be ready for the end user testers.

    D.   Escalate the issue of the system test delay to the sponsor, and let her decide what action to take.

3. Your $5,000,000 application development project includes the purchase of two new servers, which are currently listed in the cost baseline as $50,000 each for a total of $100,000. Between the time the estimate was made and the time the equipment was purchased, there was a 10 percent price increase. The bill for the servers will be a total of $110,000. What action should you take? Choose the best answer.

    A.   Use the new figure to revise your cost estimate, and communicate the change to the project team and other stakeholders as part of your ongoing performance reporting.

    B.   Add the server costs as an agenda item for the next project team meeting, and work with the project team to develop a recommendation to take to the sponsor on scope reduction to cover the increased cost of the server.

    C.   Review the scope statement and the schedule baseline for adjustments to make because of the impact of the server cost.

    D.   Schedule a performance review meeting with the project team member responsible for the estimate.

4. You are the project manager for a new address verification system. The development phase has experienced some delays, and you are meeting with the development team to look at alternatives to get back on schedule. A suggestion is made by the development manager to skip unit testing and go right to the system test. What is the best response to this suggestion?

   A. The development lead has the most information about the complexity of the individual modules. You decide to accept the suggestion, because you already have three weeks scheduled for the system test. That should be more than enough time to find any problems.

   B. You agree to accept the suggestion but make it clear to the development lead that she is accountable if this decision leads to rework or problems as a result of the system test.

   C. You need to request more information from both the development lead and the test manager regarding the complexity of the unit tests and the potential impacts to the system test if this step is omitted.

   D. You should explain to the development lead that no quality activities can be removed from the schedule, but you can agree to a scaled-back version of what is reviewed during testing.

5. The system test results of your address verification system have uncovered a problem with the screen flow that is presented to the end user. Fixing the problem will involve a major rewrite of a portion of the screen flow logic. The end user can still access the "missing" screens, but this involves additional user training on commands to manually request a specific screen. What is the best course of action?

   A. You should send a memo to the customer and copy the stakeholder team explaining both the problem and the action required of the end user. Ask the customer to determine whether there are any schedule changes related to end user training.

   B. You should review the test results with the stakeholder team and provide estimates on the impact to the schedule and the budget if the rework is done. This information should be compared with the cost of additional user training and the impact of the manual override on productivity of the customer experience.

   C. You should escalate the problem to your sponsor for resolution.

   D. You should call an emergency meeting with the team that developed the screen flow logic. Let them know that the problem must be fixed without any impact to the schedule regardless of the hours they must put in. They are salaried employees and are not eligible for overtime, so there will not be any impact to the budget.

6. Which of the following is *not* a type of change request?

   A. Corrective actions

   B. Defect repairs

   C. Performance corrections

   D. Preventive actions

7. The project you are currently managing requires a new piece of equipment that has only been available in limited quantity in a beta test mode. The manufacturer has assured you that the device will be in production mode in time to meet the committed delivery on your project schedule. Delivery of this device was identified as a high-priority risk during risk planning. Because you have no authority to impact the production of the device, your team designed a contingency plan that uses a different device that will allow the project to move forward with reduced functionality. Which of the following is the best example of a trigger that indicated that you need to implement the contingency plan?

   A. A major trade magazine has just printed a story quoting informed sources predicting the resignation of the manufacturer's CIO.

   B. Several of your project team members have come to you to express concern regarding the dependency on this one vendor.

   C. Rumors are circulating that testing of the device is not progressing as planned and major rework will be required.

   D. The vendor is scheduled to ship the first set of devices on March 1. It is February 3, and you have not received the required written confirmation from the vendor regarding the shipping date. Written confirmation was due February 1.

8. This entity is responsible for reviewing change requests, reviewing the analysis of the impact of the change, and determining whether the change is approved, denied, or delayed.

   A. CAB

   B. CCB

   C. CRB

   D. TRB

9. The Scope Control process is responsible for all of the following except which one?

   A. Formally accepting completed deliverables

   B. Monitoring the status of the project scope

   C. Monitoring changes to project scope

   D. Ensuring work results match expected outcomes

10. The scope baseline documents consists of all of the following except which one?

   A. Scope statement

   B. WBS

   C. Scope management plan

   D. WBS dictionary

11. Changes to project scope require changes to these as well. Choose two.

   A. Budget

   B. Quality

   C. Schedule

   D. Resources

   E. Product scope

12. This type of change request is implemented to help reduce the probability of a negative risk event.

    A. Contingency plan

    B. Corrective action

    C. Risk response plan

    D. Preventive action

13. Which of the following should be established as part of the change control system in the event the change control board (CCB) cannot meet in a timely manner?

    A. Emergency change request procedures

    B. Procedures for analyzing the impacts of change and preestablished criteria for determining which changes can be implemented

    C. Process for documenting the change in the change request log

    D. Coordination and communication with stakeholders

14. After a change request is submitted, all of the following steps occur prior to being reviewed by the change control board except for which one?

    A. The change request is recorded in the change log.

    B. Analysis of the impacts of the change is performed.

    C. Specific elements of the project, such as additional equipment needs, resource hours, quality impacts, and more, are analyzed.

    D. Update the appropriate project planning document to reflect the change.

15. Stakeholders have come to you to tell you they want to change the scope. Before agreeing to the scope change, what things should you do? Choose two.

    A. Determine which project constraint (time, budget, quality) is most important to stakeholders.

    B. Discuss the proposed scope change with the sponsor.

    C. Ask team members what they think about the scope change.

    D. Define alternatives and trade-offs that you can offer the stakeholders.

16. This change is the type of change made to the project schedule that's part of the ongoing work involved with managing the project.

    A. Schedule revision

    B. Schedule update

    C. Rebaselining

    D. Schedule change

17. When substantial changes to the project schedule have occurred, which of the following might you perform to provide a new means of measuring performance?

    A. Rebaselining

    B. Schedule revision

    C. Schedule update

    D. Schedule change

18. What types of corrective actions might you consider when trying to shorten the project schedule? Choose two.

    A. Request additional budget

    B. Implement contingency plan

    C. Fast tracking

    D. Crashing

19. All of the following are true regarding dashboards except for which one?

    A. They are a type of performance report.

    B. They are a type of status report.

    C. They document work expected to be completed during the next reporting period.

    D. They usually have indicators such as red-yellow-green for a quick, at-a-glance status check.

20. This type of risk occurs as a result of implementing a risk response or of another risk event occurring, and it's the responsibility of the risk owner to monitor for this.

    A. Risk trigger

    B. Contingency risk

    C. Residual risk

    D. Secondary risk

Answers to Review Questions

1. D. The customer or a stakeholder may have requested the new features. If these are required features that were omitted from the original scope statement, you need to analyze the impact to the project and obtain approval for the change. If you just make adjustments to the budget and schedule without any analysis, not only do you risk being late and over-budget, but there may be impacts to other areas of the plan or risks associated with this change. Removing the new features may add cost and time to the schedule as well as create a potentially hostile relationship with the customer. Unless this is a situation where the programmer has repeatedly changed scope outside of the approval process, requesting a replacement resource is not an appropriate response.

2. B. Any time you have a projected delay in a major deliverable, you want to immediately determine what is causing the delay, because you may determine steps to bring the deliverable back on track. If you determine that there are no options to prevent the delay, you should meet with the customer to develop a workable solution to providing testing resources at a later time. Setting an arbitrary finish date for a deliverable that is already behind will almost assure incomplete testing and a potentially poor-quality product. Given the magnitude of the impact to the customer, this is not a situation that should be communicated in a memo. You need to be part of the solution.

3. A. A price increase of that magnitude has a negligible impact on a project with a $5,000,000 budget. The change needs to be documented and communicated, but it does not warrant a scope reduction. The estimate was made with the best information available at the time, so the project team member who provided the estimate did nothing wrong. An equipment cost increase alone will not impact the scope or the schedule baseline.

4. C. Even reducing the number of planned quality activities or the scope of an activity can be risky. Leaving out the unit test could result in defects that could have been corrected early on not being found until the system is being tested end to end. You do not have enough information at this point to assess the impact of that suggestion, and you need to involve the test manager. Regardless of what you may say to the development lead, you are accountable for the entire project and would take the blame if this approach backfires.

5. B. This is a classic case of the need to evaluate trade-offs with the stakeholder. There is no perfect solution in this case. Making unreasonable demands on the project team will not resolve the situation; it may even make it worse. This is not an issue that should be decided in a vacuum by the project manager or even the sponsor; it requires input and consensus from the stakeholder team, particularly the customer, regarding the best course of action.

6. C. Corrective actions, defect repairs, and preventive actions are all types of change requests.

7. D. The vendor has missed a key milestone date—the written confirmation of the device shipping date. The team member concerns may be valid, but the risk associated with a new device produced by only one vendor was accepted when the project was authorized. The speculation regarding the status of device testing may indicate that the device will not be available, but you need to contact the vendor and ask specific questions. The other answers may all warrant further investigation, but you would not want to implement your contingency plan based on unconfirmed rumors.

8. B. The change control board (CCB) is responsible for reviewing change requests; analyzing the impact the of the change; and approving, denying, or delaying the change request.

9. A. Formally accepting the completed deliverables is the primary purpose for the Scope Verification process.

10. C. The scope management plan is not part of the scope baseline. The scope baseline consists of the scope statement, WBS, and WBS dictionary.

11. C, E. Changes to project scope require a change to both the product scope and the project schedule.

12. D. Preventive actions are implemented to help reduce the probability of a negative risk event. Contingency plans and risk response plans are not change requests. The purpose of a corrective action is to bring the work of the project into alignment with the project plan.

13. A. Emergency change request procedures should be documented so that changes that must be made on an emergency basis prior to the next CCB meeting can be made. All changes should be documented and reported at the next CCB meeting.

14. D. After options A–C are conducted, the change request and analysis are given to the CCB to make a decision. The appropriate project planning document is not updated until the CCB makes a decision regarding the disposition of the change request. If it's denied, there's no need to update the project plans.

15. A, D. Determining the constraint that stakeholders think is driving the project will help you determine the kinds of trade-offs or alternatives you can propose to lessen the effect of the proposed scope change.

16. B. A schedule update is any change made to the project schedule as part of the ongoing work involved with managing the project. A revision is an update to the approved start or end date of the schedule baseline.

17. A. Rebaselining may occur when a schedule change is substantial and impacts dates for multiple milestones or for major deliverables. Schedule updates occur as part of the ongoing work involved in managing the project, and schedule revision is an update to the approved start or end date of the schedule baseline.

18. C, D. Fast tracking and crashing are two examples of schedule compression techniques. Schedule compression techniques are a type of corrective action. Fast-tracking starts two tasks in parallel that were originally scheduled to start sequentially. Crashing is adding resources to the critical path tasks in order to shorten duration.

19. C. Dashboards are a type of performance report and a type of status report that typically use indicators like red-yellow-green to display status for previous period results. Dashboards do not report work expected to be completed during the next reporting period.

20. D. A secondary risk can occur after the originally identified risk event occurs or as a direct result of an implemented risk response. The risk owner is responsible for monitoring risk events for this potential. Risk triggers are indicators that a risk is about to occur. Residual risks are leftover risks from a risk event or risk assessment.

Controlling the Project

THE COMPTIA PROJECT+ EXAM TOPICS COVERED IN THIS CHAPTER INCLUDE:

✓ **4.5 Explain the appropriate steps to ensure quality of project deliverables**

- Monitor work performance

- Analyze performance information

- Identify variances

- Generate change requests

- Implement change requests

✓ **4.6 Identify potential tools to use when a project deliverable is out of specification as defined in the quality baseline**

- Pareto charts

- Histograms

- Run charts

- Ishikawa diagram

✓ **4.7 Given a scenario, calculate and interpret the results of Earned Value Measurement (EVM)**

- EV

- PV

- CPI

- SPI

- EAC

- ETC

- VAC

- BAC

✓ **4.8 Given a scenario, manage and implement information distribution based on communications plan**

- Manage stakeholders expectations
- Schedule effective project meetings
- Periodic stakeholders updates

✓ **4.9 Recognize the special communication needs of remote and/or indirect project team members**

- Time zones
- Communication preferences
- Functional or hierarchical barrier
- Language barriers
- Technology barriers
- Cultural differences

We'll examine the last of the Monitoring and Controlling processes in this chapter, including Quality Control, Cost Control, Managing Stakeholder Expectations, and Distributing Information.

Quality Control monitors the project deliverables against the project requirements and the quality baseline to ensure that the project is delivering according to plan.

Cost Control monitors the expenses on the project and assures costs stay in alignment with the performance baseline. We'll also cover earned value measurements in this chapter. Variance analysis, trend analysis, and earned value are used to monitor and report project performance regarding costs, schedule, and estimated completion times.

Managing Stakeholder Expectations concerns satisfying the communication needs of the stakeholders. Distributing information is one way to manage communication needs and involves conducting project status meetings, reporting the earned value measurements and performance reporting information gathered for the time period, and managing the expectations of the stakeholders. In this chapter, we'll also cover the communication needs of the team members and the barriers that they may face.

Controlling Quality

Although quality is one of the common constraints all projects share, it is an area that does not always receive the same amount of focus as the scope, budget, or time constraints. However, lack of quality management can have as many adverse impacts to the project as ignoring controls for cost, budget, or schedules may have. *Quality Control* is the process of reviewing project results and determining whether they comply with the standards documented in the quality management plan and making any appropriate changes to remove the causes of unacceptable quality when the standards are not met. The quality management plan discussed in Chapter 6, "Defining the Cost, Quality, and Risk Plans," is the foundation for the specific activities carried out during Quality Control. The quality activities, the procedures used to complete the quality activities, and the resources required are documented in the quality management plan.

Quality Control is performed throughout the project. As we have mentioned in earlier chapters, milestones are often included in the project schedule to mark the completion of a project phase or major deliverable. Quality tools and techniques are used to determine compliance with a minimum standard, and quality activities are often a key part of the formal process of approving the completion of a phase.

We will focus on the use of testing to monitor the project work results, as well as mention some other tools and techniques that are used in Quality Control. The results of your Quality Control activities may require rework, process changes, or acceptance of defects that are found.

Inspecting and Preventing Errors

Inspection is a Quality Control tool that involves examining, measuring, or testing work results to determine whether they conform to the quality standards and plan. Inspection may occur at intervals throughout the project, at the end of a project phase, or when the work is completed. When inspection occurs at any point in the project, a decision is made whether to accept or reject the work. When the work is rejected, it may have to go back through the process for rework.

Some of the costs associated with inspection include rework, labor costs, material costs, and potential loss of customers.

Inspection typically involves taking measurements or using metrics to compare results to the plan. When measurements fall within a specified range, they are called *tolerable results*. For example, the requirement might state that the measurements must be within plus or minus 2 inches. Any work result that falls within this range is tolerable and would be accepted.

Another inspection technique is *attribute sampling*. This method determines whether the results are conforming or nonconforming to the requirements. Conforming results meet the requirements and are accepted; nonconforming results do not. This is also sometimes known as a *pass/fail* or *go/no-go* decision.

Whether you choose to inspect or perform attribute sampling for every part or work result produced for the project will depend on the type of project you're working on. Inspection can be costly and time-consuming and probably isn't necessary when producing hundreds or thousands of parts. In this case, inspection or attribute sampling is performed on a sampling of parts where every x number of parts is tested for conformity.

Prevention is different from inspection. Inspection occurs after the work is complete (or at certain points during the process). Prevention keeps errors from reaching the customers or from occurring in the first place. It always costs less to prevent problems than to find them later and have to fix the problem.

Inspection tells you where problems exist and gives you the opportunity to correct them, but there's generally a cost associated with the fix. Prevention keeps mistakes from occurring or reaching the customer, and it's usually less costly, less time-consuming, and more efficient to correct errors before they reach the customer.

In the computer programming industry, testing is used as a form of inspection to tell you where problems may exist with the code. Testing is usually a boring job—someone has to run the code over and over again, testing different things in different modules and making notes about its performance. But it must be done in order to assure the program is functioning as it should. There are several methods used when testing programs. Unit testing, module testing, system testing, and user acceptance testing are some of the most common.

Unit testing   Unit testing involves testing sections of code as they're written to verify they operate properly.

Module testing   Module testing involves testing discreet units or sections of programming code. For example, you might test the printing functions or an order-entry form.

System testing   Next, the entire system as a whole is tested. This testing makes sure the system flows as expected, that all the functionality works and is accurate, and that it delivers what the customer is expecting.

User acceptance testing (UAT)   This testing involves people who will be the end users of the system. They test features, functionality, calculations, and so on, to assure the system meets the requirements laid out in the scope statement.

Testing is an important step in confirming the quality of an IT project. There are several other Quality Control tools you can use on the project, and we'll cover them next.

Using Other Quality Control Tools and Techniques

Several other tools and techniques can be used alone or in some combination to address quality defects. Don't forget you can also use these tools along with inspection and attribute sampling. Let's look at each of them now:

Histogram   A *histogram* is a bar chart that depicts variables on the horizontal and vertical axes. A Pareto diagram, which we'll discuss next, is a type of histogram. If you look at Figure 9.1, you'll see that the bars in the Pareto diagram represent a typical histogram arranged by order of frequency.

Pareto diagram   A *Pareto diagram* is used to rank the importance of a problem based on its frequency of occurrence over time. This diagram is based on the Pareto principle, which is more commonly referred to as the *80/20 rule*. The Pareto principle is named after Vilfredo Pareto, an Italian sociologist and economist, who observed that 80 percent of the wealth in Italy was held by 20 percent of the population. This principle has been applied to many disciplines since Pareto first discovered it. Applying the principle to Quality Control, it says that the majority of the project defects are caused by a small set of problems. A Pareto diagram helps isolate what the major problems are so that you can take the action that will have the greatest impact. A bar graph is used to display problems in decreasing order of occurrence so that priorities for improvement can be established.

The purpose of a Pareto diagram is twofold:

- It displays the relative importance of the defects.
- It directs the improvement efforts to those areas that will have the biggest impact.

Let's take a look at how this works. A Pareto diagram typically starts with a table that lists information regarding the frequency of the defects or failures uncovered during testing. Table 9.1 shows the frequency of failure for items A–E, the number of occurrences, the percent of defects that this item represents, and a cumulative percent.

TABLE 9.1   Frequency of Failures

Item	Defect Frequency	Percent of Defects	Cumulative Percent
A	800	.33	.33
B	700	.29	.62
C	400	.17	.79
D	300	.13	.92
E	200	.08	1.0

With this data in hand, you can create a Pareto diagram, as shown in Figure 9.1. The bars are ordered from left to right based on frequency. The bars depict the defect numbers, and the cumulative percentages are plotted using the circles. By looking at the data in Figure 9.1, you can see that the most significant problems you want to focus on are A and B. Fixing these two items will resolve more than half the defects.

FIGURE 9.1   Pareto diagram

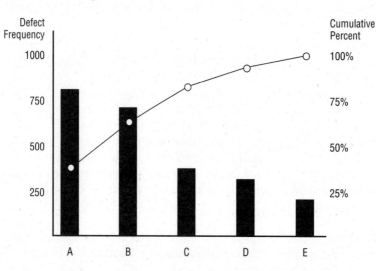

Control charts   A *control chart* measures and displays the variance of several samples of the same process over time. It is most commonly used in manufacturing. A control chart is based on a mean, an upper control limit, and a lower control limit. The upper control limit is the point beyond which preventing additional defects becomes cost-prohibitive. The lower level is the limit at which the customer or end user will reject the product because of the defects. The goal is to stay in the middle area (the mean), where the best product for the lowest cost is obtained. Figure 9.2 shows an example of a control chart.

FIGURE 9.2   Control chart

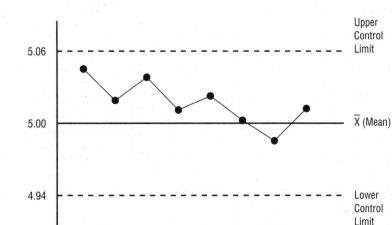

Statistical sampling   If you have numerous work results that require inspection or testing, you may decide to use *statistical sampling*, where you gather a subset of all the applicable work results and randomly select a small number for testing or examination. The results for this subset represent the whole. Statistical sampling can be very cost-effective, especially in projects where multiple versions of the same product are produced.

Flowcharting   *Flowcharting* was discussed in Chapter 6 as a means to create the process that produces the product. Flowcharts are diagrams that show the logical steps that must be performed in order to accomplish an objective. They can also show how the individual elements of a system interrelate. Flowcharting can be an effective tool during Quality Control to help determine how the problem occurred.

Trend analysis   *Trend analysis* is a mathematical technique that can be used to predict future defects based on historical results.

Run charts   *Run charts* are used to show variations in the process over time or to show trends (such as improvements or the lack of improvements) in the process. They are similar to control charts in that they plot the result of a process over time, although a run chart does not depict acceptable limits. Differences in results will occur because there is no such thing as a perfect process. When processes are considered in control, differences in results might occur because of common causes of variances.

Ishikawa diagram   An Ishikawa diagram (named after its developer, Kaoru Ishikawa) is also known as a *cause-and-effect diagram*, which shows the relationship between the effects of problems and their causes. This diagram depicts every potential cause and subcause of a problem and the effect that each proposed solution will have on the problem. This diagram is also called a *fishbone diagram*. Figure 9.3 shows an example cause-and-effect diagram.

FIGURE 9.3   Cause-and-effect diagram

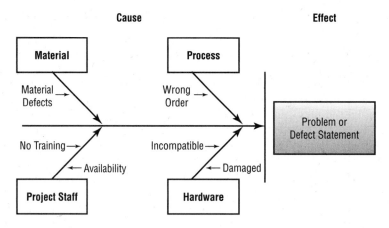

Variance measurements are a common theme in Quality Control tools. Schedule Control and Cost Control may also measure variances to determine deviations from the plan. For example, in the Cost Control processes, variance analysis examines the difference between the performance cost baseline and actual performance. *Common causes of variances* come about as a result of circumstances that are relatively common to the process you're using and are easily controlled at the operational level. Three types of variances make up the common causes of variances that you should be familiar with.

Random variances   *Random variances* might be normal, depending on the processes you're using to produce the product or service of the project, but they occur, as the name implies, at random.

Known or predictable variances   *Known or predictable variances* are variances that you know exist in the process because of particular characteristics of the product, service, or result you are processing. These are generally unique to a particular application.

Variances that are always present in the process   The process itself will have inherent variability that is perhaps caused by human mistakes, machine variations or malfunctions, the environment, and so on, which are known as *variances that are always present in the process*. These variances generally exist across all applications of the process.

Common causes of variances that do not fall within the acceptable range are difficult to correct and usually require a reorganization of the process. This has the potential for significant impact, and decisions to change the process always require management approval.

Once the results you obtain from testing or other Quality Control tools and techniques are completed, you'll use them to determine whether any action should be taken to correct poor quality. We'll look at the actions needed to correct poor quality next.

Taking Action on Quality Control

As you implement your Quality Control activities, you need to make decisions on the appropriate course of action based on the results received. Any action taken to resolve quality problems has trade-offs, so you will need to involve other stakeholders in the decision process. The most common actions taken as a result of quality activities are rework, process adjustments, and acceptance.

Rework

Rework is any action that is taken as a result of quality activities to correct a defect. A module test may result in the rewrite of a section of code from the module tested.

Rework sounds like the ideal solution to any quality problem that is found. If you discover a problem, you should fix it, right? In an ideal world with no time and budget constraints, that would be true, but rework often impacts both the project schedule and the budget. The time to complete the deliverable will be longer than estimated to account for the time it takes to fix the problem, and the people doing the rework will be billing additional hours to your project.

 There may be exceptions to the increase in billable hours if you are working with a vendor and have quality standards written into the contract. However, you should always consider the possible financial impacts.

A decision on rework is often tied to the severity of the defect and its impact on the ability of the end user to use the product. Your client, sponsor, and other impacted stakeholders need to be involved in rework decisions.

Process Adjustments

Changing a process can have a ripple effect throughout the rest of the project. Unless it is very clear that a process change is contained to a small work group or a few team members with no downstream effects, it is best to use the change control process to analyze the impacts of a process change and obtain formal approval before making any changes.

Acceptance

Acceptance is the decision to agree to any defects that are found as a result of the quality testing. Acceptance is a common action based on the analysis of the severity and frequency of the defects uncovered during testing. For example, some commercially available software products are released for sale to the public with known defects that will be fixed with an upgrade later. Meeting the publicized release date for the product is more important than fixing defects; in other words, the schedule takes priority over quality. The overall impact of accepting a defect should be analyzed and communicated to project stakeholders. You should obtain stakeholder sign-off to accept defects.

Quality Control takes different forms depending on the industry you're working in, the type of project, and whether the end goal of the project is a tangible product, a service, or a result of some other type. Remember that according to CompTIA, quality is one of the triple constraints, so careful attention should be paid to these processes throughout the course of any project.

Controlling Cost with Earned Value Measurement

The *Cost Control* process includes measuring the project spending to date, determining that a change to the cost baseline has occurred, and taking the appropriate action to deal with the change. In a nutshell, this process monitors the project budget and manages changes to the cost baseline.

Project management software is useful in tracking project spending. You can run reports that show spending to date vs. projected spending, and you can also use software to look at the impact of adding new tasks using what-if scenarios.

Major changes to the project plan that impact costs should include a process for securing additional funding as part of the change process. Adding requirements to the project and starting work on new tasks prior to securing funding is a sure way to overrun your budget.

Earned value measurement (EVM) is a tool and technique of the Cost Control process. EVM compares what you've received or produced to what you've spent by monitoring the planned value, earned value, and actual costs expended to produce the work of the project. There are EVM measurements we'll look at regarding the schedule and estimates at completion as well as those involving costs and budgets. When variances that result in changes are discovered (including schedule variances and cost variances), those changes should be managed using the project change control system.

The primary functions of this analysis technique are to determine and document the cause of the variance, to determine the impact of the variance, and to determine whether a corrective action should be implemented as a result.

NOTE   EVM results are reported as part of the performance reporting process. We talked about performance reporting in the previous chapter.

Earned Value Measurement

EVM looks at schedule, cost, and scope project measurements together and compares them to the actual work completed to date. It is the most often used performance measurement method. EVM is performed on the work packages and the control accounts of the WBS. To perform the EVM calculations, you need to first gather these three measurements: planned value, actual cost, and earned value.

Planned value   The *planned value (PV)* is the cost of work that has been authorized and budgeted for a schedule activity or WBS component during a given time period or phase. These budgets are established during the Planning processes. PV is also known as the *budgeted cost of work scheduled* (BCWS).

Actual cost   *Actual cost (AC)* is the actual cost of completing the work component in a given time period. Actual costs might include direct and indirect costs but must correspond to what was budgeted for the activity. If the budgeted amount did not include indirect costs, do not include them here. Later you'll see how to compare this to PV to come up with variance calculation results. AC is also known as the *actual cost of work performed* (ACWP).

Earned value   *Earned value (EV)* is the value of the work completed to date as it compares to the budgeted amount (PV) for the work component. EV is typically expressed as a percentage of the work completed compared to the budget. For example, if our budgeted amount is $1,000 and we have completed 30 percent of the work so far, our EV is $300. Therefore, EV cannot exceed the PV budget for the activity. EV is also known as the *budgeted cost of work performed* (BCWP).

PV, AC, and EV are really easy to mix up. In their simplest forms, here's what each means:

PV   The approved budget assigned to the work to be completed during a given time period

AC   Money that's actually been expended during a given time period for completed work

EV   The value of the work completed to date compared to the budget

PV, AC, and EV all include a cost component. When costs are displayed graphically, they form an S curve. The reason for this is that at the beginning of the project, spending is minimal; then it picks up once the work of the project is underway, and it tapers off at the end of the project as the work wraps up. Since earned value measurements include a cost component, they are also displayed in an S curve.

Cost Variance

Cost variance is one of the most popular EVM variances that project managers use. It tells you whether your costs are higher than budgeted (with a resulting negative number) or lower than budgeted (with a resulting positive number). It measures the actual performance to date against what's been spent.

The *cost variance (CV)* formula is as follows:

CV = EV – AC

For the purposes of the remainder of this section, we'll use some example figures so we can show how to calculate each of these measures. As of December 1 (our measurement date), the performance measurements are as follows:

PV = 75,000

AC = 71,000

EV = 70,000

Now let's calculate the CV using these numbers:

70,000 – 71,000 = –1,000

The result is a negative number, which means that costs were higher than what was planned for the work that was completed as of December 1. These costs are usually not recoverable. If the result was a positive number, it would mean that you spent less than what you planned for the work that was completed as of December 1.

Schedule Variance

Schedule variance, another popular EVM variance, compares an activity's actual progress to date to the estimated progress and is represented in terms of cost. It tells you whether the schedule is ahead of or behind what was planned for this period. This formula is most helpful when you've used the critical path methodology to build the project schedule. The *schedule variance (SV)* is calculated as follows:

SV = EV – PV

Plug in the numbers:

70,000 – 75,000 = –5,000

The resulting schedule variance is negative, which means you are behind schedule or behind where you planned to be as of December 1.

Together, the CV and SV are known as *efficiency indicators* for the project and can be used to compare the performance of all the projects in a portfolio.

Performance Indexes

Cost and schedule performance indexes are primarily used to calculate performance efficiencies, and they're often used to help predict future project performance.

The *cost performance index (CPI)* measures the value of the work completed at the measurement date against the actual cost. It is the most critical of all the EVM measurements according to the *PMBOK Guide* because it tells you the cost efficiency for the work completed to date or at the completion of the project. If CPI is greater than 1, you are spending less than anticipated at the measurement date. If CPI is less than 1, you are spending more than anticipated for the work completed at the measurement date.

The cost performance index (CPI) is calculated this way:

CPI = EV / AC

Plug in the numbers to see where you stand:

70,000 / 71,000 = .99

Since the result is less than one, it means cost performance is worse than expected.

The *schedule performance index (SPI)* measures the progress to date against the progress that was planned. This formula should be used in conjunction with an analysis of the critical path activities to determine whether the project will finish ahead of or behind schedule. If SPI is greater than 1, your performance is better than expected, and you're ahead of schedule. If SPI is less than 1, you're behind schedule at the measurement date.

The schedule performance index (SPI) is calculated this way:

SPI = EV / PV

Again, let's see where you stand with this example:

70,000 / 75,000 = .93

Schedule performance is not what you expected as of December 1.

Estimate at Completion

As your project progresses, you'll be asked to predict the total cost of the budget. An *estimate at completion (EAC)* is a forecast of the total cost of the project based on both the current project performance and the remaining work. To understand how EAC works, you need to know two more terms:

- *Budget at completion (BAC)* is the total amount of the budget for a work package, a control account, a schedule activity, or the project.

- *Estimate to complete (ETC)* is the cost estimate for the remaining project work. This is typically provided by the team members actually working on the project activities.

EAC is calculated as follows:

EAC = AC + ETC

If you assume your BAC is 300,000 and your ETC is 230,000, then you can calculate EAC as follows:

71,000 + 230,000 = 301,000

As of December 1, our estimate at completion is $301,000, which is $1,000 more than the budgeted amount (BAC). At this point in the project, the variance is minimal but should still be a signal to the project manager to keep a close eye on spending and assure the value delivered matches the spending to date.

NOTE   A comparison of your EAC figure to your BAC figure provides you with a current estimate of any deviation from the original budget.

To-Complete Performance Index

To-complete performance index (TCPI) is the projected performance level that the remaining work of the project must achieve in order to meet the stated financial or schedule goals. It's calculated by dividing the work that's remaining by the funds that are remaining.

The formula for TCPI is as follows:

(BAC − EV) / (BAC − AC)

Given the measurements as of December 1, here's the formula:

(300,000 − 70,000) / (300,000 − 71,000) = 1.0

This means you'll need to keep performing at the same CPI rate you've experienced to date in order to meet the BAC goal. If the result is less than one, future work does not have to be performed as efficiently as past performance. If the result is more than one, future work will have to be performed more efficiently than past performance in order to meet the BAC goal.

Variance Analysis

Variance analysis is the comparison of planned project results with actual project results. Variance analysis is most frequently used to examine the project schedule and project budget. In the Cost Control process, variance analysis looks at the difference between the performance cost baseline and actual performance. The variance at completion (VAC) formula is often used in this process. It calculates the difference between the budget at completion and the estimate at completion. The formula is as follows:

VAC = BAC − EAC

Managing Stakeholder Expectations

Managing Stakeholder Expectations concerns satisfying the needs of the stakeholders by managing communications with them, resolving issues, improving project performance by implementing requested changes, and managing concerns in anticipation of potential problems.

It's the project manager's responsibility to manage stakeholder expectations. By doing so, you will decrease the potential for project failure. Managing the expectations of your stakeholders will also increase the chance of meeting the project goals because issues are resolved in a timely manner and disruptions during the project are limited.

Stakeholders need lots of communication in every form you can provide, and their communication preferences should be documented within the communications management plan. If you are actively engaged with your stakeholders and interacting with them, providing project status, and resolving issues, your chances of a successful project are much greater than if you don't do these things. Communicating with stakeholders occurs throughout the project and is part of the Distribute Information process.

Distributing Information

The Distribute Information process is concerned with getting stakeholders information about the project in a timely manner. This can come about in several ways: status reports, project meetings, review meetings, and so on. We talked about status reports in Chapter 8, "Processing Change Requests," as part of the report performance process. Status reports inform stakeholders about where the project is today in regard to the project schedule and budget, for example. They also describe what the project team has accomplished to date. This might include milestones completed to date, the percentage of schedule completion, and what remains to be completed. The Distribute Information process also describes how this report, and other information, is distributed and to whom.

In the Distribute Information process, the communications management plan is put into action. Besides status reports, several other types of information are managed through this process. Let's take a look at each:

Project reports   *Project reports* include the project status reports and minutes from project meetings, lessons learned, closure reports, and other documents from all the processes throughout the project. If you're keeping an issues log, the issues would be included with the project reports as well.

Project presentations   *Project presentations* involve presenting project information to the stakeholders and other appropriate parties when necessary. The presentations might be formal or informal and depend on the audience and the information being communicated.

Project records   *Project records* include, as you might guess, memos, correspondence, and other documents concerning the project. The best place to keep information like this is in a project notebook or in a set of project notebooks, depending on the size of the project. The project notebooks are ordinary three-ring binders where project information gets filed. They are maintained by the project manager or project management office and contain all the information regarding the project. You could also keep the information on a project website, the company intranet, or CDs. If you're keeping the information electronically, make certain it's backed up regularly. These records serve as historical information once the project is closed.

Lessons learned documentation   *Lessons learned* documentation is information that you gather and document throughout the course of the project that can be used to benefit the current project, future projects, or other projects currently being performed by the organization. Lessons learned might include positive as well as negative lessons. We'll talk about lessons learned in more depth in Chapter 10, "Closing the Project."

Feedback from the stakeholders that can improve future performance on this project or future projects should be captured and documented as well. Typically, this is included as part of the lessons learned documentation, but you may receive feedback prior to a formal lessons learned session. If the information you receive has an impact on the current project, distribute it to the appropriate team members so that future project performance can be modified to improve the results.

Team members will provide you with information on status, project changes, and many other aspects of the project throughout its life. Some of this information will help you in managing stakeholder expectations and will be included in status reports. The project manager is responsible for ensuring the communication channels with team members are open. We've talked about managing teams in past chapters. Next we'll cover a few more key issues you should be aware of.

Managing Team Members

It's important to keep the lines of communication open with team members so that you're attuned to issues or conflicts that may be brewing. In an ideal world, this is easy to accomplish if your teams are small in number and all the team members have office space right outside your door. You'd know each of them by name and have the opportunity for water-cooler chats to help you all get to know each other better.

In today's global world, it's more likely you have team members in various geographical locations. That means several things for the project manager. First, you'll have to be aware of time-zone issues when scheduling meetings so that some team members are not required to be up in the middle of the night. Due dates may have to be adjusted in some cases to account for the various time zones. Communication preferences and language barriers also come into play. You may have team members who speak different languages. If so, you'll have to determine the best method for communication. In our experience, it's worked well to use two or three forms of communication, especially for critical information, so that there's less chance for misunderstanding.

Cultural differences can have an impact on teams whether they are collocated or dispersed. If you are used to working in the United States, for example, you know that the culture tends to value accomplishments and individualism. U.S. citizens tend to be informal and call each other by their first names, even if they've just met. In some European countries, people tend to be more formal, using surnames instead of first names in a business setting, even when they know each other well. Their communication style is also more formal than in the United States, and although they tend to value individualism, they also value history, hierarchy, and loyalty. Japanese people, on the other hand, tend to communicate indirectly and consider themselves part of a group, not as individuals. Japanese people value hard work and success, as most of us do. You should take the time to research the cultural background of your team members and be aware of the customs and practices that will help them succeed and help you in making them feel like part of the team.

Technology barriers can have impacts that are unexpected. For example, one of the authors has been working recently with some people in Brazil. It's not an uncommon occurrence for the electricity to go out for hours at a time or for Internet connections to drop for no reason. These issues can have significant impacts on the project if you're in the midst of a deliverable or troubleshooting a problem. Team members may also have different levels of proficiency with software programs and other technology you're using during the course of the project. Make certain that training is available where needed, or include questions in the interview process about proficiency with the technology used on the project. It wouldn't be a bad idea to add some buffer time to the schedule to account for unforeseen issues with technology.

Last but not least, remember that the organizational structure itself may also have an impact on the way you manage teams and the way they interact with each other. Functional organizations that are hierarchical in nature can have impacts on the team because there is another manager (or more) involved in their career and performance evaluation. Loyalty issues, politics, power struggles, and more may come into play in this type of organization.

Real World Scenario

Chaptal Wineries

You've been evaluating the project for quality, budget, and timeliness.

Budget   Comparing the actual expenses to date with the estimated expenses shows that you're almost $3,000 over budget, or about 3 percent of the overall $100,000 cost of the project.

Category	Actual	Estimated	Difference
Servers	79,124	80,000	$876.00
Network	21,478	20,000	$(1,478.00)
France circuit	2,980	2,000	$(980.00)
Australia circuit	2,480	2,000	$(480.00)
Chile circuit	2,730	2,000	$(730.00)
California circuit	1,990	2,000	$10.00
		Total	$(2,782.00)

You decide to visit Kate Cox and brief her on the overage. Kate tells you that she had a +/- 5 percent variance in mind for the budget, so she's OK with the fact that the budget is slightly over the estimate. However, you should closely monitor spending from this point forward so that corrective actions can be taken if costs are not staying under control.

Quality The overall quality of the various elements of the project has been high. Signal strength for the circuits is good throughout the network—the Chilean telecommunications contractor was able to fix the problem (after you asked for a replacement for the first person who did the configuration). Customer response on the contractor's part was excellent.

You're also especially pleased with your intranet developer. She has produced high-quality pages at a rapid rate. Although she'll use up every bit of the allotted time you've given her, she has committed to not going over and has made all of her deadlines so far. You're quite pleased with the responsiveness and completeness of the pages.

Timeliness With the exception of the two days wasted waiting on the Chilean telecommunications contractor to produce someone else who could figure out what was wrong with the circuit configuration, there have been no timeliness issues.

Managing team members This project involved contractors from several different locations. You ran into some issues in Chile with staff, but they were quickly resolved. Communications occurred in English, and the French and Chilean staff translated for the contracting staff where necessary.

Summary

Quality Control is the process of reviewing project results and determining whether they comply with the standards documented in the quality management plan and making any appropriate changes to remove the causes of unacceptable quality when the standards are not met. Quality Control is performed throughout the life of the project. You can use several tools and techniques to perform Quality Control, including inspection, prevention, histograms, Pareto diagrams, control charts, statistical sampling, flowcharting, trend analysis, run charts, and Ishikawa diagrams.

Quality Control concerns identifying variances in the process or results. There are three common causes of variance: random variances, known or predictable variances, and variances that are always present in the system.

Cost Control involves managing changes to the project cost baseline. It's also concerned with monitoring project budgets to prevent unauthorized or incorrect costs from getting included in the cost baseline.

Earned value measurement is a tool and technique that measures the value of the work completed to date by comparing what you've received or produced to what you've spent as of the measurement date by using measurements such as CV, SV, CPI, SPI, ETC, and EAC.

Managing Stakeholder Expectations involves making sure certain communication needs and expectations of the stakeholders are met, managing any issues stakeholders might raise that could become future issues, and resolving previously identified issues. One of the ways to manage expectations is to manage the information distribution process. The Distribute Information process is concerned with making certain project information is available to stakeholders at the right time and in the appropriate format. Distribute Information is performed throughout the life of the project.

Managing team members involves being aware of barriers and differences that may impact communication and the productivity of the team, including different time zones, communication and language barriers, cultural differences, technology barriers, and hierarchical barriers.

Exam Essentials

Be able to name the purpose of the Quality Control process.   The purpose of the Quality Control process is to monitor work results to determine whether they comply with the standards set in the quality management plan.

Name the three common causes of variance.   These are random variances, known or predictable variances, and variances that are always present in the process.

Name the tools and techniques for Quality Control.   These are histograms, Pareto diagrams, control charts, statistical sampling, flowcharting, run charts, and Ishikawa diagrams.

Be able to describe earned value measurement techniques.   Earned value measurement (EVM) monitors the planned value (PV), earned value (EV), and actual costs (AC) expended to produce the work of the project. Cost variance (CV), schedule variance (SV), cost performance index (CPI), and schedule performance index (SPI) are the formulas used with the EVM technique.

Define estimate to complete (ETC), estimate at completion (EAC), and budget at completion (BAC).   Estimate to complete (ETC) is a forecast of the cost of all remaining project work and is usually provided by the project team members. Estimate at completion (EAC) is a projection of final project costs obtained by adding the ETC to the actual project costs to date. Budget at completion (BAC) is the total amount of the budget for the work package, control account, schedule activity, or project.

Define the purpose for the Managing Stakeholder Expectations process.   Managing Stakeholder Expectations involves communicating, resolving issues, improving project performance by implementing change requests, and managing concerns.

Explain the purpose for the Distribute Information process.   Distribute Information is concerned with getting stakeholders information about the project in a timely manner.

This is accomplished using status reports, project meetings, review meetings, and so on, depending on their communication preferences.

Name the types of barriers a project manager might face when managing teams.   Time zones, language and communication barriers, cultural differences, hierarchical barriers, and technology barriers are all types of barriers.

Key Terms

Before you take the exam, be certain you are familiar with the following terms:

Acceptance	inspection
actual cost (AC)	Ishikawa diagram
budget at completion (BAC)	Pareto diagram
cause-and-effect diagram	planned value (PV)
common causes of variance	prevention
control chart	Quality Control
Cost Control	rework
cost performance index (CPI)	run chart
cost variance (CV)	schedule performance index (SPI)
earned value (EV)	schedule variance (SV)
earned value measurement (EVM)	to-complete performance index (TCPI)
estimate at completion (EAC)	trend analysis
estimate to complete (ETC)	variance analysis

Review Questions

1. You are working on a project that was proceeding well until a manufacturing glitch occurred that requires corrective action. It turns out the glitch was an unintentional enhancement to the product, and the marketing people are enthused about its potential. The corrective action is canceled, and you continue to produce the product with the newly discovered enhancement. As the project manager, you know that a variance has occurred. Which of the following is not true?

    A. Common causes of variance are situations that are unique and not easily controlled at the operational level.

    B. Random variances, known or predictable variances, and variances that are always present in the process are known as common causes of variance.

    C. Inspection determines whether measurements fall within tolerable results.

    D. Scatter diagrams display the relationships between an independent variable and a dependent variable to show variations in the process over time.

2. Your project concerns producing a product that must meet a specific quality standard. You are periodically pulling completed components of the product and determining whether the components have tolerable results. What tool and technique are you using?

    A. Prevention

    B. Histogram

    C. Inspection

    D. Module testing

3. This tool, used to help monitor and control quality results, ranks the importance of a problem based on its frequency of occurrence over time.

    A. Control chart

    B. Flowcharting

    C. Ishikawa diagram

    D. Pareto diagram

4. This tool and technique is used primarily for monitoring quality and is also known as a cause-and-effect diagram.

    A. Control chart

    B. Flowcharting

    C. Ishikawa diagram

    D. Pareto diagram

5.   What are the three types of variances that make up common causes of variances? Choose three.

   A. Random

   B. Tolerable

   C. Trends

   D. Known or predictable

   E. Acceptable

   F. Variances that are always present

6.   This is an action taken as a result of quality activities to correct a defect.

   A. Process adjustments

   B. Rework

   C. Acceptance

   D. Prevention

7.   This technique, used for monitoring and controlling the costs of the project, compares what was received or produced to what was spent.

   A. ETC

   B. EAC

   C. BAC

   D. EVM

8.   This is the value of the work completed to date as it compares to the budgeted amount assigned to the work component.

   A. PV

   B. EV

   C. AC

   D. EVM

9.   This is the cost of work that has been authorized and budgeted for a schedule activity or WBS component during a given time period or phase.

   A. PV

   B. EV

   C. AC

   D. EVM

10.   This is the cost of completing the work component in a given time period.

   A. PV

   B. EV

   C. AC

   D. EVM

11. If CPI is less than one, which of the following is true?

   A. You are spending less than anticipated at the measurement date.

   B. You are behind schedule at the measurement date.

   C. You are spending more than anticipated at the measurement date.

   D. You are ahead of schedule at the measurement date.

12. What are the EVM measurements for schedule variances?

   A. SV = (EV – PV) and SPI = (EV / PV)

   B. SV = (EV – AC) and SPI = (EV / AC)

   C. SV = (EV – BAC) and SPI = (EV / BAC)

   D. SV = (PV – EV) and SPI = (PV / EV)

13. Which of the following is considered the most critical EVM metric?

   A. CPI

   B. CV

   C. SPI

   D. SP

14. Which calculation will show you the ratio of remaining work compared to the remaining budget and is represented as a percentage?

   A. TCPI

   B. EVM

   C. SPI

   D. CPI

15. You're preparing some variance figures for your project, and you want to show the variance between a task's estimated progress vs. its actual progress. What variance formula should you use?

   A. SV = EV / PV

   B. SV = EV – AC

   C. SV = EV – PV

   D. SV = EV / AC

16. This is the formula for the forecast of the total cost of the project based on current project performance and the remaining work.

   A. AC + ETC

   B. ETC

   C. (BAC – EV) / (BAC – AC)

   D. BAC – EAC

17. You are comparing planned project results with actual project results. Which formula will you use?

    A. BAC

    B. VAC

    C. EAC

    D. ETC

18. You know that EV = 230, PV = 230, AC = 250, BAC = 260, and ETC is 30. What is the CPI?

    A. 280

    B. 1

    C. 3

    D. .92

19. Status reports, project meetings, and review meetings are examples of which of the following?

    A. Managing Stakeholder Expectations, which puts the communication management plan into action

    B. Distribute Information, which uses the stakeholder distribution matrix

    C. Distribute Information, which puts the communication management plan into action

    D. Managing Stakeholder Expectations, which uses the stakeholder distribution matrix

20. You are working on a project that is being implemented in a country different from your country of origin. You also have team members in several locations around the globe. You should consider all of the following specifically in regard to managing teams in this situation except for which one?

    A. Time zones

    B. Project presentation methods

    C. Cultural differences

    D. Communication styles

Answers to Review Questions

1. **A.** Common causes of variance are situations that are common to the process you're using and are easily controlled at the operational level.

2. **C.** Inspection involves physically looking at the product results to determine whether the results are tolerable. Prevention keeps errors from reaching the customers or occurring in the first place, histograms plot information on a bar chart, and module testing is used in the information-technology industry to test programming code.

3. **D.** Pareto diagrams rank the importance of problems based on their frequency of occurrence over time. Control charts display the variance of several samples of the same process over time. Flowcharts depict the logical steps that must be performed to accomplish an objective, and Ishikawa diagrams show the relationship between cause and effect.

4. **C.** Ishikawa diagrams show the relationship between cause and effect and are also known as cause-and-effect diagrams or fishbone diagrams. Control charts display the variance of several samples of the same process over time. Flowcharts depict the logical steps that must be performed to accomplish an objective. Pareto diagrams rank the importance of problems based on their frequency of occurrence over time.

5. **A, D, F.** The three types of variances that make up common causes of variance are random variances, known or predictable variances, and variances that are always present in the process.

6. **B.** Rework is an action that is taken as a result of quality activities to correct a defect. Process adjustments are made when there are quality problems as a result of a bad process, acceptance accepts the quality results, and prevention keeps errors from getting into the hands of the customers.

7. **D.** EVM, or earned value measurement, compares what was produced to what was spent. It monitors the planned value, earned value, and actual costs on the project. ETC is the estimate to complete, EAC is the estimate at completion, and BAC is the budget at completion.

8. **B.** EV is the earned value: the value of the work completed to date, as it compares to the budgeted amount assigned to the work component. PV is the planned value, AC is the actual cost, and EVM is the earned value measurement.

9. **A.** PV is the planned value or the cost of work that has been authorized and budgeted for a given time period or phase. EV is the earned value: the value of the work completed to date because it compares the budgeted amount assigned to the work component. AC is the actual cost, and EVM is the earned value measurement.

10. **C.** AC is the actual cost of completing the work component in a given time period. EV is the earned value: the value of the work completed to date as it compares the budgeted amount assigned to the work component. PV is the planned value, and EVM is the earned value measurement.

11. C. CPI is the cost performance index, and it depicts whether spending is ahead or behind at the measurement date. Values less than one indicate you are spending more than anticipated, and values greater than one indicate you are spending less than anticipated.

12. A. Schedule variance is (EV – PV), and schedule performance index is (EV / PV).

13. A. CPI is considered the most critical EVM metric. It measures the cost efficiency of the project work completed at the measuring date.

14. A. The to-complete performance index measures remaining work to remaining budget and is the projected performance level that the remaining work of the project must achieve in order to meet the stated objectives.

15. C. The schedule variance (SV) is calculated by subtracting the planned value from the earned value. Option A is the formula for SPI, option B is the formula for CV, and option D is the formula for CPI.

16. A. This question is asking about the estimate at completion (EAC) formula, which is AC + ETC. Option B is the ETC formula, option C is the TCPI formula, and option D is the VAC formula.

17. B. Variance at completion (VAC) compares the planned project results with actual project results. BAC is the budget at completion, EAC is the estimate at completion, and ETC is the estimate to complete.

18. D. The formula for CPI is EV / AC. 230 / 250 = .92

19. C. The Distribute Information process uses status reports, project meetings, review meetings, and more to communicate with the stakeholders. The Distribute Information process puts the communication management plan into action.

20. B. Managing team members in geographically dispersed areas can be challenging. You'll need to consider several factors, including time zones, cultural differences, communication styles, technological barriers, and hierarchical structures when managing teams like this. Project presentations are part of the Distribute Information process and don't really have an impact on the way you manage a team.

Chapter

10

Closing the Project

THE COMPTIA PROJECT+ EXAM TOPICS COVERED IN THIS CHAPTER INCLUDE:

✓ **5.1 Explain the importance and benefits of formal project closure**

- Confirm and document objectives that were completed/not complete

- Release resources

- Provide historical information for future projects

- Close contracts

- Standards compliance

  - Document retention compliance

- Post-project review

  - Meeting to review what went right/what went wrong

✓ **5.2 Identify circumstances in which project/phase closure might occur and identify steps to take when closure occurs**

- Phase closure

- Project completion

- Stage completion

- Component completion

- Project cancellation

✓ **5.3 Identify the components and purpose of closing documentation**

- Lessons learned
  - Strengths/weaknesses
- Close report
  - Historical data
  - Summary of costs
- Post mortem analysis
  - Documents reasons for early closure and impact
- Final individual performance appraisal
  - Final review of performance
- Transition plan

Your project is winding down, and the end date is in sight. But the project doesn't end when the last deliverable of the project is completed. Your project plan should also include all the tasks required to transition the project to an ongoing operation.

Project managers follow processes to formally close the project. The good news regarding these additional tasks is that much of the work you do during project closure will help you do a better job managing future projects.

Project closure activities apply regardless of the reason the project is ending and regardless of what point you are at in the project life cycle. Even if your project is canceled, there is still a closeout process to perform. One of the elements of project closure involves contract closeout, where there is a formal acceptance (or rejection) of the vendor's work.

Administrative closure involves finishing and archiving project documentation, obtaining formal sign-off from the customer, conducting a comprehensive review of the project to document lessons learned, turning over the project to operations and maintenance, and releasing project team members to their functional organizations.

Preparing for Project Closure

You've made it to the end of the project and to the end of the project life cycle. The Closing process group is the last set of processes you'll perform for the project. Two processes are involved in the Closing process group: Close Project or Phase and Close Procurements. Before we get into the specifics of the processes, we'll cover some of the common characteristics of project closure and the types of project endings.

Characteristics of Closing

A few characteristics are common to all projects during the Closing processes. You've already completed the majority of the work of the project—if not all of the work—so the probability of not finishing the project is very low. Risk is very low in this process group also because the work is completed. There's little chance that a risk would occur at the very end that would derail the project.

Stakeholders have the least amount of influence during the Closing processes, while project managers have the greatest amount of influence. Costs are significantly lower during this process because the majority of the project work and spending has already occurred. One last common characteristic of projects during closing is that weak matrix organizations tend to experience the least amount of stress during the Closing processes. This is because, in a weak matrix organization, the functional manager assigns all tasks (project-related tasks, as well) so the team members have a job to return to once the project is completed and there's no change in reporting structure.

All projects eventually come to an end, and there are several types of project endings we'll cover next.

Project Endings

We usually think of a project coming to an end when all the deliverables are completed. Ideally, this is what you'll experience most of the time. There are several reasons that a project might end, and the authors have experienced all of them:

- They're completed successfully.
- They're canceled or killed prior to completion.
- They evolve into ongoing operations and no longer exist as projects.
- Their budgets are slashed.
- The project resources are redirected to other activities or projects.
- The customer goes out of business or is merged with another entity.

In our experience, we've probably worked on as many projects that were canceled as those that were completed. Cancelation can occur for any number of reasons: project sponsors move on to other assignments, budgets are cut, new management comes into power and changes direction, vendors don't perform as anticipated, and many more. The important thing to remember about cancelation is that all the steps of project closeout should be performed when a project is canceled so that the records are archived and the reasons for cancelation are documented.

All the reasons for project endings we listed in this section, including cancelation, are incorporated into four formal types of project endings that you should know for the exam:

- Addition
- Starvation
- Integration
- Extinction

We'll look at each of these ending types in detail in the following sections.

Addition

Projects that evolve into ongoing operations are considered projects that end because of *addition*; in other words, they become their own ongoing business unit. An example of this is the installation of an enterprise resource planning system. These systems are business management systems that integrate all areas of a business, including marketing, planning, manufacturing, sales, financials, and human resources. After the installation of the software, these systems can develop into their own business unit because the ongoing operations, maintenance, and monitoring of the software require full-time staff. These systems usually evolve into an arm of the business reporting system that no one can live without once it's installed.

A project is considered a project when it meets these criteria: it is unique, has a definite beginning and ending date, and is temporary in nature. When a project becomes an ongoing operation, it is no longer a project.

Starvation

When resources are cut off from the project or are no longer provided to the project, it's starved prior to completing all the requirements, and you're left with an unfinished project on your hands. *Starvation* can happen for any number of reasons:

- Other projects come about and take precedence over the current project, thereby cutting the funding or resources for your project.
- The customer curtails an order.
- The project budget is reduced.
- A key resource quits.

Resource starving can include cutting back or withholding human resources, equipment and supplies, or money. In any case, if you're not getting the people, equipment, or money you need to complete the project, it's going to starve and probably end abruptly.

This is one of those cases where documentation becomes your best friend. Organizations tend to have short memories. As you move on to bigger and better projects, your memory regarding the specifics of the project will fade. Six months from now when someone important wonders why that project was never completed and begins the finger-pointing routine, the project documents will clearly outline the reasons why the project ended early. That's one of the reasons why project documentation is such an important function. We'll talk more about documenting project details shortly.

Integration

Integration occurs when the resources of the project—people, equipment, property, and supplies—are distributed to other areas in the organization or are assigned to other projects. Perhaps your organization begins to focus on other areas or other projects, and the next thing you know, functional managers come calling to retrieve their resources for other, more important things. Again, your project will come to an end because of a lack of resources because they have been reassigned to other areas of the business or have been pulled from your project and assigned to another project.

 The difference between starvation and integration is that starvation is the result of staffing, funding, or other resource cuts, while integration is the result of reassignment or redeployment of the resources.

Again, good documentation describing the circumstances that brought about the ending of a project because of integration should be archived with the project records for future reference.

Extinction

This is the best kind of project end because *extinction* means the project has been completed and accepted by the stakeholders. As such, it no longer exists because it had a definite ending date, the goals of the project were achieved, and the project was closed out.

> **NOTE** Sometimes, closing out a project is like finishing a great book. You just don't want it to end. The team is working at peak performance, deliverables are checked off at record pace, and camaraderie is high. If you practice good project management techniques and keep the communication channels open, most of your projects can fall into this category.

The majority of this chapter and the processes associated with the Closing process group are discussed from the perspective that the work of the project is complete. But there are other situations where you'll use the Closing process group processes. You may have projects performed in phases or stages. You'll perform the steps and processes we talk about in this chapter at the completion of each phase. You may also decide that the product of the project is easily broken down into components so that when each component is delivered and completed, you can perform the Closing processes and move on to producing the next major component.

Now that you've determined the reason for your project ending, it's time to examine the steps in project closeout and obtain formal written acceptance of the project.

Steps in Closing Out a Project

Closing out a project involves several steps that we'll be covering throughout the remaining sections of this chapter:

- Obtaining formal sign-off and acceptance of the project
- Transferring the results of the project to operations and maintenance
- Releasing project resources
- Closing out contracts
- Performing administrative closure
- Documenting historical information for future projects
- Conducting a post-mortem
- Conducting a post-project review and capturing lessons learned
- Preparing the project close report

Phase closure occurs at the end of each project phase and involves all the steps listed here. You'll obtain acceptance and sign-off at the completion of each phase as well as at the end of the project. The transfer that occurs in phase completion is the official hand-off to the next phase of the project, not to an operations or maintenance group.

The project isn't finished until the sponsor or the customer signs on the dotted line. We'll cover obtaining sign-off next.

Obtaining Sign-Off

Project closeout involves accepting the final product, service, or result of the project and then turning over the product to the organization. Obtaining formal written sign-off and acceptance of the project is the primary focus of the Closing process group.

Documenting formal acceptance is important because it signals the official closure of the project, and it is your proof that the project was completed satisfactorily. Formal acceptance includes distributing notice of the acceptance of the project results to the stakeholders.

Ideally, obtaining sign-off should just be a formality. If you've involved the sponsor and stakeholders in the verification and acceptance of the deliverables during the Executing and Monitoring and Controlling processes, it should be easy to obtain sign-off on the project.

The sponsor is the person who has the authority to end the project or accept the final outcome of the project. In cases where you are working on a project that involves an external customer, the sponsor typically is the customer.

Transferring the Product of the Project

Another function of sign-off is that it kicks off the beginning of the warranty period and/or the transfer of the product to maintenance and operations. Sometimes project managers or vendors will warranty their work for a certain time period after completing the project. Projects that produce software programs, for example, might be warranted from bugs for a 60- or 90-day time frame from the date of implementation or the date of acceptance. Typically in the case of software projects, bugs are fixed for free during the warranty period. Watch out, because users will try to squeeze new requirements into the "bug" category mold. If you offer a warranty, it's critical that the warranty spells out exactly what is covered and what is not.

You should document a transition plan for transferring the product or result of the project to the organization. Set up a meeting—or a series of meetings, depending on the complexity of the project—with the manager who will be responsible for the ongoing upkeep of the product or result you're turning over. Provide them with user documentation for the product. Document special skills, training, maintenance issues and costs, licensing costs, warranty periods, and so on. Make certain the new manager understands any special requirements for maintaining the product as well.

Releasing Team Members

Releasing team members may occur once or several times throughout the project. Projects that are divided into phases will likely release team members at the end of each phase.

Other times, team members are brought on for one specific activity and are released when that activity is completed. No matter when the team members are released, you'll want to keep the functional managers or other project managers informed as you get closer to project completion so that they have time to adequately plan for the return of their employees. This gives the other managers the ability to start planning activities and scheduling activity dates.

Team members may also become anxious about their status, especially if people are rolling off the project at different times. You should explain to team members that as various deliverables are completed, team members who have completed their assignments are released. Unless you are prevented from doing so by labor contract terms or human resource guidelines, provide your team members with as much information as you can on anticipated release dates.

You should perform a final performance appraisal when releasing team members from the project. If you work in a functional organization, you should coordinate this with the employee's functional manager and make certain your review is included as part of their final, annual review.

Closing Out the Contract

Close Procurements is the process of completing and settling the terms of the contract and documenting acceptance. This process determines whether the work described in the procurement documentation or contract was completed accurately and satisfactorily. Projects that have multiple deliverables may have procurements for some of the deliverables but not all. Obviously, this process applies only to those phases, deliverables, or portions of the project that were performed under some form of procurement.

As we discussed in Chapter 9, "Controlling the Project," you should perform quality control activities on vendor deliverables as you receive them and provide feedback regarding acceptance throughout the project life cycle.

Close Procurements updates records and archives the information for future reference. These records detail the final results of the work of the project. Procurement documents might have specific terms or conditions for completion and closeout. You should be aware of these terms or conditions so that project closure isn't held up because you missed an important detail. If you are not administering the procurement yourself, be certain to ask your procurement department whether there are any special conditions that you should know about so that your project team doesn't inadvertently delay contract or project closure.

The procurement department needs to provide the vendor formal written notice that the deliverables have been accepted and the contract has been completed. This letter will be based on your approval of the work. *Product verification* determines whether the work has been completed accurately and satisfactorily according to the stakeholders. It's the project manager's responsibility to make certain that the deliverables meet the acceptance criteria. Once the contract has been completed, you may have no recourse if you find missing deliverables or poor-quality work.

You should retain a copy of the completed contracts to include in the project archives, which we'll discuss next in the Administrative Closure process.

Administrative Closure

The *Administrative Closure* process involves gathering and centralizing project documents, performing a post-project review, and writing the final project close report. This is where project records and files are collected and archived, including the project-planning documents (project scope statement, budget, schedule, risk responses, quality plan and baselines, and so on), change records and logs, issue logs, lessons learned, and more. You'll also collect and archive documentation showing that the project or phase is completed and that the transfer of the product of the project to the organization (or department responsible for ongoing maintenance and support) has occurred. This process is also where the notice of final project acceptance and closure is sent to the stakeholders. Let's get started with archiving project documents.

Archiving Project Documents

You have created a lot of documents over the course of your project, particularly in the Planning phase. The purpose for archiving those documents is twofold. First, it's to show you have completed the work of the project and that you can produce sign-offs, and other legal documents, should the need arise. The second primary benefit of archiving the project documentation is that it can be used to help you or other project managers on future projects. Your planning documents can be a reference for cost and time estimates or used as templates for planning similar projects in the future.

You can create a project archive in a variety of ways. First check with your project management office (PMO). They likely have a centralized project archive or storage area for project documents. They will tell you what the guidelines are for documentation and how to file, organize, and store it.

If you don't have a PMO, you'll need to create your own archiving solution. Check with your organization regarding standards compliance and document retention policies. For example, the organization may require all documents to be numbered or named in a certain fashion. Part of your archiving process will include the retention period. Your organization may have guidelines regarding when certain types of documents can be destroyed or what information must be retained. There are also laws regarding retaining some types of documents, so make certain you are familiar with them when creating your archiving system.

Electronic archives are the easiest way to store your project documents. Back in the "old days," project managers used to create project binders that contained all the project information in one or more three-ring binders. These binders were stored on a shelf, usually in the project manager's office, and as soon as someone asked to borrow the binder, it disappeared forever. That defeated the purpose of collecting the information in the first place.

Electronic storage allows anyone to access the information in a convenient manner, and it's not likely to disappear. There is a host of solutions on the market to help you with this. Microsoft SharePoint is a great tool for not only archiving project documents but for managing, sharing, and distributing them throughout the course of the project.

Performing the Post-Project Review and Documenting Lessons Learned

A *post-project review* is conducted at the conclusion of the project. The primary purpose for the post-project review is to collect and document lessons learned. The size and complexity of the project will help you decide whether you need to hold one or more review meetings. You'll want to include any key project team members, the project sponsor, and the key stakeholders at a minimum.

The purpose for this review is to assess the good and the not-so-good aspects of the project. During this meeting, you'll evaluate each phase of the project in order to determine the things that went right and the things that could be improved.

 Conducting post-project reviews and documenting lessons learned give you the opportunity to improve the overall quality of your project management processes on the next project and benefit projects currently underway.

Documenting Lessons Learned

Lessons learned describe the successes and failures of the project. As an example, lessons learned document the reasons why specific corrective actions were taken, their outcomes, the causes of performance variances, unplanned risks that occurred, mistakes that were made and could have been avoided, and so on.

Lessons learned help you assess what went wrong and why, not so you can point fingers at the guilty parties but so that you can improve performance on the next project by avoiding the pitfalls you encountered on this one. It also helps you determine what went right so that you can repeat these processes on the next project. Lessons learned involves analyzing the strengths and weaknesses of the project management process, the project team, and, if you dare, the project manager's performance.

Unfortunately, sometimes projects do fail. You can learn lessons from failed projects as well as from successful projects, and you should document this information for future reference. Most project managers, however, do not document lessons learned. The reason for this is that employees don't want to admit to making mistakes or learning from mistakes made during the project. And they do not want their name associated with failed projects or even with mishaps on successful projects.

You and your management team will have to work to create an atmosphere of trust and assurance that lessons learned are not reasons for dismissing employees but are learning opportunities that benefit all those associated with the project. Lessons learned allow you to carry knowledge gained on this project to other projects you'll work on going forward. They'll also prevent repeat mistakes in the future if you take the time to review the project documents and lessons learned prior to undertaking your new project.

Lessons learned can be some of the most valuable information you'll take away from a project. We can all learn from our experiences, and what better way to have even more success on your next project than to review a similar past project's lessons learned document? But lessons learned will be there only if you document them now.

The following is a partial list of the areas you should review in the post-review process. This is by no means a complete list but should give you a good starting point. You should document everything you learn in these sessions in the lessons learned document. Lessons learned are included with all the other project documentation and go into the project archive when completed.

- Review each process group (Initiating, Planning, Executing, Monitoring and Controlling, and Closing).
- Review the performance of the project team.
- Document vendor performance.
- Examine sponsor and key-stakeholder involvement.
- Review the risks that occurred and the effectiveness of the risk response plans.
- Document risks that occurred that were not identified during the project.
- Evaluate the estimating techniques used for costs and resources.
- Evaluate the project budget vs. actual performance.
- Review the schedule performance, critical path, and schedule control.
- Review the effectiveness of the change management process.

Real World Scenario

Involving Project Team Members in Lessons Learned

Although you can evaluate the various components of the project on your own using the project plan and the project results, to get a more comprehensive lessons-learned document, you should involve the team members.

One way to organize a project review session is to make the session interactive. Let the team members know in advance which aspects of the project the review will focus on, and ask them to be prepared to contribute input on both what went well and what did not. You could also distribute some questions ahead of the meeting for them to consider. One question you'll always want to ask the team members is, "If you could change one thing about this project, what would it be?"

You should always set ground rules before you start. You want to stress that the purpose of this session is not to assign blame but to assess the project so that both this team and other project teams can learn from your experience.

Prepare the meeting room in advance with easel paper listing all the areas of the project you want to cover, and provide each team member with a pad of sticky notes. For each topic, ask the team members to post one positive occurrence and one negative. Each negative comment needs a plan for improvement. If they encounter this situation on a future project, what would they do differently?

Requiring a plan for improvement serves two purposes: it engages the team members in the review by making them part of the problem-solving process, and it helps keep those few team members who may only want to whine under control. This is not the time or place to complain.

When you have concluded the session, collect all the notes, and use them as input for your written report.

Performing Post-Mortem Analysis

A *post-mortem analysis* is performed for projects that are canceled or end prematurely. A post-mortem goes hand in hand with lessons learned because in it you examine the project from the beginning to the ending point and look at what went right and what went wrong.

Post-mortem analysis should examine and document the reasons for early closure and the impacts this has on the organization. You should also include a plan for transferring any completed deliverables to the organization and determine how to treat partially completed deliverables.

Preparing the Project Close Report

A finalized project assessment needs to be prepared and distributed to all of the project stakeholders. This is the final status report for the project and should include at least the following:

- Recap of the original goals and objectives of the project
- Statement of project acceptance or rejection (and the reasons for rejection)
- Summary of project costs
- Summary of project schedule
- Lessons learned and historical data

This report is usually prepared after the post-project review meeting so that lessons learned and other historical data can be included in the report. You'll distribute this to the stakeholders after they have accepted and signed off on the project.

⊕ **Real World Scenario**

Chaptal Wineries

Closeout of the Chaptal project is straightforward. You validated that all the email servers are up and running and that email is working between the sites. The intranet is working well, and everyone is satisfied with the information it provides. Kate Cox authorizes the final acceptance of the project.

You hold a post-project review and document the lessons learned on the project. You interview Kate Cox, the international stakeholders, and the project team members regarding what could have been improved on the project and what went well from their perspective. The most important lesson learned from this project was to perform more thorough reference checks on vendors' skills and abilities. After documenting the lessons learned, you prepare the final project report and distribute it to the stakeholders.

Then you begin work on your next project, the Chaptal Internet site. This project will involve designing and building an Internet site that includes information about all of Chaptal's wineries worldwide.

Summary

Project closeout should be performed when the project ends, when a phase of a project ends, or when a project is killed or canceled. The Closing process group is the most often skipped on projects because project managers and team members are anxious to move on to their next assignments. It's important to take the time to perform the steps in the Closing process group so that you can obtain sign-off on the project, turn over the product to the organization, release project resources, close out the contract, perform a post-project review, document lessons learned, and create a final project report.

Four types of project endings encompass the majority of reasons a project comes to an end. They are addition, starvation, integration, and extinction.

Close Procurements involves completing and settling the terms of the contract and documenting its acceptance. Product verification occurs here that determines whether the work was completed accurately and satisfactorily.

Administrative Closure involves gathering and centralizing all the project documents, performing the post-project review, and writing the final project report.

The post-project review is conducted at the conclusion of the project, and its primary purpose is to collect and document lessons learned. Perhaps the most important element of project closure is the lessons learned document. This entails identifying where things went wrong, what things went well, and the alternatives you considered during the course of the project. Lessons learned are an extremely useful reference for future projects regarding what worked and what didn't, for estimating techniques, for establishing templates, and more.

Post-mortem analysis is performed on projects that are canceled or end prematurely. This is much like the lessons learned process where information is gathered and recorded regarding what went wrong, the decisions for cancelation, and the plan for turning over completed deliverables.

The project close report is distributed to the stakeholders and includes several elements, including the project's goal, the statement of acceptance, a summary of costs and schedule data, and lessons learned data.

Exam Essentials

Name the four reasons for project endings.   They are addition, starvation, integration, and extinction.

Understand the steps involved in closing a project or phase.   The steps include obtaining sign-off and acceptance, transferring the product to the organization, releasing project resources, closing out contracts, performing Administrative Closure, documenting historical information, conducting post-mortem analysis, and conducting post-project reviews.

Explain the purpose of obtaining formal customer or stakeholder sign-off.   The formal sign-off documents that the customer accepts the project work and that the project meets the defined requirements. It also signals the official closure of the project and the transfer of the final product of the project to the organization.

Describe transferring the project results to the organization.   Transferring the project results occurs once sign-off has been obtained. There should be a documented transition plan for transferring the project results, including describing the type of training or skills needed to maintain the product. License costs, warranty coverage and time period, user documentation, and any other materials needed by the organization should be included in the transfer.

Understand the key elements of the Close Procurements process.   Contract closeout verifies that all the work described in the contract was completed satisfactorily per the contract terms and conditions. It includes notifying the vendor in writing that the work of the contract was accepted.

Name the procedures involved in Administrative Closure.   Administrative Closure involves gathering and centralizing project documents, performing a post-project review, writing the final project close report, archiving project documents, and documenting lessons learned and historical information.

Describe lessons learned.   Lessons learned describe the successes and failures of the project.

Key Terms

Before you take the exam, be certain you are familiar with the following terms:

Addition	lessons learned
Administrative Closure	post-mortem analysis
Close Procurements	post-project review
Extinction	product verification
Integration	starvation

Review Questions

1. Your project is winding down, and you are eager to get started on your next project. An outside company was responsible for completing several of your deliverables. There are acceptance test activities for each of these deliverables on the project schedule. The procurement manager wants to know whether the project deliverables have been accepted or rejected. This information must be provided in writing to the vendor in four days according to the terms of the contract. What action should you take?

   A. You should forward the procurement manager's message to the person assigned to the vendor acceptance test.

   B. You need more time to complete testing, so tell the procurement manager there are problems with some of the test results.

   C. You should confirm that the vendor acceptance testing included all aspects of the vendor deliverables and that all testing has been completed with satisfactory results.

   D. You can ignore the procurement manager's message for now, because you should have the final test results with a week. Procurement always thinks they need an answer right away.

2. You have just left a meeting with the project sponsor where you were advised that your project has been canceled because of budget cuts. You have called the project team together to fill them in and to review the remaining activities to close out the project. Several of your team members question the benefit of doing a lessons learned review on a project that has been canceled. What should your response be?

   A. Advise the team that part of the review time will be spent on documenting the failure of the lack of clear requirements from the customer.

   B. Tell the team they need to do this to be able to stay on the project payroll another week while they look for a new assignment.

   C. Inform the team that a final report is a requirement from the PMO, regardless of how the project ends.

   D. Explain that there is value both to the team and for future projects in analyzing the phases of the project that have been completed to date to document what went right, what went wrong, and what you would change.

3. You have just left a meeting with the project sponsor where you were advised that your project has been canceled because of budget cuts. You have called the project team together to fill them in and to review the remaining activities to close out the project. Which of the following describes the type of project ending this project experienced?

   A. Extinction

   B. Starvation

   C. Addition

   D. Integration

4. You are gathering documents to work on your comprehensive post-project review. What aspects of the project should you focus on?

   A. The review should focus on the technical aspects of the project.

   B. All phases of the project, from planning through execution, should be included in the review.

   C. The review should focus on the project schedule with an emphasis on the accuracy of the original estimates.

   D. The review should be limited to the positive aspects of the project. This will help all the team members get better assignments in the future.

5. Which of the following is the "best" type of project ending?

   A. Extinction

   B. Addition

   C. Integration

   D. Starvation

6. What is the primary purpose of a formal sign-off at the conclusion of the project work?

   A. The sign-off allows the project manager to start a new assignment.

   B. The sign-off means the project team is no longer accountable for the product of the project.

   C. The sign-off is the trigger for releasing team members back to their functional organization.

   D. The sign-off indicates that the project meets the documented requirements and the customer has accepted the project deliverables.

7. Your project was canceled because of the redeployment of project resources. All of the following are true regarding this situation except for which one?

   A. All of the steps of project closeout should occur even though the project was canceled.

   B. A post-mortem should be conducted to determine the cause of the project cancelation and to document any lessons learned.

   C. This project ended because of addition.

   D. Any completed deliverables should be turned over to the organization.

8. What is the focus of the lessons learned report resulting from the comprehensive project review session?

   A. The report should cover both the positive and negative aspects of the project, with suggestions for improvement.

   B. The report should primarily summarize the results of the project schedule, the budget, and any approved scope changes.

   C. The report should focus on the IT deliverables and any issues that were created by the customer.

   D. The report should cover what went well during the project. If the project was canceled, blame for the failure needs to be established.

9. Your project is winding down, and some of your team members are anxious about their status. What is the best way to deal with their concerns?

   A. Explain to the team members that they will be released when the project is done.

   B. Let the team members know that you can only discuss their release date with the functional managers.

   C. Establish the same release date for all the team members, even if their work is completed. If some people start leaving, others may try to jump ship as well.

   D. Review the team member release plans from the staffing management plan. Keep team members and functional managers informed based on the status of the project schedule.

10. Your client has suddenly produced a list of items that they want fixed prior to final sign-off on the project. You suspect they are attempting to add functionality to the system. What is the best approach to deal with the client's request?

    A. Let the client know that this is too late in the process to be bringing these issues to your attention. Any user issues should have been formally documented during user acceptance testing.

    B. Advise the client you will forward the list to the operations manager after turnover to provide time and cost estimates for each item.

    C. Request that the client map the fixes to specific requirements in the project scope document, and explain what the problem is. Review the results of acceptance testing to determine whether any bugs were identified.

    D. Escalate this to the project sponsor so they can decide whether these new enhancements should be added to the project.

11. When performing Close Procurements, this procedure determines whether the work performed on contract was accurate and satisfactory.

    A. Post-project review

    B. Product verification

    C. Post-mortem

    D. Closeout report

12. Centralizing documents, archiving project documents, performing post-project reviews, writing the final closeout report, and distributing the notice of project acceptance occur during which process?

    A. Administrative Closure

    B. Project close

    C. Close Procurements

    D. Post-mortem Review

13. Your project evolved over time into an ongoing operation. What type of project ending is this, and what are your next steps? Choose two.

    A. The project ending is because of addition.

    B. The next step is to inform the project sponsor and stakeholders the project has ended.

    C. The project ending is because of integration.

    D. The next step is to write the project close report.

    E. The next step is to perform a post-mortem analysis.

14. The primary purpose of this activity is to collect and document lessons learned.

    A. Post-mortem analysis

    B. Post-project review

    C. Project closeout review

    D. Administrative Closure

15. This document is produced at the end of the project and reports the final project outcomes.

    A. Lessons learned

    B. Final status report

    C. Project close report

    D. Post-mortem analysis

16. You're a project manager for a large, complex IT project. You're in the middle of the executing phase. The project sponsor has decided to cancel the project because of unexpected cost overruns and resource shortages. What are your next steps? Choose two.

    A. Change vendors to obtain a lower bid for hardware and software components.

    B. Prepare project closure documents, including lessons learned.

    C. Perform a post-mortem analysis, and release resources.

    D. Ask the sponsor to allow you to redesign the project with fewer deliverables.

    E. Ask for a new sponsor.

17. The Closing process group should be performed for all of the following except for which one?

    A. When projects are canceled

    B. When a project phase is concluded

    C. When projects complete successfully

    D. When the feasibility study for a project is concluded

18. All of the following are true regarding the release of team members except for which one?

   A. Team members are released after lessons learned are documented.

   B. The project manager should perform a final performance appraisal for team members when they're released from the project.

   C. The project manager should inform the functional managers well in advance of the team members' release date.

   D. The project manager should communicate with the team members about their upcoming release date.

19. When should Close Procurements be performed?

   A. It should be performed for all projects.

   B. It should be performed for projects that are canceled.

   C. It should be performed for projects that are carried out on contract.

   D. It should be performed in conjunction with Administrative Closure for all projects.

20. Who is responsible for authorizing the closure of the project?

   A. Stakeholders

   B. Project manager

   C. Executive team members

   D. Sponsor

Answers to Review Questions

1. C. Acceptance of deliverables is a key part of the vendor contract. Failure to accept or reject deliverables according to the terms of the contract could put your company in breach of contract. You should immediately confirm the status of vendor deliverable acceptance testing and ensure that all results are completed and meet the deadline. This is not something that should be pushed aside or handed off to someone else.

2. D. There is valuable information to be gained from a review of any project, even projects that do not complete. The assessment should focus on those phases of the project that did finish, as well as a look at whether anything could have been done differently to make the project a success. The purpose of lessons learned is not to assign blame, even for projects that are canceled.

3. B. Starvation is a project ending caused by resources being cut off from the project. Extinction occurs when the project work is completed and is accepted by the stakeholders. Addition occurs when projects evolve into ongoing operations, and integration occurs when resources are distributed to other areas of the organization.

4. B. A post-project review is most beneficial to future projects if it covers all aspects of the project and includes both the negative and the positive of each phase.

5. A. Extinction occurs when the project work is completed and is accepted by the stakeholders. This is the best type of project ending. Starvation is a project ending caused by resources being cut off from the project. Addition occurs when projects evolve into ongoing operations, and integration occurs when resources are distributed to other areas of the organization.

6. D. A sign-off is the formal acceptance of the project. Its primary purpose is the customer's acceptance of the product of the project. Team members are released after sign-off, but this isn't the primary purpose of a formal sign-off. Both the project manager and the project team members may continue to be involved in the project until all closure activities are complete.

7. C. This project ended because of integration, not addition. All the steps of project closeout should occur for projects that are completed as well as those that are canceled. A post-mortem analysis is conducted for canceled projects to determine the cause of the cancelation or failure and to document lessons learned. Any completed deliverables should be turned over to the organization.

8. A. Both the successes and failures of a project need to be documented in the lessons learned report. Successes will provide blueprints to follow on future projects, and failures will alert teams on what to avoid. A good lessons learned document covers all aspects of the project from all participants. It should include all project information, not just schedule, budget, and changes, and it should never place blame for the things that went wrong.

9. D. The procedures for releasing project team members should be documented in your staffing management plan. Both team members and functional managers need to know in advance when you think a team member will be released. Team members may roll off the project at different times, so you need to discuss the release with each team member individually.

10. C. You need to determine whether there is a valid issue here. If the system does not perform according to the requirements, the client has every right to expect fixes to be made. By asking the client to map the fixes to specific requirements, you can both determine whether you are dealing with a fix or an enhancement. Escalation to the project sponsor would be premature at this point, as would passing the list to operations before you have determined the appropriate category for each item on the list.

11. B. Product verification ensures the work performed on contract was completed accurately and satisfactorily.

12. A. Administrative Closure involves centralizing and archiving documents, performing post-project reviews, and writing the final project close report.

13. A, E. Addition occurs when the project evolves into ongoing operations. Integration occurs when the resources on the project are reassigned to other projects or activities. When a project fails, is canceled, or otherwise ends before completion, the next step is performing a post-mortem review.

14. B. The primary purpose of the post-project review is to collect and document lessons learned. A post-mortem analysis occurs when a project is canceled or ends prematurely. Lessons learned are part of the Administrative Closure process, but other activities are involved in this process besides lessons learned.

15. C. The project close report is produced at the end of the project, and it serves as the final status report. It summarizes the project goals, costs, schedule, lessons learned, and historical data.

16. B, C. If you have a sponsor who opts to cancel the project, you will still perform project closing procedures. During this process, you'll assemble the closure documents, perform a post-mortem analysis, and release any resources working on the project.

17. D. A feasibility study is conducted to determine whether the project is worth undertaking. A feasibility study is not typically considered a project and does not need to be closed out.

18. A. Team members can be released prior to the lessons learned session. If your team members are leaving the organization or are located at a different geographical location, you could perform a lessons learned session with them before they leave, or you could include them in the final lessons learned session using video conferencing or similar technology.

19. C. Close Procurements should be performed for any project that is carried out on contract or any project that has certain deliverables produced on contract.

20. D. The sponsor is the one who signs off on the closure documents. As the project manager, you create them, providing supporting documentation that illustrates that all deliverables have been successfully completed.

Appendix

About the Companion CD

IN THIS APPENDIX:

✓ What you'll find on the CD

✓ System requirements

✓ Using the CD

✓ Troubleshooting

What You'll Find on the CD

The following sections are arranged by category and summarize the software and other goodies you'll find on the CD. If you need help with installing the items provided on the CD, refer to the installation instructions in the "Using the CD" section of this appendix.

Sybex Test Engine

For Windows

The CD contains the Sybex test engine, which includes all of the assessment test and chapter review questions in electronic format, as well as two bonus exams located only on the CD.

PDF of Glossary of Terms

For Windows

We have included an electronic version of the text in .PDF format, as well as the glossary. You can view the electronic version of the book with Adobe Reader.

Adobe Reader

For Windows

We've also included a copy of Adobe Reader so you can view PDF files that accompany the book's content. For more information on Adobe Reader or to check for a newer version, visit Adobe's website at www.adobe.com/products/reader/.

Electronic Flashcards

These handy electronic flashcards are just what they sound like. One side contains a question or fill-in-the-blank question, and the other side shows the answer.

System Requirements

Make sure your computer meets the minimum system requirements shown in the following list. If your computer doesn't match up to most of these requirements, you may have problems using the software and files on the companion CD. For the latest and greatest information, please refer to the ReadMe file located at the root of the CD-ROM.

- A PC running Microsoft Windows 98, Windows 2000, Windows NT4 (with SP4 or later), Windows Me, Windows XP, Windows Vista, or Windows 7
- An Internet connection
- A CD-ROM drive

Using the CD

To install the items from the CD to your hard drive, follow these steps:

1. Insert the CD into your computer's CD-ROM drive. The license agreement appears.

The interface won't launch if you have autorun disabled. In that case, click Start ➢ Run (for Windows Vista or Windows 7, Start ➢ All Programs ➢ Accessories ➢ Run). In the dialog box that appears, type **D:\Start.exe**. (Replace *D* with the proper letter if your CD drive uses a different letter. If you don't know the letter, see how your CD drive is listed under My Computer.) Click OK.

2. Read the license agreement, and then click the Accept button if you want to use the CD.

The CD interface appears. The interface allows you to access the content with just one or two clicks.

Troubleshooting

Wiley has attempted to provide programs that work on most computers with the minimum system requirements. Alas, your computer may differ, and some programs may not work properly for some reason.

The two likeliest problems are that you don't have enough memory (RAM) for the programs you want to use or you have other programs running that are affecting installation or running of a program. If you get an error message such as "Not enough memory" or "Setup cannot continue," try one or more of the following suggestions and then try using the software again:

Turn off any antivirus software running on your computer.   Installation programs sometimes mimic virus activity and may make your computer incorrectly believe that it's being infected by a virus.

Close all running programs.   The more programs you have running, the less memory is available to other programs. Installation programs typically update files and programs, so if you keep other programs running, installation may not work properly.

Have your local computer store add more RAM to your computer.   This is, admittedly, a drastic and somewhat expensive step. However, adding more memory can really help the speed of your computer and allow more programs to run at the same time.

Customer Care

If you have trouble with the book's companion CD-ROM, please call the Wiley Product Technical Support phone number at (800) 762-2974. Outside the United States, call +1(317) 572-3994. You can also contact Wiley Product Technical Support at `http://sybex` `.custhelp.com`. John Wiley & Sons will provide technical support only for installation and other general quality-control items. For technical support on the applications themselves, consult the program's vendor or author.

To place additional orders or to request information about other Wiley products, please call (877) 762-2974.

Glossary

A

A Guide to the Project Management Body of Knowledge (PMBOK Guide)   The project management standard developed by the Project Management Institute.

acceptance   The decision to tolerate the defects that are found as a result of the quality testing. This is also a tool for risk response planning.

acceptance criteria   The process and the criteria that will be used to determine whether the deliverables are acceptable and satisfactory.

activity definition   Identifying the activities of the project that need to be performed to produce the product or service of the project.

activity duration   Assessing the number of work periods needed to complete the project activities. Work periods are usually expressed in hours or days. Large projects might express duration in weeks or months.

activity list   A list of all the activities required to complete the work of the project that also includes an identifier code and the WBS code it's associated with. Activities are broken down from the work package level of the WBS.

activity sequencing   Sequencing activities in logical order and determining whether dependencies exist among the activities.

actual cost (AC)   The cost to complete a component of work in a given time period. Actual costs include direct and indirect costs.

addition   A type of project ending that occurs when projects evolve into ongoing operations.

Administrative Closure   A process that involves gathering and disseminating information to formalize project closure. The completion of each project phase requires Administrative Closure also. The primary purpose of this process is to gather lessons learned and distribute the notice of acceptance.

analogous estimating   An estimating technique that uses the actual duration of a similar, completed activity to determine the duration of the current activity. This is also called *top-down estimating*.

appraisal costs   Costs of quality that cover the activities that keep the product defects from reaching the client, including inspection, testing, and formal quality audits.

assumption   An event or action believed to be true for planning purposes. Project assumptions should always be documented.

avoiding   A conflict-resolution technique that occurs when one party refuses to talk anymore about the issue and physically leaves. This is an example of a lose-lose conflict-resolution technique. This technique is also known as *withdrawal*.

B

backward pass   Calculating late start and late finish dates by starting at the end of a network diagram and working back through each path until reaching the start of the network diagram. This is part of critical path method (CPM), which is a mathematical technique to develop the project schedule.

benchmarking   Compares previous similar activities to the current project activities to provide a standard to measure performance against. It's often used to derive ideas for quality improvements for the project.

benefit measurement methods   A type of decision model that compares the benefits obtained from a variety of new project requests by evaluating them using the same criteria and comparing the results.

bidder conference   A meeting held by the buyer with potential vendors during the procurement process to allow vendors to ask questions and get clarification on the project.

bottom-up estimating   Individually estimating each work package, all of which are then rolled up, or added together, to come up with a total project estimate. This is a very accurate means of estimating, provided the estimates at the work package level are accurate.

budget at completion (BAC)   The total amount of the project budget for a work package, control account, or schedule activity, or for the project.

business analyst   The person in charge of understanding the business unit's needs when assessing a project request. The business analyst might be assigned directly from the business unit itself or may be part of the IT organization.

business case   Formally documents components of the project assessment, including a description of the analysis method and the results.

business process reengineering   Applying changes to an IT system and putting those elements into place based on a project request and a business analyst's examination of the workflow—how people handle their work relative to the request.

business requirements   The requirements that describe how the business objectives of the project will be met.

C

cause-and-effect diagram   A Quality Control technique that shows the relationship between the effects of problems and their causes. This is also known as an *Ishikawa diagram* and a *fishbone diagram*.

change control board (CCB)   A board responsible for reviewing and approving, denying, or delaying change requests. The change control board is usually made up of stakeholders, managers, project team members, and others who might have an interest in the project.

Close Procurements   A process that concerns completing and settling the terms of the contract and documenting its acceptance.

Closing   A process that documents the final delivery and acceptance of the project and is where hand-off occurs to the operational unit. Lessons learned are performed during this process, and project team members are released.

collocated   When team members work together at the same physical location.

commercial off-the-shelf (COTS)   Describes a software application that is purchased from a reseller, vendor, or manufacturer.

common causes of variances   Variances that come about as a result of circumstances that are common to the process you're performing and are easily controlled at the operational level. The three types of common cause variances are random, known or predictable, and variances that are always present in the process.

communications management plan   Documents the types of information needs the stakeholders have, when the information should be distributed, and how the information will be delivered.

communications planning   Determines the communication needs of the stakeholders, when and how the information will be received, and who will receive the information.

comprehensive project plan   Integrates all planning data into one document that the project manager can use as a guidebook to oversee the project work during the Executing and Controlling phases.

compromise   A conflict-resolution technique where each party involved gives up something to reach a resolution. This is not generally a permanent solution.

configuration management   Describes the characteristics of the product of the project and ensures the description is accurate and complete. Controls changes to the characteristics of an item and tracks the changes made or requested and their status. It is usually a subset of the change control process in most organizations, or it may serve as the change control system.

confronting   A conflict-resolution technique that is also known as *problem solving*. This is the best way to resolve conflicts and involves fact finding to bear out the solution. This is a win-win conflict-resolution technique.

constrained optimization models   Decision models that use complex principles of statistics and other mathematical concepts to assess a proposed project.

constraint   Anything that either restricts the actions of the project team or dictates the actions of the project team.

contingency reserve   An amount of money or time set aside and dedicated to the project to be used to cover unforeseen costs or time that was not identified as part of the planning process.

contract   A legally binding document that describes the work that will be performed, how the work will be compensated, and any penalties for noncompliance.

contract administration   The process of monitoring vendor performance and ensuring all the requirements of the contract are met.

contract closeout   The process of completing and settling the terms of the contract and determining whether the work described in the contract was completed accurately and satisfactorily.

control chart   A graph of the variance of several samples of the same process over time based on a mean, an upper control limit, and a lower control limit.

corrective actions   A type of change request that typically occurs during the Monitoring and Controlling processes. Corrective actions bring the work of the project back into alignment with the project plan.

cost baseline   The total approved, expected cost of the project created in the planning process. It's used as a comparison to actual project expenses throughout the remainder of the project.

cost-benefit analysis   A commonly used benefit measurement method that calculates the cost of producing the product, service, or result of the project and compares this to the financial gain the project is expected to generate.

cost budgeting   Assigning cost estimates to activities and creating the cost baseline, which measures the performance of the project throughout the project's life.

Cost Control   A process that measures the project spending to date, determines whether changes have occurred to the cost baseline, and takes action to deal with the changes. This process monitors the budget and manages changes to the cost baseline.

cost estimating   Developing an estimation of the cost of resources needed for each project activity.

cost of quality   The cost of all of the work required to assure the project meets the quality standards. The three costs associated with the cost of quality are prevention costs, appraisal costs, and failure costs.

cost performance index (CPI)   Measures the value of the work completed at the measurement date against actual cost. This is the most critical of all EVM measurements. The formula is $CPI = EV / AC$.

cost-reimbursable contract   Provides the seller with payment for all costs incurred to deliver or produce the product or service requested.

cost variance   The difference between a task's value at the measurement date and its actual cost. The formula is $CV = EV - AC$.

crashing   This is a schedule compression technique that adds resources to the project to reduce the time it takes to complete the project.

critical path (CP)   The longest path through the project. Activities with zero float are considered critical path tasks.

critical path method (CPM)   A schedule development method that determines a single early and late start date, early and late finish date, and the float for each activity on the project.

critical success factor   Elements that must be completed in order for the project to be considered complete. Critical success factors that are not satisfactory can lead to project failure.

customer   The recipient of the product or service created by the project. In some organizations this stakeholder may also be referred to as the *client*.

D

decision model   A formal method of project selection that helps managers make the best use of limited budgets and human resources. Includes benefit measurement methods and constrained optimization models.

decomposition   The process of breaking project deliverables down into smaller, manageable components of work so that work packages can be planned and estimated.

defect repairs   A type of change request that typically comes about during the Monitoring and Controlling process group. Defect repairs either correct or replace components that are substandard or are malfunctioning.

definitive estimate   An estimating technique that assigns a cost estimate to each work package in the project WBS. This is the most accurate of the cost estimating techniques, which typically falls within −5 percent and +10 percent of the actual budget.

deliverable   An output or result that must be completed in order to consider the project complete or to move forward to the next phase of the project. Deliverables are tangible and can be measured and easily proved.

dependencies   The relationship between project activities.

dependency relationships   The type of dependency between two activities and the specific relationship between the activities.

discounted cash flow (DCF)   Compares the value of the future cash flows of the project to today's dollars.

discretionary dependency   A type of dependency that the project manager and project team choose to impose on the project schedule, such as the use of an established corporate practice.

Document control process   Defines how revisions are made, the version numbering system, and the placement of the version number and revision date.

duration compression   The use of techniques such as fast-tracking or crashing to shorten the planned duration of a project or to resolve schedule slippage.

E

early finish   The earliest date an activity may finish as logically constrained by the network diagram.

early start   The earliest date an activity may start as logically constrained by the network diagram.

earned value (EV)   The value of the work completed to date as it compares to the budgeted amount for the work component.

earned value measurement (EVM)   EVM is a tool and technique of the Cost Control process that compares what you're received or produced as of the measurement date to what you've spent. The three measurements needed to perform earned value measurement are planned value (PV), actual cost (AC), and earned value (EV).

economic model   A type of benefit measurement method. It is a series of financial calculations that provide data on the overall financials of the project and is generally used as a project selection technique.

enterprise project   A project that will be used by users throughout the enterprise.

equipment   (a) Resources such as servers, specialized test equipment, or additional PCs that are required for a project. (b) One of the categories of project resources. It includes test tools, servers, PCs, or other related items required to complete the project.

estimate at completion (EAC)   A forecast of the total cost of the project based on both current project performance and the remaining work. The formula is EAC = AC + ETC.

estimate to complete (ETC)   The cost estimate for the remaining project work. This estimate is provided by the project team members.

executing   This project process group is where the work of the project is performed.

expert judgment   A technique used in project selection, determining estimates, and determining other related project information that relies on the knowledge of those with expertise on the requested subject matter. Expert judgment can come from stakeholders, other departments, consultants, team members, vendors, or industry groups.

external dependency   A type of dependency where a relationship between a project task and a factor outside the project, such as weather conditions, drives the scheduling of that task.

extinction   This is a type of project ending that occurs when the project is completed and accepted by the stakeholders.

F

failure costs   The cost if the product fails, including downtime, user support, rework, and scrapping the project.

fast-tracking   A schedule compression technique where two activities that were previously scheduled to start sequentially start at the same time. Fast-tracking reduces schedule duration.

feasibility study   Undertaken to determine whether the project is a viable project, the probability of project success, and the viability of the product of the project.

finish-to-finish   A project task relationship in which the finish of the successor task is dependent on the finish of the predecessor task.

finish-to-start   A project task relationship in which the successor task cannot begin until the predecessor task has completed.

fixed-price contracts   A contract that states a fixed fee for the work that the vendor will perform.

float time   The amount of time the early start of a task may be delayed without delaying the finish date of the project. Also known as *slack time*.

flowchart   A diagram that shows the logical steps that must be performed in order to accomplish an objective. It can also show how the individual elements of a system interrelate.

forcing   This is a conflict-resolution technique where one party forces their solution on the others. This is an example of a win-lose conflict resolution technique.

formal communications   Planned communications such as project kickoff meetings, team status meetings, written status reports, or team-building sessions.

forward pass   The process of working from the left to the right of a network diagram in order to calculate early start and early finish dates for each activity.

functional organization   A form of organizational structure. Functional organizations are traditional organizations with hierarchical reporting structures.

functional requirements   These define what the product of the project will do by focusing on how the end user will interact with the product.

H

high-level requirements   These explain the major characteristics of the product and describe the relationship between the business need and the product requested. This is also referred to as a *product description*.

human resources   The people with the background and skills to complete the tasks on the project schedule.

human resources planning   Defining team member roles and responsibilities, establishing an appropriate structure for team reporting, securing the right team members, and bringing them on the project as needed for the appropriate length of time.

I

impact   The consequences imposed if a risk event occurs on the project.

informal communications   Unplanned or ad hoc communications, including phone calls, emails, conversations in the hallway, or impromptu meetings.

information distribution   Providing stakeholders with information regarding the project in a timely manner via status reports, project meetings, review meetings, email, and so on. The communications management plan is put into action during this process.

initiating   The first process in a project life cycle and the first of the five project process groups. This is the formal acknowledgment that the project should begin. The primary result of this process is the project charter.

inspection   A quality control technique that includes examining, measuring, or testing work results.

integrated change control   A process that influences the factors that cause change, determines that a change is needed or has happened, and manages and monitors change. All other change control processes are integrated with this process.

integration   A type of project ending where the resources of the project are reassigned or redeployed to other projects or other activities within the organization.

internal rate of return (IRR)   The discount rate when the present value of the cash inflows equals the original investment. Projects with higher IRR values are generally considered better than projects with lower IRR values. Assumes that cash inflows are reinvested at the IRR value.

Ishikawa diagram   A Quality Control technique that shows the relationship between the effects of problems and their causes. This is also known as a *cause-and-effect diagram* and *fishbone diagram*.

iterative process   Any process that is repeated more than once. The five process groups are repeated throughout the project's life because of change requests, responses to change, corrective action, and so on.

K

key performance indicators (KPIs)   Help you determine whether the project is on track and progressing as planned by monitoring the project against predetermined criteria.

L

late finish   The latest date an activity can complete without impacting the project end date.

late start   The latest date an activity can start without impacting the project end date.

lessons learned   Information gathered throughout the project (and again at the end of a project phase or the end of the project) that documents the successes and failures of the project. This information is used to benefit the current project and future projects.

lines of communication   A mathematical formula that determines the number of lines of communication between participants in a meeting. The formula is n (n − 1) / 2, where *n* represents the number of participants.

loaded rate   A rate used for cost estimating of human resources that includes a percentage of the salary to cover employee benefits, such as medical, disability, or pension plans.

logical relationships   The dependency relationships that may exist between tasks. Finish-to-start is the most common logical relationship.

M

make-or-buy analysis   Determines the cost effectiveness of producing goods or services in-house vs. procuring them from outside the organization.

managerial reserve   An amount of money set aside by upper management to cover future expenses that can't be predicted during project planning.

mandatory dependency   A type of dependency where the relationship between two tasks is created by the type of work the project requires.

materials   A catchall category of project resources that includes software, utility requirements such as electricity or water, any supplies needed for the project, or other consumable goods.

mathematical analysis   Calculating theoretical early and late start and finish dates for all project activities.

matrix organization   An organizational structure where employees report to one functional manager and at least one project manager. Functional managers assign employees to projects and carry out administrative duties, while project managers assign tasks associated with the project to team members and execute the project.

metric   A standard of measurement that specifically defines how something will be measured.

milestone   A major deliverable or key event in the project used to measure project progress.

Monitoring and Controlling   This project process group is where activities are performed to monitor the progress of the project and determine whether there are variances from the project plan. Corrective actions are taken during this process to get the project back on course.

multiple business unit project   A project that is initiated by multiple business units.

N

negotiating   Negotiating is a leadership technique and a conflict-resolution technique. Negotiating is the act of two or more parties explaining their needs and coming to a mutual agreement on a resolution.

net present value (NPV)   Evaluation of the cash inflows using the discounted cash flow technique, which is applied to each period the inflows are expected. The total present value of the cash flows is deducted from the initial investment; this assumes that cash inflows are reinvested at the cost of capital. It is similar to discounted cash flows.

network diagram   A depiction of project activities and the interrelationships between these activities.

O

operations   Operations typically involve ongoing functions that support the production of goods or services. They don't have a beginning or an end.

order of magnitude   A high-level estimate of the time and cost of a project based on the actual cost and duration of a similar project.

organizational planning   The process of addressing factors that may impact how to manage a project team, defining roles and responsibilities for project team members, identifying how the project team will be organized, and documenting a staffing management plan.

P

parametric estimating   A quantitatively based estimating technique that is typically calculated by multiplying rate times quantity.

Pareto diagram   A Quality Control technique used to rank importance of a problem based on its frequency of occurrence over time. This diagram is based on the Pareto principle, more commonly referred to as the *80/20 rule*, which says that the majority of defects are caused by a small set of problems.

payback period   The length of time it takes a company to recover the initial cost of producing the product or service of the project.

performance reporting   Collecting information regarding project progress and project accomplishments and reporting it to the stakeholders, project team members, management team, and other interested parties. It also makes predictions regarding future project performance.

planned value (PV)   The cost of work that's been budgeted for an activity during a certain time period.

planning   The process group where the project plans are developed that will be used throughout the project to direct, monitor, and control work results. The primary result of this process is the project plan.

post-mortem analysis   Performed when a project is canceled or ends prematurely. It describes the reasons for cancellation or failure and documents the deliverables that were completed.

post-project review   Conducted at the end of the project to document lessons learned.

precedence diagramming method (PDM)   A network diagramming method that places activities on nodes, which connect to dependent activities using arrows. Also known as *activity on node*.

predecessor   A task on the network diagram that occurs before another task.

preliminary investigation   An investigation at project request time to determine the costs and benefits of the project, as well as examine alternatives to the proposed solution in order to determine the feasibility of carrying out the project.

preventive action   A type of change request that usually occur during the Monitoring and Controlling process group. Preventive actions are implemented to help reduce the probability of a negative risk event.

prevention   A Quality Control tool and technique that keeps errors from reaching the customer. Prevention is less expensive than having to fix problems after they've occurred.

prevention costs   The cost of activities performed to avoid quality problems, including quality planning, training, and any product or process testing.

probability   The likelihood a risk event will occur. Probability is expressed as a number between 0.0 and 1.0.

procurement planning   The process of identifying what goods or services will be purchased from outside the organization. It uses make-or-buy analysis to determine whether goods or services should be purchased outside the organization or produced internally.

product description   Explains the major characteristics of the product and describes the relationship between the business need and the product. This is also referred to as *high-level requirements*.

product verification   Occurs in the Close Procurements process and determines whether the work of the contract is acceptable and satisfactory.

program   A grouping of related projects that are managed together to capitalize on benefits that couldn't be achieved if the projects were managed separately.

program evaluation and review technique (PERT)   Calculates the expected value, or weighted average, of critical path tasks to determine project duration by using three estimates: most likely, pessimistic, and optimistic. The PERT calculation is (optimistic + pessimistic + (4 × most likely)) / 6.

progress reports   Reports from project team members listing the tasks each team member is working on, the current progress of each task, and the work remaining.

project   Temporary in nature, with a definite start and end date; creates a unique product, service, or result. It is completed when the goals and objectives of the project have been met and signed off on by the stakeholders.

project-based organization   An organizational structure focused on projects. Project managers generally have ultimate authority over the project, and sometimes supporting departments such as human resources and accounting might report to the project manager. Project managers are responsible for making project decisions and acquiring and assigning resources.

project champion   The person who fully understands, believes in, and espouses the benefits of the project to the organization. This is the cheerleader for the project.

project charter   An official, written acknowledgment and recognition that a project exists. It's signed by the project sponsor and gives the project manager authority to assign organizational resources to the work of the project.

project closure   The formal acceptance of a project and the activities required to formally end the project work.

project description   Documents the key characteristics of the product or service that will be created by the project.

project execution   Carrying out the project plan. Activities are clarified, the work is authorized to begin, resources are committed and assigned to activities, and the product or service of the project is created. The largest portion of the project budget will be spent during this process.

project justification   Documentation in the project charter that includes the reason the project is being undertaken and the business need the project will address.

project life cycle   The grouping of project phases in a sequential order from the beginning of the project to the close.

project management   Applying skills, knowledge, and project management tools and techniques to fulfill the project requirements.

Project Management Institute (PMI)   The world's leading professional project management association.

project management knowledge areas   The nine project management groupings, or Knowledge Areas, that bring together common or related processes. They are Integration, Scope, Time, Cost, Quality, Human Resource, Communications, Risk, and Procurement.

project management office (PMO)   Established by organizations to create and maintain procedures and standards for project management methodologies to be used throughout the organization.

project manager   The person responsible for applying the skills, knowledge, and project management tools and techniques to the project activities to successfully complete the project objectives.

project performance indicators   Measures that the project manager uses to determine whether the project is on track, such as any deviation from the baseline schedule or the baseline budget.

project plan   A document, or assortment of documents, that constitutes what the project is, what the project will deliver, and how all the processes will be managed. Used as the guideline throughout the project Executing and Controlling phases to track and measure project performance and to make future project decisions. Also used as a communication and information tool for stakeholders, team members, and management.

project review   A formal presentation by the project manager or project team members to the sponsor, the client, and the other executive stakeholders.

project schedule   Determines the start and finish dates for project activities and assigns resources to the activities.

project selection   Used to determine which proposed projects are approved to move forward.

proof of concept   A project that undertakes to prove that a specific activity can be done or an idea can be accomplished.

Q

qualitative risk analysis   Determining the impact of identified risks on the project and the probability they'll occur. Aligns risks in a priority order according to their effect on the project objectives.

quality control   Monitoring work results to see whether they fulfill the quality standards set out in the quality management plan; determines whether the end product conforms to the requirements and product description defined during the planning processes.

quality management plan   Describes how the project management team will enact the quality policy and documents the resources needed to carry out the quality plan. It describes the responsibilities of the project team in implementing quality and outlines all the processes and procedures the project team and organization will use to satisfy quality requirements.

quality planning   Identifying the quality standards applicable for the project and how they'll be fulfilled.

quantitative risk analysis   A complex analysis technique that uses a mathematical approach to numerically analyze the probability and impact of risk events.

quantitatively based durations   A duration estimate obtained by applying a productivity rate of the resource performing the task.

R

RACI chart   A type of responsibility assignment matrix that describes the resources needed for the task and their role for that task using the following descriptors: responsible, accountable, consult, or inform.

rebaselining   Setting a new project baseline because of substantial changes to the schedule or the budget.

Report Performance   This process is where the project manager gathers and documents the collection of baseline data for the project. Baseline data includes cost, schedule, scope, and quality data. Performance report information is delivered to the stakeholders at project status meetings and steering committee meetings.

request for proposal (RFP)   A document that is sent out to potential vendors requesting them to provide a proposal on a product or service.

requirement   The specifications and characteristics of the goal or deliverable.

resource planning   A process that defines and documents all the resources needed and the quantity of resources needed to perform project activities, including human, material, and equipment resources.

resource pool description   A listing of all the job titles within a company or department with a brief description of the job. It may also identify the number of people currently employed in each job title.

resource requirements   A document containing a description of the resources needed from all three resource types for work package items from the WBS.

responsibility assignment matrix (RAM)   A resource chart that defines the WBS identifier, the resource type needed for the WBS element, and the quantity of resources needed for the task. A WBS is displayed in chart form.

revision   An update to the approved start or end date of the schedule baseline, typically a result of approved scope changes.

rework   An action that is taken as a result of quality activities to correct a defect.

risk   A potential future event that can have either negative or positive consequences.

risk analysis   The process used to identify and focus on those risks that are the most critical to the success of your project.

risk identification   Identifying the potential project risks and documenting their characteristics.

risk list   A numbered list of risks that are produced during the risk identification process and that are documented within a risk register.

risk management plan   Details how risk management processes will be implemented, monitored, and controlled throughout the life of the project. It does not define responses to individual risks.

risk monitoring and control   The process that involves implementing the risk response plan, tracking and monitoring identified risks, and identifying and responding to new risks as they occur.

risk planning   Identifying, analyzing, and determining how risk events will be managed for a project.

risk response planning   A process that describes how to reduce threats and take advantage of opportunities, documents the plan for negative and positive risk events, and assigns owners to each risk.

risk trigger   An event that warns a risk is imminent and a response plan should be implemented.

run chart   A Quality Control tool and technique that shows variation in the process over time or shows trends such as improvements or the lack of improvements in the process.

S

schedule baseline   The final, approved project schedule that is used during project execution to monitor project progress.

schedule control   The process of documenting and managing changes to the project schedule.

schedule development   Calculating and preparing the schedule of project activities, which becomes the schedule baseline. It determines activity start and finish dates, finalizes activity sequences and durations, and determines activity duration estimates.

schedule performance index (SPI)   Measures the progress to date against the progress that was planned. The SPI indicator acts as an efficiency rating. If the result is greater than one, performance is better than expected, and you're ahead of schedule. If it's less than one, performance is less than expected, and you're behind schedule. The formula is $SPI = EV / PV$.

schedule update   Any change that is made to the project schedule as part of the ongoing work involved with managing the project.

schedule variance (SV)   The difference between a task's progress as compared to its estimated progress represented in terms of cost. The formula is $SV = EV - PV$.

scope   The description of the work involved to complete the project. It defines both what is included in the project and what is excluded from the project.

scope control   The process of documenting and managing changes to project scope. Any modification to the agreed-upon WBS is considered a scope change. Changes in product scope will require changes to project scope, and scope changes always require schedule changes.

scope creep   The minor changes or small additions that are made to the project outside of a formal scope change process that cause project scope to grow and change.

scope definition   Per the *PMBOK Guide*, the process of breaking down the major deliverables from the scope statement to create the WBS. For purposes of the CompTIA objectives and exam, scope definition is used in a much broader sense to cover several scope planning elements, including the scope statement and the scope management plan.

scope management plan   Defines the process for preparing the scope statement and the WBS. This also documents the process that manages project scope and changes to project scope.

scope planning   The process of defining the scope management plan, the scope statement, and the WBS and WBS dictionary.

scope statement   Documents the product description, key deliverables, success and acceptance criteria, key performance indicators, exclusions, assumptions, and constraints. The scope statement is used as a baseline for future project decisions.

scope verification   A process that concerns formally accepting the deliverables of the project and obtaining sign-off that they're complete.

scoring model   One of the benefit measurement methods used for project selection. It contains a predefined list of criteria against which each project is ranked. Each criterion has a scoring range and a weighting factor. A scoring model can also be used as a tool to select from among competing vendors.

sequencing   Putting the project activities in the order in which they will take place.

slack time   The amount of time allowed to delay the early start of a task without delaying the finish date of the project. This is also known as *float time*.

sole source   A requirement that a product or service must be obtained from a single vendor in government work; also includes justification.

solicitation   Obtaining bids and proposals from vendors in response to RFPs and similar procurement documents prepared during the solicitation planning process.

sponsor   An executive in the organization with authority to allocate funds, assign resources, and enforce decisions regarding the project.

staff acquisition   Obtaining human resources and assigning them to the project. Human resources may come from inside or outside the organization.

staffing management plan   Documents when and how human resources will be added to and released from the project team and what they will be working on while they are part of the team.

stakeholder   A person or an organization that has something to gain or lose as a result of the project. Most stakeholders have a vested interest in the outcomes of the project.

start-to-finish   A task relationship where the finish of the successor task is dependent on the start of its predecessor.

start-to-start   A project task relationship where the start of the successor task depends on the start of the predecessor task.

starvation   A type of project ending where resources are cut off from the project.

statement of work (SOW)   Contains the details of a procurement item in clear, concise terms and includes the project objectives, a description of the work of the project, and concise specifications of the product or services required.

status date   The date when the project manager measures how much has been spent on a specific task.

success criteria   See *acceptance criteria*.

successor   A task on the network diagram that occurs after another task.

T

team building   A way to get diverse groups of people to work together efficiently and effectively. This is the responsibility of the project manager. It can involve activities performed together as a group or individually designed to improve team performance.

team development   Creating an open, encouraging environment for stakeholders to contribute, as well as developing the project team into an effective, functioning, coordinated group.

technical requirements   Also known as *nonfunctional requirements*, the product characteristics needed for the product to perform the functional requirements. Technical requirements typically refer to information technology–related projects. They are typically the elements and functions that happen behind the scenes of a program to meet the client's request.

time and materials contract   A type of contract where the buyer and the seller agree on a unit rate, such as the hourly rate for a programmer. The total cost is unknown and will depend on the amount of time spent to produce the product.

to-complete performance index (TCPI)   The projected performance level that must be achieved in the remaining work of the project in order to satisfy financial or schedule goals. The formula is TCPI = (BAC – EV) / (BAC – AC).

top-down estimating   An estimating technique that uses actual durations from similar activities on a previous project. This is also referred to as *analogous estimating*.

trend analysis   A mathematical technique that can be used to predict future defects based on historical results.

triple constraint   According to CompTIA, time, cost, and quality. Other sources site scope rather than quality in their definitions of the triple constraints.

V

variance analysis   The comparison of planned project results with actual project results. The formula is VAC = BAC – EAC.

W

work breakdown structure (WBS)   A deliverables-oriented hierarchy that defines the total work of the project. Each level has more detailed information than the previous level.

work breakdown structure (WBS) dictionary   A document that describes the deliverables and their components, the code of accounts identifier, estimates, resources, criteria for acceptance, and any other information that helps clarify the deliverables.

work effort   The total time it takes for a person to complete a task if they did nothing else from the time they started until the task was complete.

work package   The lowest level in a WBS. Team assignments, time estimates, and cost estimates can be made at this level. On very large projects, this level is handed off to subproject managers who develop their own WBS to fulfill the requirements of the work package deliverable.

Index

Note to the Reader: Throughout this index **boldfaced** page numbers indicate primary discussions of a topic. *Italicized* page numbers indicate illustrations.

T

The Absolute CompTIA Project+ Book/CD Package on the Market!

Get ready for your CompTIA Project+ certification with the most comprehensive and challenging sample tests anywhere!

The Sybex test engine features the following:

■ Challenging questions representative of those you'll find on the real exam

■ Two full-length bonus exams, available only on the CD

■ An assessment test to narrow your focus to certain objective groups.

■ Access the entire *CompTIA Project+ Study Guide*, complete with figures and tables, in electronic format.

■ Search the *CompTIA Project+ Study Guide* chapters to find information on any topic in seconds.

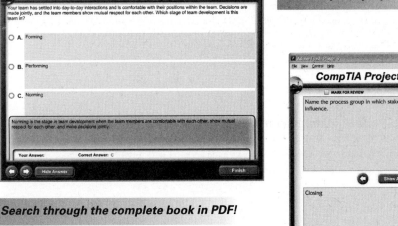

Use the electronic flashcards to jog your memory and prep last-minute for the exam!

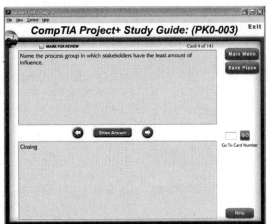

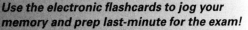

Search through the complete book in PDF!

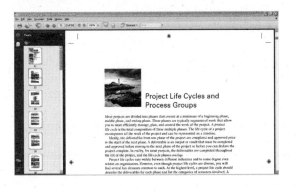

■ Reinforce your understanding of key concepts with these hardcore flashcard-style questions.

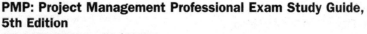

CompTIA Project+ Study Guide (PK0-003)

Exam Objectives

OBJECTIVE	CHAPTER
1.0 Pre-Project Setup/Initiating	
1.1 Explain the requirements to complete a pre-project setup	1
• Identify the project	1
• Validate the project	1
• Prepare a project charter	1
• Obtain approval (signature) for project charter	1
1.2 Identify the characteristics of a project	1
• Temporary endeavor	1
• Delivers a unique product or service	1
• Constrained by time	1
• Resources and quality	1
1.3 Summarize the steps required to validate a project	1
• Validate business case (Feasibility analysis, Justification for project, Alignment to strategic plan)	1
• Identify and analyze stakeholders	1
1.4 Explain the components of a project charter	2
• Key project deliverables	2
• High level milestones	2
• High level cost estimates	2
• Identify stakeholders	2
• General project approach	2
• Problem statement	2
• High level assumptions	2
• High level constraints	2
• High level risks	2
• Project objectives	2
1.5 Outline the process groups of the project life cycle	2
• Initiating/Pre-Project Setup	2
• Planning	2
• Executing	2
• Monitoring/controlling	2
• Closing	2
1.6 Explain the different types of organizational structures	1
• Functional	1
• Weak matrix	1
• Matrix	1
• Strong matrix	1
• Project Based	1
2.0 Project Planning	
2.1 Prepare a project scope document based on an approved project charter	3
• Key Performance Indicators (KPIs)	3
• Scope boundaries	3
• Constraints	3
• Assumptions	3
• Detailed objectives	3
• Final project acceptance criteria	3
• Validate scope statement with stakeholders	3

Sybex®
An Imprint of
WILEY

OBJECTIVE	CHAPTER
2.2 Use a Work Breakdown Structure (WBS) and WBS dictionary to organize project planning	3
• Explain the benefits of WBS	3
• Explain the levels of a WBS	3
• Explain the purpose of a WBS	3
• Identify the planning processes which utilize the WBS as an input	3
• Critique a given WBS	3
• Explain the purpose of a WBS dictionary	3
2.3 Outline a process for managing changes to the project	6
• Approvals required	6
• Forms needed	6
• Turnaround times	6
• Document routing	6
• Communication flow	6
2.4 Develop a project schedule based on WBS, project scope and resource requirements	4
• Schedule to milestones	4
• Analyze Gantt chart	4
• Identify dependency types	4
• Determine the critical path of a project schedule	4
• Establish schedule baselines	4
2.5 Given a desired deliverable, apply the appropriate tool and/or method to produce the appropriate outcome	4
• Tools (PERT, Gantt)	4
• Methods (CPM)	4
2.6 Given a scenario, interpret the results of using the following tools and/or methods	4
• Tools (GERT)	4
• Methods (CPMNetwork diagram: ADM, PDM, CDM, CCM)	4
2.7 Identify components of an internal/external communication plan	5
• Frequency	5
• Format (formal, informal, written and verbal)	5
• Method of distribution	5
• Distribution list	5
2.8 Outline the components of a risk management plan	6
• Initial risk assessment	6
• Risk matrix	6
• Risk register	6
• Risk response strategies	6
• Stakeholder risk tolerance	6
2.9 Identify roles and resource requirements based on WBS and resource availability	5
• Identify existing resource availability	5
• Identify training needs/outsourcing requirements	5
• Assign resources to scheduled tasks	5
2.10 Identify components of a quality management plan	6
• Quality metrics, control limits, and frequency of measurement	6
• Quality assurance processes	6
• Quality control processes	6
• Quality baseline	6
2.11 Identify components of a cost management plan	6
• Control limits	6
• Assign costs	6
• Chart of accounts	6
• Project budget	6
• Cost estimates (bottom up, top down, parametric, expert judgment, analogous)	6
• Cost baseline	6
2.12 Explain the procurement process in a given situation	5
• Project needs assessment/gap analysis	5
• Make or buy decision	5
• RFI, RFQ, RFP (Request for: Information, Quote, Proposal)	5

Sybex®
An Imprint of
WILEY